THE CRADLE SONG

G. MARTÍNEZ SIERRA

THE CRADLE SONG

And Other Plays

BY

G. MARTINEZ SIERRA

IN ENGLISH VERSIONS WITH AN
INTRODUCTION BY

JOHN GARRETT UNDERHILL

NEW YORK
E. P. DUTTON & CO., INC.

FIRST PRINTING..........NOVEMBER, 1922
SECOND PRINTING.........FEBRUARY, 1929
THIRD PRINTING.........SEPTEMBER, 1929
FOURTH PRINTING........DECEMBER, 1931
FIFTH PRINTING..............APRIL, 1938

CONTENTS

Translated in collaboration with
May Heywood Broun

INTRODUCTION

Gregorio Martínez Sierra was born at Madrid March 6, 1881, María de la O Lejárraga at San Millán de la Cogolla, a mountain village in the fertile wine-growing district of the Rioja, one year previously. They were married in 1899. Gregorio Martínez Sierra is not only a name but a pen-name, and the works which have appeared under it are the result of a collaboration that began even before marriage and has continued through all their books and plays ever since.

Precocious in talent, Gregorio attended the University of Madrid where he came to grief in history, doubtless, as he says, because of a settled aversion to battles. His affinity for formal study was slight. María, however, early associated herself with the educational system and was already established as a teacher in the public normal schools. Together they soon abandoned all thought of academic preferment and turned to literature as a career.

At seventeen, with the manuscript of his first book, *El poema del trabajo* ("The Song of Labor"), he presented himself to Jacinto Benavente, who furnished an introduction and arranged its publication which took place in 1898. Two series of prose poems, or pastels, as they were called in that day, followed, besides a collection of short stories, *Cuentos breves,* issued independently and attributed to María. In 1900 a novelette, *Almas ausentes* was awarded the prize in a contest conducted by the *Biblioteca Mignon.* This and other tales of the sort, subsequently appearing separately, have been reprinted in three volumes, *Abril melancólico* ("Melancholy April"), *El diablo se ríe* ("The Devil

Laughs"), and *La selva muda* ("The Silent Wood"). The most notable work in the shorter form, however, is contained in *Sol de la tarde,* or "Declining Sun," which established their reputation beyond cavil in 1904. To the same year belongs the first of two novels, "The Humble Truth," while a second and more popular venture in the field of fiction, "Peace" (*Tú eres la paz*), was composed two years later.

In the beginning an intellectual by temperament and a word-painter by inclination, Martínez Sierra may be characterized as an impressionist, well-versed in the procedure of the modern French schools. Perhaps the principal personal influence of his formative period was that of the poet Juan Ramón Jiménez, with whom he kept bachelor hall at Madrid. Other associations of these days were likewise predominantly literary, and leaders of the modern movement such as Antonio and Manuel Machado and the Catalan, Santiago Rusiñol, painter of gardens, proved themselves kindred spirits. Under their friendly stimulus, he published a volume of verse, *La casa de la primavera,* a chance excursion into an alien domain, as well as a prose poem upon "Hamlet in the Person of Sarah Bernhardt." With these works his "Dream Theatre" may be coupled, a quartet of symbolic, mystical dialogues with pronounced Maeterlinckian tendencies.

The first decade of the productivity of Martínez Sierra suggests little of the theatre. It was quietistic in feeling, essentially contemplative, a communion with idyllic and elegiac poets. Yet through these days another influence had been active, although less conspicuously, which in the end was to prove decisive. In the year immediately following the publication of "The Song of Labor," the Art Theatre was founded at Madrid by Benavente. The coöperation of the more promising of the younger generation was enlisted, among whom was Martínez Sierra, who played the rôle of Manuel in support of Benavente in the latter's comedy

"A Long Farewell" at the opening performance. The ensuing months were months of intimate association with a remarkable mind. "As I listened to him talk, the fundamental laws of the modern theatre were revealed to me, and I have profited by his instruction unceasingly." So, properly, Martínez Sierra had already served an apprenticeship in the theatre before he began to write plays. His début as a playwright was delayed for ten years, and was then made in collaboration with Rusiñol, with whom he composed a comedy entitled *Vida y dulzura,* presented at the Teatro de la Comedia, Madrid, in 1907. This was followed by *Aucells de pas,* also in collaboration with Rusiñol, produced in Catalan at Barcelona in 1908, and, after a further interval of two years, by *Cors de dona,* in Catalan by the same hands. Meanwhile, during the spring of 1909, Martínez Sierra attained his first independent success with the comedy in two acts, *La sombra del padre,* presented at the Lara Theatre, one of the favorite houses of the capital. *El ama de la casa,* ("The Mistress of the House,") was acted at the same theatre in 1910, and in 1911 he achieved a definitive and permanent triumph with the production of "The Cradle Song," (*Canción de cuna*). A companion piece *Los pastores,* ("The Two Shepherds"), was brought out in 1913, also at the Lara. As Martínez Sierra's non-dramatic prose becomes most nicely expressive, most pictorial and most imaginative in *Sol de la tarde,* his comedy attains perfection in these beautiful idyls of the religious life. Radiant with the bland charm and luminosity of the Andalusian sketches of the Quinteros, these comedies possess, nevertheless, a quality which is distinctive and personal, at once richer and humanly more significant than the work of any competitors in the *genre.* No other plays convey so convincingly, or with equal grace, the implications of environment as it interprets itself in terms of character, not symbolically nor in any didactic way, but directly and visually so that the ambient becomes the protagonist rather than the individual, and the spirit

of the *milieu* is felt to express more clearly than words the
fundamentals which condition its life.

"The Cradle Song" has been translated into many
languages, and has been played and imitated widely throughout the civilized world. Ten years after the Madrid pre-
miere Augustin Duncan hazarded four special matinees in
English at the Times Square Theatre, New York, beginning in February, 1921, without, however, attracting support. A play in two acts was held to be revolutionary by
the consensus of experts, and was thought to fall wholly
without the purlieus of drama. During the same season
a slighter piece, "The Romantic Young Lady" (*Sueño de
una noche de agosto*), reached the London stage with Dennis
Eadie, achieving a *succès d'estime*. The publication of the
plays in translation fortunately attracted general attention,
and it was not long before the wisdom of the pioneers had
been justified. On November 2, 1926, "The Cradle Song"
reappeared at the Fortune Theatre, London, with Miss
Gillian Scaife, to be later transferred to the Little Theatre,
where it completed a run of 109 performances, while Miss
Eva LeGallienne brought her singularly fine and sensitive
interpretation to the Civic Repertory Theatre, New York,
during the following January, where it has been repeated
125 times. A special company headed by Miss Mary Shaw
later travelled throughout the United States. Productions
at the Playhouses of Oxford and Liverpool and the Abbey
Theatre, Dublin, also deserve mention. Meanwhile "The
Romantic Young Lady" was revived at the Neighborhood
Playhouse, New York, with Miss Mary Ellis, "The Lover"
presented at the Fortune Theatre and on tour through
England and Scotland, and "Madame Pepita" at the Playhouse, Oxford and the Festival Theatre, Cambridge. "Love
Magic," the first piece by Sierra to be acted in English
(Waldorf-Astoria, New York, March 1918), "Poor John",
"The Two Shepherds" and "Wife to a Famous Man" are
all familiar in the little theatres of Great Britain and

America. Finally, during the fall of 1927, Miss Scaife and Mr. Eadie brought "The Kingdom of God" to the Strand Theatre, and the same play, staged and directed by Miss Ethel Barrymore, was recently chosen to inaugurate the new Ethel Barrymore Theatre in this city in December, 1928.

Martínez Sierra has now written some forty-six original plays which have been acted, in addition to the three composed in collaboration with Rusiñol. He has translated and adapted forty-seven plays, chiefly from the French, English and Catalan, besides making occasional excursions into German. Perhaps the most important translation is a five-volume edition of Maeterlinck. His non-dramatic works occupy thirty-two volumes to which six others of translations must be added. In the intervals of composition, he established and edited *Helios,* a short-lived literary periodical, and founded and directed the *Biblioteca Renacimiento,* one of the most prosperous and progressive publishing houses of the capital. He has also edited a library for the world's classics in translation, and more recently has established a publishing house of his own, the *Biblioteca Estrella.* In 1916 he assumed the management of the Teatro Eslava, Madrid, installing there a stock company, the *Compañía Lírico-Dramática Gregorio Martínez Sierra,* for the presentation of the modern repertory, prominently featuring his own plays. Whether from the point of view of acting or of *mise en scène,* this company must be accounted one of the most complete and satisfying in the peninsula. A Parisian engagement was undertaken successfully in 1925, and the company has since twice visited America, appearing first in a repertory of eighteen plays upon a tour extending from Buenos Aires to New York, terminating at the Forrest Theatre in May 1927. An admirably printed and illustrated selection of monographs, *Un teatro de arte en España,* records the story of Sierra's tenancy of the Eslava and renders adequate tribute to Catalina Bárcena, the gifted and versatile actress around whom from the beginning the company has been built.

An artist who is subjected continually to the distractions of business, sacrifices with his leisure opportunity for detachment. Already, previous to the production of *Los pastores,* Martínez Sierra had manifested a tendency to approximate the main currents of the modern popular theatre. An improviser of unusual facility, he composed the slightest of musical comedies in *Margot* and *La Tirana;* a charming light opera libretto, *Las golondrinas* ("The Swallows"), based upon an earlier play, *Aucells de pas;* grand opera libretto in *La llama,* and the scenario of a dancing suite with music by Manuel de Falla for the gypsy *bailarina* Pastora Imperio. He remade old comedies, reworked juvenilia, republished forgotten stories, and dramatised his novel *Tú eres la paz* as *Madrigal.* He contrived pantomime. The lesser plays of this miscellaneous epoch become an epitome of the activities of the contemporary Madrid stage, broadened, however, by a thorough cosmopolitanism. They are eclectic, light-hearted, persistently gay, and, upon the more serious side, progressive documents considered from the sociological point of view. As he has grown older, Martínez Sierra has come to be interested not so much in the picturesque, in the life which is about to pass, as it lies inert in the present with all the remoteness of objective art, as he is in the future with its promise of the amelioration of the life which he formerly portrayed. He is an apostle of the new order, which is to be assured in his conception through the dissemination of a wider and more complete knowledge, a more truly international culture and sympathy, a keener social consciousness, and, more precisely and immediately, through the promotion of certain reforms. The more significant of the recent comedies, "The Kingdom of God" and *Esperanza nuestra* ("The Hope That is Ours") are indicative of this development. Although by no means didactic, they are purely social in genesis and in trend. Even his *Don Juan de España,* a re-embodiment of the traditional libertine celebrated by Tirso de Molina and by Zorrilla, is a Don Juan redeemed. Yet Sierra remains essentially a man of the theatre. As a social thinker, his ideas are general, by no chance controversial, rising little beyond a broad humanitarianism, temperately and engagingly expressed. "Letters to the Women of Spain," "Feminism, Femininity and the Spanish Spirit," and "The Modern Woman," all volumes of frankly confessed propaganda, are more effective because they persuade rather than provoke, avoiding partisan commitments or advocacies of any sort. They are quite as dispassionately impersonal as the plays. In these maturer works, as in those of Linares Rivas and Benavente, the modern movement, which during the earlier years of the century had been predominantly intellectual and aesthetic, turns toward the practical and political sphere, and fixes its attention upon results. It is the completion of the cycle which began in 1898.

Thirty years have slipped by since the publication of "The Song of Labor." Martínez Sierra is no longer a young man of promise. Soon he will be counted among the elders whose art has matured and attained its full extension, consolidated and ripened by experience. It is now possible to appraise his accomplishment and to determine with relative certainty his contribution to the contemporary theatre.

In this task, the secrets of a collaboration as intimate as it has been enduring, must of necessity be respected. We have no work avowedly solely by Martínez Sierra. Only one has been acknowledged by his wife as her own. Obviously, the letters and lectures in promotion of feminism are at least in great part by a feminine hand. Beyond question she is responsible for the major share of translation. An increasing proportion of the later output, also, may safely be attributed to her, more especially the collaborations with the poet Marquina and the actor Sassone,

carried on during the absence of the Sierra troupe in America.
Then "The Cradle Song" is a reminiscence of María's
youth in Carabanchel, a town in which her father was convent doctor and where her sister took the veil, the Sister
Joanna of the Cross of the play. Her intervention here
has been confessed publicly. Yet these facts, though con-
ceded, shed no light upon the basic problem, and provide
no data for the identification of individual styles. A study
of the earlier poems and stories might seem, indeed, to in-
dicate that the elaboration and the subsequent simplification
of the style are predominantly to be credited to Gregorio,
while the bulk of actual composition—and to an increasing
extent with the passing years—has been done by María.

Like the Quinteros, Sierra is primarily an optimist, a
child of the sun. This is fundamental in his theatre and
has not escaped the attention of the Spanish humorists:
"Glory to God in the highest,
    On earth peace, good will toward men!
    All's well with the world, says Martínez Sierra,
    And then says it again."
He is not, however, an optimist by virtue of high spirits
or uncommon enthusiasms, or because he has found life
pleasant and easy, but through his sensitiveness. It is an
optimism that is partly aesthetic, partly emotional. His
sympathies have led him to hope. He has faith in the human
equation, trust in men rather than in measures. The law
he esteems very little in face of the gentle wisdom whose
increment is sure with the years. Social progress is individual progress and individual progress is spiritual progress whose conquests are recorded first in the heart. This,
of course, is no new doctrine, but it is the core of Martínez
Sierra's philosophy and the main-spring of his art. In so
far as the Church is a liberating and humanizing force he
is a Christian, but he is a dissenter from all creeds and
doctrines which restrict and inhibit the upward march of
man.

Curiously enough, as a playwright, Sierra, for all his tenderness, has little concern with the individual. This is the source of his calm. One of the most sensitive of men, he is also one of the most detached. His drama is expository, chiefly for the reason that the inception of his plays is invariably generic and abstract. They are illustrative each of some general axiom or principle, whether human or social. He is no apostle of personal causes. Every man must be suffered, none the less, to shape his own career—"Live Your Own Life." The old virtues are destined to make way before the advance of the new—"The Two Shepherds." Sometimes, again, he has paused to probe some universal passion or emotion, devotion as in "The Lover", or, as in "The Cradle Song", to echo the cry of the eternal mother instinct which has been stifled and denied. Sometimes, as in "Fragile Rosina", in a sportive mood, he is content to parade mere temperament or an idle trait. Plays like "The Cradle Song" and "The Kingdom of God" are eloquent too, above the plane of feeling, of a social scheme, a new, a better life. The course of the story is the setting forth of the idea, the impelling emotion in all its significant phases, now by direct statement, now through contrast, but, in whatever way it may be effected, the content is plainly implicit in the theme from the beginning to become evident in detail as the action proceeds. For this reason the volitional element, in so far as it passes beyond mere childish caprice, is almost wholly lacking. Sierra draws no villains, creates no supermen, heroically imposing their wills, inherits no complexes, and cherishes small love for the tricks of display. His taste is unfailingly nice. Mystery, however veiled, he abhors, complication of plot, all thrill of situation. He even flees those internal crises of character which are so absorbing to the great dramatists, through whose struggles personality is built up and self-mastery won. These savor always of violence and conflict, no matter how subjective or subtle they may be. They are drama of action, and Sierra's drama is static drama. He is content to sacrifice movement to visual quality, excitement to charm.

Although indubitably theatre of ideas, characteristically and fundamentally this is emotional theatre. It is live and warm. Naturally the spectacular ardors which have been associated time out of mind with the so-called emotional play have been discarded. Yet there is no more skilful purveyor of tears. The feeling is always direct, the presentation transparently clear. The playwright displays the intuitive grace of simple truth. The spectator sees and is persuaded without argument at sight. Life is depicted as a process of adjustment, a pervading harmony which influences the characters and tempers them to its key, so that they are never suffered to become intellectualized. This is the most extraordinary of Sierra's gifts. His men and women remain spontaneously human, unchilled by the ideas in which they have previously been conceived. Standing by themselves, it is true, they betray a tendency to pale and grow thin, because, like the action, they have been born of the theme, and acquire substance and vitality only as they fit into the general plan and merge themselves with the incidents and scenes which reflect their life history. It is an art compact of simplicities, so delicate and frail that it can exist authentically only at propitious moments. Every element must concur in the perfection of the whole. Absolute unity is indispensable. Character must synchronize with theme, dialogue with action, situation with background, until each at last becomes articulate in the other, through every shade of feeling and the concord of smiles and tears. Otherwise the spell is shattered and ceases to be. Comedy and pathos join as one. Sierra's art is a blending of the more tractable emotions, of technical elements and all the ingredients which go to make up a play, that is so complete as not to stop short of interpenetration. To achieve less for him means failure. In the rehearsal of memory, the people of the plays do not recur to the mind, nor the stories, nor any fragments nor striking features, but the atmosphere, the feeling, the impression of the ensembles. The plays live as emotion, pictures.

When posterity comes to assess the fame of Martínez Sierra, the non-dramatic works, despite their undoubted merits, beyond peradventure will be set to one side. Time will ignore, also, as it has already done in large measure, the purely theatrical, occasional pieces contrived to meet the needs of aspiring actors or to tide over the exigencies of importunate companies, including specifically his own. There will remain a body of plays, considerable in bulk, and notable, at least superficially, in variety. A surprising amount of the best work must be assigned to the plays in one-act. Few have wrought more happily in miniature, or have qualified more instinctively in the lesser *genre*. The briefer pieces are without exception deft and tenuous, by their very nature peculiarly congenial to a temperament that is shy and retiring and a method that is tactful and restrained. Sierra's success has been unquestioned in this field. In two acts, he has shown equal facility, profiting in addition by the superior dignity and weight which are corollaries of the larger scale. "The Cradle Song" is Martínez Sierra, the epitome of his virtues and the confutation of his detractors, while into this group fall also the major number of his more serious efforts often, perhaps, only by limitation of subject inferior to those better known. In drama of greater extension and presumably more profound import, prolonged through three or more acts, he has been less impressive. The expository method here becomes treacherous, for either the play or the audience in the end is obliged to move. Confronted by this dilemma, Sierra falls back upon episode, and takes refuge in devices which temporize to sustain the interest, and at best are purely conventional. The most noteworthy of the longer plays such as "The Kingdom of God", are in consequence properly sequences of one-act units, carefully assembled and held together by a common subject or related, it may be, by a single character which runs its course through them all. Still they preserve unity of atmosphere, still they plead unobtrusively their causes and retain the freshness of their visual appeal, but the problem at full length is more complex, position and juxta-position of incident are not so potent nor so suggestive, while even the most skilfully graduated emotion proves unable ex-cept in the rarest instances to dispense with progressive action and a continuous story artfully unrolled. These are multiple dramas, spoken pageants. They are chronicles of the modern stage.

In the history of the theatre, only two names, Ramón de la Cruz and Quiñones de Benavente, both countrymen of Sierra's, have lived as creators of one-act plays. Sierra's title to fame has a broader basis. He has produced the pop-ular masterpiece of the two-act style, already secure as an international classic. He has written also more perfectly than his contemporaries the Spanish realistic comedy of at-mosphere, that gently sentimental, placid communion with patience and peace whose quiet falls like a benediction upon a restless world.

JOHN GARRETT UNDERHILL.

THE CRADLE SONG

COMEDY IN TWO ACTS
WITH AN
INTERLUDE IN VERSE

TEATRO LARA, MADRID
1911
TIMES SQUARE THEATRE, NEW YORK
1921

FORTUNE THEATRE, LONDON
1926

CIVIC REPERTORY THEATRE, NEW YORK
1927

TO JACINTO BENAVENTE

CHARACTERS

SISTER JOANNA OF THE CROSS, *18 years of age.*

TERESA, *aged 18.*

THE PRIORESS, *aged 40.*

THE VICARESS, *aged 40.*

THE MISTRESS OF NOVICES, *aged 36.*

SISTER MARCELLA, *aged 19.*

SISTER MARÍA JESÚS, *aged 19.*

SISTER SAGRARIO, *aged 18.*

SISTER INEZ, *aged 50.*

SISTER TORNERA, *aged 30.*

THE DOCTOR, *aged 60.*

ANTONIO, *aged 25.*

THE POET.

A COUNTRYMAN.

Also a Lay Sister, Two Monitors, and several other Nuns, as desired.

ACT I

A room opening upon the cloister of a Convent of Enclosed Dominican Nuns. The walls are tinted soberly; the floor is tiled. Three arches at the rear. In the right wall a large door with a wicket in it, leading to a passage communicating with the exterior. A grilled peephole for looking out. Above the door a bell which may be rung from the street. Beside the door an opening containing a revolving box, or wheel, on which objects may be placed and passed in from the outside without the recipient's being seen, or a view of the interior disclosed. Not far from this wheel, a pine table stands against one of the piers of the cloister. Ancient paintings relieve the walls. Through the arches the cloister garden may be seen, with a well in the middle; also a number of fruit trees, some greenery and a few rose bushes. Beneath the arches, potted flowers— roses, carnations, sweet basil, herb Louisa and balsam apple —together with a number of wooden benches and rush-seated chairs, and three arm chairs.

As the curtain rises THE PRIORESS *is discovered seated in the largest of the arm chairs, and* THE MISTRESS OF NOVICES *and* THE VICARESS *in the smaller ones, the former on the right, the latter on the left, well to the front. The other* NUNS *are grouped about them, seated also. The novices,* SISTER MARCELLA, SISTER JOANNA OF THE CROSS, SISTER MARÍA JESÚS *and* SISTER SAGRARIO *stand somewhat to the right,* SISTER JOANNA OF THE CROSS *occupying the centre of the stage. The* LAY SISTER *and* SISTER TORNERA *remain standing by the table at the rear.*

It is broad day light. The scene is one of cheerfulness and animation.

SISTER SAGRARIO. Yes, do! Do! Do let her read them!

5

SISTER MARCELLA. Yes, do Mother! Do say yes!

PRIORESS. Very well. You may read them then, since you have written them.

SISTER JOANNA OF THE CROSS. I am very much ashamed.

MISTRESS OF NOVICES. These are the temptations of self-love, my child.

VICARESS. And the first sin in the world was pride.

SISTER JOANNA OF THE CROSS. They are very bad. I know you will all laugh at me.

VICARESS. In that way we shall mortify your vanity.

MISTRESS OF NOVICES. Besides, since we are not at school here, all that our Mother will consider in them will be the intention.

PRIORESS. Begin. And do not be afraid.

SISTER JOANNA OF THE CROSS. [*Reciting.*] To our Beloved Mother on the day of her Blessed Saint—her birthday:

> Most reverend Mother,
> On this happy day
> Your daughters unite
> For your welfare to pray.
> We are the sheep
> Who under your care
> Are seeking out Heaven—
> The path that leads there.
> On one side the roses,
> On the other the thorn,
> On the top of the mountain
> Jesus of Mary born.
> To Jesus we pray
> Long years for your life,
> And of the Virgin María
> Freedom from strife;
> And may the years vie
> In good with each other,
> In holiness and joy,
> Our dearly-loved Mother!

[*The nuns applaud and all speak at once.*]

SOME. Good! Very good!

OTHERS. Oh, how pretty!

SISTER TORNERA. They are like the Jewels of the Virgin!

SISTER INEZ. [*Depreciatively.*] She has copied them out of a book.

SISTER JOANNA OF THE CROSS. [*Carried away by her triumph.*] Long live our Mother!

ALL. [*Enthusiastically.*] Long live our Mother!

PRIORESS. Come, you must not flatter me, my children. The verses are very pretty. Many thanks, my daughter. I did not know that we had a poet in the house. You must copy them out for me on a piece of paper, so that I may have them to read.

SISTER JOANNA OF THE CROSS. They are copied already, reverend Mother. If your Reverence will be pleased to accept them . . .

[*She offers her a roll of parchment, tied elaborately with blue ribbons. The verses are written on the parchment and embellished with a border of flowers, doves and hearts, all of which have been painted by hand.*]

PRIORESS. [*Taking and unrolling the parchment.*] Bless me! What clear writing and what a beautiful border! Can you paint too?

SISTER JOANNA OF THE CROSS. No, reverend Mother. Sister María Jesús copied out the verses, and Sister Sagrario painted the border. Sister Marcella tied the bows.

SISTER MARCELLA. So it is a remembrance from all the novices.

PRIORESS. And all the while I knew nothing about it! The children have learned how to dissimulate very skilfully.

SISTER JOANNA OF THE CROSS. We had permission from

Mother Anna St. Francis.   She gave us the ribbon and the parchment.

PRIORESS.   No wonder, then.   So the Mother Mistress of Novices knows also how to keep secrets?

MISTRESS OF NOVICES.   Once . . . Only for to-day. . .

SISTER JOANNA OF THE CROSS.   Today you must forgive everything.

PRIORESS.   [*Smiling.*]   The fault is not a grave one.

VICARESS.   [*Acridly.*]   Not unless it leads them to pride themselves upon their accomplishments.   The blessed mother Santa Teresa de Jesús never permitted her daughters to do fancy work.   Evil combats us where we least expect it, and ostentation is not becoming in a heart which has vowed itself to poverty and humility.

MISTRESS OF NOVICES.   Glory be to God, Mother Vicaress, but why must your Reverence always be looking for five feet on the cat?

[SISTER MARCELLA *laughs flagrantly.*]

VICARESS.   That laugh was most inopportune.

SISTER MARCELLA.   [*Pretending repentance, but still continuing to laugh in spite of herself.*]   I beg your pardon, your Reverence, I didn't mean it.   This sister has such temptations to laugh, and she can't help it.

VICARESS.   Biting your tongue would help it.

SISTER MARCELLA.   Don't you believe it, your Reverence.   No indeed it wouldn't!

PRIORESS.   [*Thinking it best to intervene.*]   Come, you must not answer back, my daughter.   Today I wish to punish nobody.

VICARESS.   [*Muttering.*]   Nor today, nor never!

PRIORESS.   [*Aroused.*]   What does your Reverence mean by that, Mother Vicaress?

VICARESS.   [*Very meekly.*]   What we all know, reverend Mother—that the patience of your Reverence is inexhaustible.

PRIORESS. Surely your Reverence is not sorry that it is so?

VICARESS. [*Belligerently.*] Not upon my account, no. For by the grace of God I am able to fulfil my obligation and accommodate myself to the letter and spirit of our holy rule. But there are those who are otherwise, who, encouraged by leniency, may stumble and even fall . . .

PRIORESS. Has your Reverence anything definite in mind to say? If so, say it.

VICARESS. I have noticed for some time—and the Lord will absolve me of malice—that these "temptations to laugh" of which Sister Marcella speaks, have been abounding in this community; and these, taken with other manifestations of self-indulgence, not any less effervescent, are signs of a certain relaxation of virtue and deportment.

PRIORESS. I hardly think we need trouble ourselves upon that account. Providence has been pleased of late to bring into our fold some tender lambs, and perhaps they do frisk a little sometimes in the pastures of the Lord. But the poor children mean no harm. Am I right in your opinion, Mother Mistress of Novices?

MISTRESS OF NOVICES. You are always right in my opinion, reverend Mother. *Gaudeamus autem in Domino!*

VICARESS. Your Reverences of course know what you are doing. I have complied with my obligation.

[*The bell rings at the entrance.* SISTER TORNERA, *who is an active little old woman, goes up to the grille and looks through it, after first having made a reverence to the* PRIORESS.]

SISTER TORNERA. *Ave Maria Purissima!*

A VOICE. [*Outside, hoarse and rough.*] Conceived without sin. Is it permitted to speak with the Mother Abbess?

SISTER TORNERA. Say what you have need of, brother.

VOICE. Then here's a present for her from my lady, the

mayor's wife, who wishes her happiness, and sends her this present, and she's sorry she can't come herself to tell her; but she can't, and you know the reason . . . [*The* PRIORESS *sighs, lifting up her eyes to heaven, and the others do the same, all sighing in unison.*] And even if she could on that account, she couldn't do it, because she's sick in bed, and you know the reason . . .

SISTER TORNERA. God's will be done! Can the poor woman get no rest? Tell her that we will send her a jar of ointment in the name of the blessed Saint Clara, and say that these poor sisters never forget her in their prayers. They pray every day that the Lord will send her comfort. [*She turns the wheel by the grille, and a basket appears, neatly covered with a white cloth.*] Ah!—and the reverend Mother thanks her for this remembrance. And may God be with you, brother. [*Approaching the others with the basket, which she has taken from the wheel.*] Poor lady! What tribulations our Lord sends into this world upon the cross of matrimony!

PRIORESS. And to her more than anybody. Such a submissive creature, and married to a perfect prodigal!

MISTRESS OF NOVICES. Now that we are on the subject, your Reverences, and have the pot by the handle, so to speak, do your Reverences know that the blasphemies of that man have completely turned his head? You heard the bells of the parish church ringing at noon yesterday? Well, that was because the mayor ordered them to be rung, because in the election at Madrid yesterday the republicans had the majority.

ALL. God bless us! God bless us!

VICARESS. Did the priest give his consent to that?

SISTER INEZ. The priest is another sheep of the same color—he belongs to the same flock, may the Lord forgive me if I lack charity! Didn't your Reverences hear the sacrilege he committed upon our poor chaplain, who is holier than God's bread? Well, he told him that he was

more liberal than the mayor, and that the next thing he
knew, when he least expected it, he was going to sing the
introitus to the mass to the music of the Hymn of Riego!

PRIORESS. Stop! Enough! It is not right to repeat
such blasphemies.

MISTRESS OF NOVICES. Yes, calumnies invented by un-
believers, the evil-minded . . .

SISTER INEZ. No such thing! Didn't Father Calixtus
tell me himself while he was dressing for mass this morning? We'll have to put a new strip pretty soon down the
middle of his chasuble.

PRIORESS. What? Again?

SISTER INEZ. Yes. It's all worn out; it looks terribly. Poor Father Calixtus is so eloquent! Pounding on
his chest all the time, he simply tears the silk to pieces.

VICARESS. God's will be done, the man is a saint!

PRIORESS. And all this while we have been forgetting
the present from the mayor's wife. Bring it nearer,
Sister.

SISTER SAGRARIO. Mercy! What a big basket!

SISTER TORNERA. It's very light, though.

SISTER INEZ. Ha! It's easy to see what sister has a
sweet tooth!

SISTER MARÍA JESÚS. As if she didn't like sweets!
[*Aside.*]

SISTER MARCELLA. Now, Sister Inez, what did we see
you doing this morning? You know we caught you licking the cake pan yourself.

SISTER INEZ. I? Licking the pan? Your Sister licking the pan? Oh, what a slander! *Jesús!*

PRIORESS. Come, you must not be displeased, Sister
Inez; for it was said only in pleasantry. Ah, Sister Marcella! Sister Marcella! Do have a little more circum-
spection and beg your Sister's pardon.

SISTER MARCELLA. [*Kneeling before* SISTER INEZ.]
Pardon me, Sister, as may God pardon you, and give me

your hand to kiss as a penance for having offended you.

PRIORESS. That is the way my children should behave, humbly and with contrition. Sister Inez, give Sister Marcella your hand to kiss, since she begs it of you so humbly.

SISTER MARCELLA. [*Spitefully, after kissing her hand.*] *Ay!* But what a smell of vanilla you have on your fingers, Sister! Goody! We're going to have cookies for lunch. [*The others laugh.*]

SISTER INEZ. [*Irritated, almost in tears.*] Vanilla? God-a-mercy! Vanilla! Look at me! Do my fingers smell of vanilla?

PRIORESS. [*Imposing silence.*] Surely the devil must be in you, Sister Marcella, and may God forgive you for it! Go and kneel in the corner there with your face to the wall, and make the cross with your arms while you repeat a greater station. May the Lord forgive you for it!

SISTER MARCELLA. Willingly, reverend Mother.

SISTER INEZ. [*Rubbing her hands under her scapular.*] Too bad! Too bad! *Ay! Ay! Ay!*

SISTER MARCELLA. [*Aside.*] Old box of bones!
[*She goes and kneels in the corner, right, but keeps smiling and turning her head while she lets herself sink back on her heels, as if not taking the penance too seriously.*]

PRIORESS. You may uncover the basket now, Sister. Let us see what is in it.

SISTER TORNERA. With your permission, reverend Mother. Why! It's a cage!

SISTER SAGRARIO. With a canary in it!

ALL. A canary! A canary! Why, so it is! Let me see! How lovely!

MISTRESS OF NOVICES. Isn't it pretty?

SISTER MARÍA JESÚS. The dear! Isn't it cunning, though?

SISTER JOANNA OF THE CROSS. It looks as if it were made of silk.

SISTER INEZ. I wonder if it can sing?

PRIORESS. Of course it can sing. The mayor's wife would never send us a canary that couldn't sing.

SISTER SAGRARIO. What a beautiful cage! Why, there's a scroll on the front!

MISTRESS OF NOVICES. That isn't a scroll. It has letters on it.

SISTER MARÍA JESÚS. Why, so it has! Look and see what they say.

MISTRESS OF NOVICES. "The Convent of Dominican Nuns!"

SISTER INEZ. [Laughing.] I'd call that a pretty airy convent!

VICARESS. The good woman is holier than God's bread.

PRIORESS. She could not have sent me anything that would have pleased me better. I have always been anxious to have a canary.

SISTER INEZ. The Carmelite Sisters have two lovely canaries, and they say last year on Holy Thursday they hung them in the door of the tomb they have in the church for Easter, and it was like a miracle to hear them sing.

MISTRESS OF NOVICES. Then if ours sings, we can hang him in the church this year, and take the music box away.

PRIORESS. No, for the music box is a present from the chaplain, and he would rightly be offended. We will have the box and the canary there together, and when we wind up the box, it will encourage the bird to sing.

SISTER JOANNA OF THE CROSS. Oh, look at him now —he's taking his bath!

SISTER SAGRARIO. See how he jumps.

PRIORESS. What wonders God performs!

VICARESS. And yet there are misguided creatures who pretend that the world made itself!

SISTER INEZ. Sister Marcella stuck her tongue out at me.

SISTER MARCELLA. Oh, reverend Mother! I did nothing of the kind!

VICARESS. How nothing of the kind? Didn't I see it with my own eyes? And I was struck dumb!

SISTER MARCELLA. I said nothing of the kind . . . as . . . as that I had stuck my tongue out at Sister Inez. I stuck it out because there was a fly on the end of my nose, and since I had my arms out making the cross, I had to frighten him away with something.

SISTER JOANNA OF THE CROSS. Reverend Mother, since this is your Saint's day, won't you please excuse Sister Marcella this time?

SISTER MARÍA JESÚS. Yes, reverend Mother! I am sure she won't do anything that's wrong again.

PRIORESS. Sister Inez is the one who has been offended, and she is the only one who has the right to request her pardon.

NOVICES. She does! She does! You do, don't you, Sister Inez?

SISTER INEZ. [*With a wry face.*] Your Reverence will pardon her when your Reverence thinks best.

PRIORESS. Then come here, my erring daughter.—She knows that I pardon her because of the day, and so as not to spoil the pleasure of her sisters.

SISTER MARCELLA. May God reward you, reverend Mother!

PRIORESS. And set your veil straight, for this is the Lord's house, and it looks as if you were going on an excursion.—And now to your cells, every one. (*To the* NOVICES.) What are you whispering about?

SISTER SAGRARIO. We were not whispering, Mother . . . We wanted to ask you something.

SISTER MARÍA JESÚS. And we are afraid to do it.

PRIORESS. Is it as bad as that?

SISTER MARÍA JESÚS.   No, it isn't bad.   But——
SISTER JOANNA OF THE CROSS.   Your Reverence might think so.

PRIORESS.   I might?   I am not so evil-minded.

SISTER SAGRARIO.   I . . . I . . . Our Mother Mistress will tell you.

MISTRESS OF NOVICES.   They mean me.—Do you want me to?

NOVICES.   Yes!   Yes!   Do!

MISTRESS OF NOVICES.   With God's help I will try. Though I don't know for certain, I think what they want is for your Reverence to give them permission to talk a little, while they are waiting for the beginning of the *fiesta*.   Am I right?

NOVICES.   Yes!   Yes!   You are!   Do, Mother, do!

SISTER MARCELLA.   Long live our Mother!

PRIORESS.   Silence!   Silence!   What?   Haven't they had talking enough to-day after the dispensation I allowed them this morning?

VICARESS.   The appetite always grows by what it feeds on.   It is an unruly monster, and woe to her who gives it rein.   If they came under my authority, I would not give them opportunity to make a single slip, for the holy Apostle Saint James has said and well said: "He who saith that he hath not offended by his tongue, lies."

SISTER MARCELLA.   Ah, Sister Crucifixion!   Don't spoil this holiday for our Mother.

VICARESS.   Spoil it, eh?   Who pays any attention to what I say in this house?

PRIORESS.   Will you promise not to whisper nor offend the Lord with foolish talk?

NOVICES.   We promise.

PRIORESS.   Then you may talk as much as you like until the hour for prayers.

NOVICES.   Thanks, thanks!   [*The bell rings at the entrance twice.*]

SISTER TORNERA. Two rings! The doctor!

PRIORESS. Cover your faces. [*The nuns lower their veils over their faces.*] And pass out through the cloister. [*The nuns begin to file out slowly and disappear through the cloister.*]

SISTER SAGRARIO. [*Approaching the* PRIORESS.] This Sister has a felon, reverend Mother.

PRIORESS. Remain then—and you too, Sister María Jesús. [*To* SISTER TORNERA.] Open, Sister. [THE PRIORESS, SISTER TORNERA, SISTER SAGRARIO *and* SISTER MARÍA JESÚS *remain.* SISTER TORNERA *unchains, unbolts and opens the door. The* DOCTOR *enters. He is about sixty years of age.*]

SISTER TORNERA. *Ave Maria Purissima!*

DOCTOR. Conceived without sin. [*He comes in.*] Good morning, Sister.

SISTER TORNERA. Good morning, Doctor.

DOCTOR. Well, what progress are we making in holiness today?

SISTER TORNERA. [*Laughing.*] Ho, ho, Doctor!

DOCTOR. Enough! Enough! No doubt, no doubt! [*Discovering the* PRIORESS.] Congratulations, Mother.

PRIORESS. What? A heretic, and yet you remember the days of the saints?

DOCTOR. You are the saint, Mother; you are the saint.

PRIORESS. Ah! You must not scandalize me before my novices.

DOCTOR. Novices? Where, where? I said so when I came in. I smell fresh meat.

PRIORESS. Don José! Don José!

DOCTOR. But I say no more. Come! To work! To work! . . . What is the trouble with these white lambs?

SISTER SAGRARIO. Your handmaid has a felon, Doctor.

DOCTOR. Eh? On the hand? And such a lovely hand! Well, we shall have to lance it, Sister.

SISTER SAGRARIO. [*Alarmed.*] What? Not now?

DOCTOR. No, tomorrow, Sister. Tomorrow, unless it yields first to a poultice and five *Pater nosters.* Remember, not one less!

SISTER SAGRARIO. [*In perfect earnest.*] No, Doctor.

DOCTOR. And this other one, eh?

PRIORESS. Ah, Doctor! She has been giving me a great deal of worry. She falls asleep in the choir; she sighs continually without being able to assign any reason; she cries over nothing whatever; she has no appetite for anything but salads . . .

DOCTOR. How old are you?

SISTER MARÍA JESÚS. Eighteen.

DOCTOR. How long have you been in this holy house?

SISTER MARÍA JESÚS. Two years and a half.

DOCTOR. And how many more do you remain before you come to profession?

SISTER MARÍA JESÚS. Two and a half more, if the Lord should be pleased to grant this unworthy novice grace to become his bride.

DOCTOR. Let me see the face.

PRIORESS. Lift your veil. [SISTER MARÍA JESÚS *lifts her veil.*]

DOCTOR. Hm! The Lord has not bad taste. A little pale, but well rounded, well rounded.

SISTER TORNERA. Don José! But who ever heard of such a doctor?

DOCTOR. So, we have melancholy then, a constant disposition to sigh, combined with loss of appetite—well, there is nothing else for it, Sister: a cold bath every morning and afterwards a few minutes' exercise in the garden.

SISTER TORNERA. [*Somewhat scandalized.*] Exercise? Don José!

DOCTOR. Unless we write at once home to her mother to hurry and fetch her and find us a good husband for her.

SISTER MARÍA JESÚS. Oh, Don José! But this Sister has taken her vows to the Church!

DOCTOR. Well, in that case cold water. There is nothing else for it. For melancholy at eighteen, matrimony or cold water.

SISTER SAGRARIO. [*Summoning her courage.*] You always talk so much about it, Doctor, why don't you get married yourself?

DOCTOR. Because I am sixty, daughter; and it is fifteen years since I have felt melancholy. Besides, whom do you expect me to marry when all the pretty girls go into convents?

PRIORESS. Doctor, doctor! This conversation will become displeasing to me.

DOCTOR. Is this all the walking infirmary?

SISTER TORNERA. Yes, Doctor.

DOCTOR. And the invalid? How is she?

SISTER TORNERA. She is the same to-day, Doctor. Poor Sister Maria of Consolation hasn't closed her eyes all night! Don't you remember? Yesterday she said she felt as if she had a viper gnawing at her vitals? Well, today she has a frog in her throat.

DOCTOR. Goodness gracious! Come, let me see, let me see. What a continual war the devil does wage against these poor sisters!—Long life, Mother, and happy days!

PRIORESS. Long life to you, Doctor. [*To* SISTER TORNERA.] Go with him, Sister, and meanwhile these children will take care of the gate. [SISTER TORNERA *takes a bell from the table and, her veil covering her face, precedes the* DOCTOR *through the cloister, ringing solemnly in warning. They disappear.*] I must repair to the choir; I fear that today I have fallen behind in devotion and prayer.

SISTER MARÍA JESÚS. Will your Reverence give us permission to call the others?

PRIORESS. Yes, call them; but be careful that you commit no frivolity. [*The* PRIORESS *goes out.*]

SISTER MARÍA JESÚS. [*Approaching one of the arches of the cloister.*] Sister Marcella! Sister Joanna of the Cross! Pst! Come out! We are watching the grille and we have permission to talk.

[SISTER MARCELLA *and* SISTER JOANNA OF THE CROSS *re-enter.*]

SISTER SAGRARIO. What shall we talk about?

SISTER JOANNA OF THE CROSS. Let Sister Marcella tell us a story.

SISTER MARCELLA. Yes, so that you'll all be shocked.

SISTER MARÍA JESÚS. *Ay!* We are not such hypocrites as that, Sister.

SISTER MARCELLA. Or so that Sister Sagrario can run and tell on us to the Mother Mistress.

SISTER SAGRARIO. Oh, thank you, Sister!

SISTER MARCELLA. It wouldn't be the first time either.

SISTER SAGRARIO. You needn't mind me, Sisters. I am going to sit here in the corner and work, and you can talk about whatever you please. I shan't hear you.

[*She takes a pair of pincers, some beads and a piece of wire out of her pocket, and sitting down in a corner, begins to string a rosary.*]

SISTER JOANNA OF THE CROSS. Oh, come on, Sister! Don't be foolish. [*They all surround her, and finally she allows herself to be persuaded, after many expressions of protest, like a small child who says "I won't play."*]

SISTER SAGRARIO. Why! If they haven't forgotten the canary!

SISTER MARCELLA. Poor thing! How do you like to be left in this nest of silly women, little fellow? Let's open the cage.

SISTER MARÍA JESÚS. What for?

SISTER MARCELLA.   So that he can fly away, silly, if he wants to.

SISTER SAGRARIO.   No, no!

SISTER MARÍA JESÚS.   Our Mother wouldn't like that.

SISTER MARCELLA.   He would like it, though.   Come on!   [*She opens the door of the cage.*]   Fly out, sweetheart!   Fly away, the world is yours.   You are free!

SISTER JOANNA OF THE CROSS.   He doesn't fly out.

SISTER MARÍA JESÚS.   He doesn't budge.

SISTER MARCELLA.   Stupid, don't you see what a bright, sunny day it is?

SISTER JOANNA OF THE CROSS.   They say canaries are born in cages and, see, now he doesn't care to fly away.

SISTER MARÍA JESÚS.   He'd rather stay shut up all his life like us nuns.

SISTER MARCELLA.   Then you're a great fool, birdie. [*She shuts the door of the cage.*]   God made the air for wings and He made wings to fly with.   While he might be soaring away above the clouds, he is satisfied to stay here all day shut up in his cage, hopping between two sticks and a leaf of lettuce!   What sense is there in a bird?   *Ay, Mother!*   And what wouldn't I give to be a bird!

SISTER JOANNA OF THE CROSS.   Yes!   What wouldn't you give to be a bird?

SISTER MARÍA JESÚS.   They say that the swallows fly away every year over the ocean, and nobody knows where they go.

SISTER SAGRARIO.   I often dream that I am flying in the night time—that is not flying, but floating—just floating in the air without wings.

SISTER SAGRARIO.   I often dream that I am running fast—oh so fast!—and that I am skipping down stairs, without ever touching my feet to the ground, or to the stairs.

SISTER SAGRARIO.   Isn't it nice, though?   And how dis-

appointed you are when you wake up and find out after
all that it isn't so, that it was only a dream!

SISTER MARCELLA. I have dreamed that dream so many
times, that now when I wake up, I hardly know whether
it is the truth or a dream.

SISTER JOANNA OF THE CROSS. What do you suppose it
is that makes you dream the same dream so many times?

SISTER MARCELLA. I don't know, unless it is because it
is the things you want to do, and you can't, and so you
do them in dreams.

SISTER MARÍA JESÚS. What nice things you want to
do!

SISTER SAGRARIO. But then what good would it be if
you could do them? For instance, if we had wings like
birds, where would we fly?

SISTER MARCELLA. I? I would fly to the end of the
world!

SISTER MARÍA JESÚS. I? To the Holy Land, to
Mount Calvary!

SISTER JOANNA OF THE CROSS. I would fly to Bethle-
hem and to the garden of Nazareth, where the Virgin lived
with the child.

SISTER SAGRARIO. How do you know that there is a
garden at Nazareth?

SISTER JOANNA OF THE CROSS. Of course there's a garden there, with a brook running by it. The song says
so:

> "The Virgin washed his garments
>   And hung them on the rose.
> The little angels sing
>   And the water onward flows" . . .

[*Simply.*] There was a garden, too, by our house in the
village, with a big rosebush on the border of a brook that
ran by it; and I used to kneel beside the brook, and sing

that song while I washed my baby brother's clothes, for there were seven of us children, and I was the oldest. [*Feelingly.*] And that's what I miss most! [*Drying her eyes with her hands.*] *Ay,* Mother! And I always cry when I think of that baby boy! But it isn't right, I know . . . He loved me more than he did mother, and the day that they took me away to the Convent, and I left home, he cried—he cried so that he nearly broke his little baby heart!

SISTER MARCELLA. I have a brother and a sister, but they are both older than I am. My sister married two years ago, and now she has a baby. [*With an air of importance.*] She brought him here once to show me.

SISTER JOANNA OF THE CROSS. [*Interrupting her, greatly interested.*] I remember. He stuck his little hand in through the grille and your sister kissed it. Did you ever think how soft babies' hands are? Whenever I take communion I try to think I am receiving our Lord as a little child, and I take and press him like this to my heart, and then it seems to me that he is so little and so helpless that he can't refuse me anything. And then I think that he is crying, and I pray to the Virgin to come and help me quiet him. And if I wasn't ashamed, because I know you would all laugh at me, I'd croon to him then, and rock him to sleep, and sing him baby songs.

[*The bell rings by the grille.*]

SISTER SAGRARIO. The bell! I wonder who it is?

SISTER JOANNA OF THE CROSS. Better ask. That's why they left us here.

SISTER MARÍA JESÚS. Who'll do it? I won't. I'm afraid.

SISTER SAGRARIO. So am I.

SISTER MARCELLA. You're not usually so bashful, I must say. I'll ask, though I was the last to enter the house. [*Going up to the grille, she says in a timid voice:*] *Ave Maria purissima!* [*A moment's silence.*] No one answers.

SISTER JOANNA OF THE CROSS. Try again. Say it louder.

SISTER MARCELLA. [*Raising her voice.*] *Ave Maria purissima!*

SISTER SAGRARIO. Nothing this time, either.

SISTER MARÍA JESÚS. [*Summoning her courage, in a high-pitched voice.*] *Ave Maria purissima!*
[*Another silence. The Novices look at each other in surprise.*]

SISTER MARCELLA. It is very strange.

SISTER MARÍA JESÚS. It must be spirits.

SISTER SAGRARIO. Oh, I'm afraid!

SISTER JOANNA OF THE CROSS. Nonsense! It's some little boy who has rung the bell on his way home from school, so as to be funny.

SISTER MARÍA JESÚS. Peep through the hole and see if anybody is there.

SISTER MARCELLA. [*Stooping down to look.*] No, nobody. But it looks as if there was something on the wheel. Yes . . .

SISTER JOANNA OF THE CROSS. Let me see! Yes . . . Can't you turn it? [*She turns the wheel, and a second basket appears, carefully covered with a white cloth like the first.*] A basket!

SISTER SAGRARIO. Another present for our Mother.

SISTER MARÍA JESÚS. Of course it is! And here's a paper tied fast to it.

SISTER JOANNA OF THE CROSS. [*Reading, but without unfolding the paper.*] "For the Mother Prioress."

SISTER SAGRARIO. Didn't I tell you?

SISTER MARCELLA. Somebody wants to give her a surprise.

SISTER JOANNA OF THE CROSS. I wonder if it's Don Calixtus, the chaplain?

SISTER MARCELLA. Of course it is, child!

SISTER MARÍA JESÚS. Or maybe it's the Doctor.

SISTER JOANNA OF THE CROSS. No. He was just here and he didn't say anything about it.

SISTER SAGRARIO. All the same it might be from him. Maybe he wants to keep it a secret.

SISTER MARÍA JESÚS. Let's take it off the wheel.

SISTER MARCELLA. [*Lifting and carrying it to the table.*] We'd better put it here by the canary. My! But it's heavy!

SISTER SAGRARIO. I wonder what it is?

SISTER MARCELLA. Lets lift the corner and see.

SISTER MARÍA JESÚS. No, for curiosity is a sin.

SISTER MARCELLA. What of it? Come on! Let's do it. Who will ever know? [*She lifts the corner of the cloth a little and starts back quickly with a sharp cry.*] *Ay!!*

SISTER JOANNA OF THE CROSS. [*Hurrying to look.*] *Jesús!*

SISTER MARÍA JESÚS. *Ave Maria!* [*Looking too.*]

SISTER SAGRARIO. [*Following.*] God bless us!

  [*The Convent is aroused at the cry of Sister Marcella. Presently* THE PRIORESS, THE VICARESS, THE MISTRESS OF NOVICES *and the other* NUNS *enter from different directions.*]

PRIORESS. What is the matter? Who called out?

VICARESS. Who gave that shout?

MISTRESS OF NOVICES. Is anything wrong? [*The four Novices, trembling, stand with their backs to the basket, their bodies hiding it completely.*]

VICARESS. It is easy to see it was Sister Marcella.

PRIORESS. What has happened? Speak! Why are you all standing in a row like statutes?

MISTRESS OF NOVICES. Has anything happened to you?

SISTER JOANNA OF THE CROSS. No, reverend Mother, not to us; but——

SISTER MARÍA JESÚS. No, reverend Mother; it's . . .

SISTER MARCELLA. Someone rang the bell by the wheel . . . and we looked . . . and there was nobody

there . . . and they left a basket . . . this basket . . . and
. . . and your sister had the curiosity to undo it . . .

VICARESS. Naturally, you couldn't do otherwise.

SISTER MARCELLA. And it's . . .

PRIORESS. Well? What is it?

SISTER MARCELLA. It's . . . I . . . I think it would
be better for your Reverence to look yourself.

PRIORESS. By all means! Let me see. [*She goes up
to the basket and uncovers it.*] *Ave Maria!* [*In a hoarse
whisper.*] A baby!

ALL. [*Variously affected.*] A baby? [*The* VICARESS,
horrified, crosses herself.]

PRIORESS. [*Falling back.*] Your Reverences may see
for yourselves. [*The* NUNS *hurry up to the basket and surround it.*]

VICARESS. *Ave Maria!* How can such an insignifi-
cant object be so pink?

MISTRESS OF NOVICES. It's asleep.

SISTER JOANNA OF THE CROSS. See it open its little
hands!

SISTER MARÍA JESÚS. Why! It has hair under the
edge of its cap!

SISTER SAGRARIO. It is like an angel!

VICARESS. A pretty angel for the Lord to send us.

SISTER JOANNA OF THE CROSS. [*As if she had been
personally offended.*] *Ay,* Mother Vicaress! You mustn't
say that.

PRIORESS. [*Tenderly.*] Where do you come from, little
one?

VICARESS. From some nice place, you may be sure.

PRIORESS. Who can tell, Mother? There is so much
poverty in the world, so much distress.

VICARESS. There is so much vice, reverend Mother.

MISTRESS OF NOVICES. You say that there was nobody
at the grille?

SISTER MARCELLA. Nobody; no, Mother. The bell
rang; we answered . . . but there was nobody there.

SISTER SAGRARIO. [*Picking up the paper which has fallen on the floor.*] Here is a paper which came with it.

PRIORESS. [*Taking the paper.*] "For the Mother Prioress."

VICARESS. An appropriate present for your Reverence.

PRIORESS. Yes, it is a letter.

[*She unfolds the paper and begins to read.*]

"Reverend Mother:

Forgive the liberty which a poor woman takes, trusting in your Grace's charity, of leaving at the grille this new-born babe. I, my lady, am one of those they call women of the street, and I assure you I am sorry for it; but this is the world, and you can't turn your back on it, and it costs as much to go down as it does to go up, and that is what I am writing to tell you, my lady. The truth is this little girl hasn't any father, that is to say it is the same as if she didn't have any, and I—who am her mother —I leave her here, although it costs me something to leave her; for although one is what one is, one isn't all bad, and I love her as much as any mother loves her baby, though she is the best lady in the land. But all the same, though she came into this world without being wanted by anyone, she doesn't deserve to be the daughter of the woman she is, above all, my lady, of her father, and I don't want her to have to blush for having been born the way she was, nor for having the mother she has, and to tell it to me to my face, and I pray you by everything you hold dear, my lady, that you will protect her and keep her with you in this holy house, and you won't send her to some orphanage or asylum, for I was brought up there myself, and I know what happens in them, although the sisters are kind—yes, they are—and have pity. And some day, when she grows up and she asks for her mother, you must tell her that the devil has carried her away, and I ask your pardon, for I must never show myself to her, nor see her again, nor give you any care nor trouble, so you can do this good work in peace, if you will do it, for I implore you again,

my lady, that you will do it for the memory of your own
dear mother, and God will reward you, and she will live
in peace, and grow up as God wills, for what the eyes have
not seen the heart cannot understand, my lady."

VICARESS. Bless us! *Ave Maria!*

MISTRESS OF NOVICES. Poor woman!

SISTER JOANNA OF THE CROSS. Baby dear! Darling
baby!

VICARESS. What pretty mothers the Lord selects for his
children!

PRIORESS. God moves in his own ways, Sister. God
moves in his own ways.

SISTER INEZ. Is that all the letter says?

PRIORESS. What more could it say?

[THE DOCTOR *and* SISTER TORNERA *have re-entered
during the reading.*]

DOCTOR. Exactly. What more could it say?

PRIORESS. What do you think, Don José?

DOCTOR. I think that somebody has made you a very
handsome present.

PRIORESS. But what are we going to do with it? Because I . . . this poor woman . . . she has put this poor
creature into our hands, and I would protect her willingly,
as she asks, and keep her here with us . . .

NOVICES. Yes, yes, Mother! Do! Do!

MISTRESS OF NOVICES. Silence!

PRIORESS. But I don't know if we can . . . that is, if
it is right, if it is according to law . . . for, when we
enter this holy rule, we renounce all our rights . . . and to
adopt a child legally . . . I don't know whether it can be
done. How does it seem to you?

DOCTOR. I agree with you. Legally, you have no right
to maternity.

VICARESS. And even if we had, would it be proper for
our children to be the offspring of ignominy and sin?

PRIORESS. I would not raise that question, reverend
Mother, for the child is not responsible for the sin in which

she was born, and her mother, in renouncing her mother-hood, has bitterly paid the penalty.

VICARESS. Yes, it didn't cost her much to renounce it.

PRIORESS. Do we know, Mother? Do we know?

VICARESS. We can guess. It is easy enough to go scattering children about the world if all you have to do is leave them to be picked up afterwards by the first person who happens along.

DOCTOR. How easy it is might be a matter for discussion. There are aspects of it which are not so easy.

SISTER SAGRARIO. Oh! She's opened her mouth!

SISTER JOANNA OF THE CROSS. The little angel is hungry.

SISTER MARÍA JESÚS. She's sucking her thumb!

SISTER JOANNA OF THE CROSS. Make her take her thumb out of her mouth. She'll swallow too much and then she'll have a pain.

SISTER SAGRARIO. Don't suck you fingers, baby.

SISTER JOANNA OF THE CROSS. Isn't she good, though? You stop her playing, and she doesn't cry.

PRIORESS. There is another thing we must consider. What are we to do for a nurse?

SISTER JOANNA OF THE CROSS. The gardener's wife has a little boy she is nursing now.

PRIORESS. In that case I hardly think she would care to be responsible for two.

SISTER JOANNA OF THE CROSS. But it won't be any trouble—she's so tiny! Besides, we can help her out with cow's milk and a little pap. The milk will keep on the ice and we can clear it with a dash of tea.

DOCTOR. It is easy to see Sister Joanna of the Cross has had experience with children.

SISTER JOANNA OF THE CROSS. Your handmaid has six little brothers and sisters. Ah, reverend Mother! Give her to me to take care of and then you will see how strong she'll grow up.

VICARESS. Nothing else was needed to complete the

demoralization of the Novices. You can see for your-
selves how naturally they take to this dissipation.
PRIORESS. I want you to tell me frankly what you think
—all of you. [*All speak at once.*]
MISTRESS OF NOVICES. Your Sister thinks, reverend
Mother . . .
SISTER TORNERA. Your handmaid . . .
SISTER INEZ. It seems to me . . .
PRIORESS. [*Smiling.*] But one at a time.
SISTER TORNERA. It is an angel which the Lord has
sent us, and your Sister thinks that we ought to receive her
like an angel, with open arms.
MISTRESS OF NOVICES. Of course we ought. Suppose,
your Reverences, it hadn't been a little girl, but . . . I
don't know—some poor animal, a dog, a cat, or a dove,
like the one which flew in here two years ago and fell
wounded in the garden trying to get away from those
butchers at the pigeon-traps. Wouldn't we have taken
it in? Wouldn't we have cared for it? And wouldn't
it have lived happy forever afterward in its cage? And
how can we do less for a creature with a soul than for a
bird?
SISTER TORNERA. We must have charity.
VICARESS. I am glad the Mother Mistress of Novices
has brought up the incident of that bird, for it will absolve
me from bringing it up, as it might seem, with some malice.
It was against my advice that that creature was received
into this house, and afterward we had good reason to regret it, with this one saying "Yes, I caught him!" and that
one, "No, I took care of him!" and another "He opens
his beak whenever I pass by!" and another, "See him flap
his wings! He does it at me!"—vanities, sophistries, de-
ceits all of them, snares of the devil continually! And if
all this fuss was about a bird, what will happen to us with
a child in the house? This one will have to dress it, that
one will have to wash it, another will be boasting, "It is
looking at me!" another that it's at her that it googles

most . . . There is Sister Joanna of the Cross making faces at it already!

SISTER JOANNA OF THE CROSS. What did your Reverence say?

VICARESS. Dissipation and more dissipation! Your Reverences should remember that when we passed behind these bars, we renounced forever all personal, all selfish affection.

MISTRESS OF NOVICES. Is it selfish to give a poor foundling a little love?

VICARESS. It is for us. Our God is a jealous God. The Scriptures tell us so.

MISTRESS OF NOVICES. Bless us! Mercy me!

VICARESS. And this quite apart from other infractions of our order which such indulgence must involve. For example, your Reverences—and I among the first—take no account of the fact that at this very moment we are transgressing our rule. We are conversing with our faces unveiled in the presence of a man.

PRIORESS. That is true.

DOCTOR. Ladies, as far as I am concerned—Take no account of me. . . .

PRIORESS. No, Doctor, you are of no account. I beg your pardon, Don José; I hardly know what I am saying.—Your Reverence is right. Cover yourselves—that is, it makes no difference . . . The harm has been done . . . only once. . . . But comply with your consciences . . . [*The* VICARESS *covers her face. The others, hesitating, wait for the* PRIORESS, *who makes a movement to do so, but then desists. The* VICARESS, *when she is covered, cannot see that she has become the victim of the rest.*] But where were we? I confess that my heart prompts me to keep the child.

VICARESS. The Doctor already has told us that we have no right to maternity.

MISTRESS OF NOVICES. But the child is God's child, and she is returning to her father's mansion.

VICARESS.   God has other mansions for his abandoned children.

SISTER JOANNA OF THE CROSS.   Don't send her to the asylum!

SISTER SAGRARIO.   No!

PRIORESS.   Her mother entreats us.

VICARESS.   Her mother is not her mother. She has abandoned her.

PRIORESS.   She has not abandoned her. She has entrusted her to others who seemed worthier to undertake her keeping.

VICARESS.   Unholy egotism!

MISTRESS OF NOVICES.   Christian heroism!

VICARESS.   So? We are coining phrases, are we? Is this a convent, or an illustrated weekly?

MISTRESS OF NOVICES.   Life is hard to some people, and thorny.

VICARESS.   Yes, and into the details of it, it is not becoming for us to go, since by the grace of God we have been relieved from the temptations and the frailties of the world.

MISTRESS OF NOVICES.   All the more, then, we ought to have compassion on those who have fallen and are down.

VICARESS.   Compassion? Mush and sentiment!

MISTRESS OF NOVICES.   The veil of charity!

PRIORESS.   Silence! And let us not begin by rending it, irritating ourselves and aggravating each other.—Don José, I suppose this birth will have to be reported?

DOCTOR.   It will, madam. To the Register.

SISTER JOANNA OF THE CROSS.   But then they will take her away?

DOCTOR.   If nobody wants her. But if you have made up your minds you would like to keep her, I think I can propose a solution.

PRIORESS.   A solution that is legal?

DOCTOR.   Perfectly. Thanks be to God I am a single man. But, although I am not a saint, yet I cannot take to myself the credit of having augmented the population of this country by so much as a single soul. I have not a penny, that is true, but like everybody else, I have a couple of family names. They are at the service of this little stranger, if they will be of use to her. She will have no father and no mother—I cannot help that—but she will have an honorable name.

PRIORESS. Do you mean to say?——

DOCTOR. That I am willing to adopt her; exactly— and to entrust her to your care, because my own house . . . The fact is the hands of Doña Cecilia are a little rough for handling these tiny Dresden dolls, and perhaps I might prove a bit testy myself. The neighbors all say that the air grows blue if my coat rubs against me as I walk down the street.

[*All laugh.*]

DOCTOR. Besides I am sure Sister Crucifixion is better equipped for the robing of saints.

VICARESS Doctor, God help us both!

DOCTOR. Is it agreed?

PRIORESS. God reward you for it! Yes, in spite of everything. We shall notify the Superior immediately. It is not necessary that the child should live in the cloister. She can remain with the gardener's wife until she has grown older, and enter here later when she has the discretion to do so. She has been entrusted to our hands, and it is our duty to take care of her—a duty of conscience.

DOCTOR. If I cannot be of further service, I will go. And I will speak to the Register.

PRIORESS. As you go, be so kind as to ask the gardener's wife to come in. We must see if she will take charge of the child and nurse her. And tell her also to bring with her some of her little boy's clothes.

SISTER JOANNA OF THE CROSS. Yes, for we shall have to make a change immediately.

SISTER SAGRARIO. We shall?

VICARESS. Not a change, but a beginning.

DOCTOR. Good afternoon, ladies.

ALL. Good afternoon, Don José. [*The* DOCTOR *goes out.*]

          [*A pause.*]

PRIORESS. Sisters, may God pardon us if we have acted in this with aught but the greatest purity of motive. I hope and pray that His grace will absolve us of offense, nor find us guilty of having loved too much one of His poor children. The child shall be brought up in the shadow of this house, for we may say that her guardian angel has delivered her at the door. From this hour forth we are all charged with the salvation of her soul. The Lord has entrusted to us an angel and we must return to Him a saint. Watch and pray.

ALL. Watch and pray. We will, reverend Mother.

PRIORESS. And now bring her to me, Sister Joanna of the Cross, for as yet it can scarcely be said that I have seen her. [*Looking at the child.*] Lamb of God! Sleeping as quietly in her basket as if it were a cradle of pure gold! What is it that children see when they are asleep that brings to their faces an expression of such peace?

SISTER JOANNA OF THE CROSS. They see God and the Virgin Mary.

SISTER MARÍA JESÚS. Maybe the angel who watches over them whispers in their ears and tells them about heaven.

PRIORESS. Who can say? But it is a comfort to the soul to see a child asleep.

SISTER MARÍA JESÚS. It makes you want to be a saint, reverend Mother.

SISTER SAGRARIO. Will your Reverence grant me permission to give her a kiss?

SISTER MARÍA JESÚS. Oh, no! For it hasn't been baptized yet, and it is a sin to kiss a heathen!

PRIORESS. She is right. We must send for the Chaplain and have her baptized immediately.

MISTRESS OF NOVICES. What shall we call her?

SISTER INEZ. Teresa, after our beloved Mother.

SISTER TORNERA. María of the Miracles.

SISTER SAGRARIO. Bienvenida. [*A large bell rings outside.*]

PRIORESS. The summons to the choir! We can decide later. Let us go. [*The* NUNS *file out slowly, looking at the child as they go.*] Remain with her, Sister Joanna of ·the Cross—you understand children; and wait for the coming of the gardener's wife. Follow the devotions from where you are, and do not let your attention falter.

[*All the* NUNS *go out, except* SISTER JOANNA OF THE CROSS, *who bends over the basket; then sinks on her knees beside it. The choir is heard within, led by a single* NUN *in solo, the responses being made in chorus, in which* SISTER JOANNA OF THE CROSS *joins. While the* NUN *is leading,* SISTER JOANNA OF THE CROSS *talks and plays with the child; then she makes her responses with the others.*]

VOICE WITHIN. *In nomine Patri et Filio et Spiritui Sancto.* [SISTER JOANNA OF THE CROSS *crosses herself and says with the other* NUNS:]

VOICES WITHIN AND SISTER JOANNA OF THE CROSS. *Amen!*

SISTER JOANNA OF THE CROSS. [*To the child.*] Pretty one! Pretty one!

VOICE WITHIN. *Deus in adjutorium meum intende.*

VOICES WITHIN AND SISTER JOANNA OF THE CROSS. *Domine ad adjuvandum me festina.*

SISTER JOANNA OF THE CROSS. [*To the child.*] Do you love me, sweetheart? Do you love me?

VOICE WITHIN. *Gloria Patri et Filio et Spiritui Sancto.*

VOICES WITHIN IN CHORUS. *Sicut erat in principio et nunc et semper et insecula seculorum. Amen! Allelulia!*

[*But this time* SISTER JOANNA OF THE CROSS *makes no response. Instead she bends over the basket, embracing the child passionately, oblivious of all else, and says:*]

SISTER JOANNA OF THE CROSS.   Little one!   Little one! Whom do you love?

CURTAIN

INTERLUDE

You came tonight to listen to a play;
Instead into a convent you made way.
Singular hardihood! Almost profanation!
What will a poet not do to create sensation?
Pardon, good nuns, him who disturbs the rest
And troubles the serene quietude of your nest,
Kindling amid the shades of this chaste bower
The flame of love you have renounced and flower.
Nay! Do not frown because I have said love,
For you must know, chaste brides of God above,
That which you have deemed charity and pity,
The act of mercy, clemency for the pretty,
Unfriended foundling fate has brought along,
Yearning of adoption and the cradle song,
No other is than love's fire, divine and human
Passion ever brooding in the heart of woman.

Ah, love of woman, by whose power we live,
Offend so often—but to see forgive!
Whence do you draw your grace but from above?
Whence simply? Simply from maternal love!
Yes, we are children, woman, in your arms;
Your heart is bread, you soothe our wild alarms,
Like children give us the honey of your breast,
In a cradle always your lover sinks to rest
Although he prostitutes our grovelling flesh.
Mother if lover, mother if sister too,
Mother by pure essence, day long and night through,
Mother if you laugh, or if with us you cry,

36

In the core of being, in fibre and in mesh,
Every woman carries, so God has willed on high,
A baby in her bosom, sleeping eternally!

So being women, you are lovers, nuns;
Despite the ceintured diamond which runs
Across your virgin shields, showing in your lives
How to be mothers without being wives.
And in this child of all, you have poured all
The honey of your souls, and blended all
The fire of the sun, all fragrance and all light,
The first sweet morning kiss, the last good-night,
Till all her being tenderness exhales,
Her heart the home of love and nightingales.
A hundred times a woman but no saint.
The nuns pray in the choir; outside her plaint
A song; her prayer, gay rippling laughter.
Mass and the May morning slip by, she running after
Or dreaming in the garden. The roses smell
So sweetly! No child this for the hermits' cell.
She loves Heaven, but in good company;
And before the altar of the Virgin see
Her with a boy, ruddier than the candle's flame,
Who calls her "Sister," the nuns "Aunt" for name.
A smiling, bashful boy, who soon will grow
To be a strong man, learn to give a blow
And take one, conquer worlds and redress wrong,
Justice in his heart, and on his lips a song!
Sometimes she takes the cat up, calls it "Dear!"
The nuns cross themselves, religiously severe.
"The child is mad," they say. Ah! No such thing!
With her into the convent entered Spring.

This then the simple story. The poet would
Have told it day by day, if well he could,
In shining glory. But the task were vain.
The glory of our daily lives is plain.

For life builds up itself in such a way,
The water runs so clear, so bright the day,
That time is lulled to sleep within these walls.
An age or moment? Which passes? Who recalls?
The wheel turns round, but no one notes the turn.
What matter if the sisters' locks that burn
With gold, in time to silvery gray have paled?
Their hoods conceal it. And the pinks have failed
In the cheeks, and the lilies on the brow.
There are no mirrors. The sisters then as now
May walk in the garden, believe it still is May.

Among these hours which softly slip away,
This timeless time, we shyly pause at that
In which there is most warmth, the concordat
Of youth and incense, breaking of the spring.
The years have passed, the child is ripening.
The curtain rises on a soul in flower,
And a love chapter claims us for an hour.
It is quiet afternoon, quiet breeding;
The nuns are sewing and their sister reading:

CHAPTER II

Parlor of a Convent.
At the rear, a grille with a double row of bars. A
curtain of dark woolen cloth hangs over the grille and inter-
cepts the view of the outer parlor, to which visitors are
admitted. This is without decoration, and may be brightly
illuminated at the proper moment from the garden. A
number of oil paintings of saints hang upon the walls—all
of them very old and showing black stains. With them
a carved crucifix or large black wooden cross. A small
window furnished with heavy curtains, which, when drawn,
shut off the light completely, is cut in the wall of the inner
parlor on either side of the grille, high up toward the
ceiling. A pine table, a carved arm chair, two other arm
chairs, smaller chairs and benches, together with all the
materials necessary for sewing.

THE PRIORESS, THE MISTRESS OF NOVICES, SISTERS
INEZ and TORNERA, SISTER SAGRARIO, SISTER JOANNA OF
THE CROSS, SISTER MARCELLA, SISTER MARÍA JESÚS and
the other NUNS are discovered upon the rise of the curtain.
Only THE VICARESS is absent. All are seated, sewing, with
the exception of SISTER MARÍA JESÚS, who stands in the
centre, to the left of THE PRIORESS'S chair, reading. A
bride's trousseau is spread out upon the table and chairs.
It is embroidered elaborately, trimmed with lace and tied
with blue silk ribbons. A new trunk stands against the
wall on the right, the trays being distributed about the
benches and upon the floor.

Eighteen years have passed. It must be remembered
that the NUNS have changed in appearance, and those who
were novices have now professed and have exchanged the
white for the black veil.

SISTER MARÍA JESÚS. [*Reading and intoning.*] "The Treasury of Patience, the Meditations of an Afflicted Soul in the presence of its God."

SISTER MARCELLA. [*Sighing.*] *Ay!*

SISTER MARÍA JESÚS. [*Reading.*] "First Meditation: The Sorrows of an Unhappy Spirit, Submerged in a Sea of Woe."

[*Outside,* TERESA'S *voice is heard, singing gaily.*]

TERESA.   "Come singing and bringing
            Flowers from the field,
            Flowers from the field,
            Sweet gardens, to Mary.
            Flowers you must yield
            For Love's sanctuary!"

[*The reader stops, and, smiling, glances in the direction of the window through which the voice is heard. The other* NUNS *smile also, complacently.*]

PRIORESS. [*With affected severity.*] The child interrupts us continually.

SISTER INEZ. And a day like to-day!

SISTER JOANNA OF THE CROSS. [*Sympathetically.*] She sings like a lark.

MISTRESS OF NOVICES. [*Indulgently.*] She is so young!

SISTER MARCELLA. *Ay,* Mother!

PRIORESS. Continue reading, Sister María Jesús.

SISTER MARÍA JESÚS. [*Reading.*] "The Sorrows of an Unhappy Spirit, Submerged in a Sea of Woe. My God, O my God, save me, for every moment I die! Overwhelmed, I sink in the midst of this terrible storm. Every moment I am buffeted and borne down. I am sucked into the uttermost depths, and there is no health in me!"

TERESA. [*Singing.*]
            "From the glory of your brightness,
                Radiantly sweet,
            O, let me stoop and bend me
                To kiss your feet!

> Let me stoop and bend me
>   To kiss your feet!"

[*Again the reader stops. The* NUNS *smile again.*]

PRIORESS. Sister Sagrario, will you step out into the garden and ask the child not to sing? We are reading.

[SISTER SAGRARIO *goes out, right, after making the customary reverence.*]

Continue, Sister, continue.

SISTER MARÍA JESÚS. [*Reading.*] "There is no health in me. I cannot support myself; I cannot resist the shock of the horrible onrushing waves."

TERESA. [*Singing.*]

> "You too were happy, Mary,
>   Happy in his love,
> Flowers of love and springtime
>   That bloom above!"

[*The song is broken off suddenly, as if the* NUN *had arrived and commanded* TERESA *to stop. A moment later, there is a sound of light laughter.*]

PRIORESS. It cannot be helped. [*Smiling.*] The child was born happy and she will die so. [*To the reader.*] Continue.

SISTER MARCELLA. *Ay,* Lady of Sorrows!

PRIORESS. But Sister Marcella, my daughter, why do you sigh like this? Are you unwell?

SISTER MARCELLA. No, reverend Mother. But your daughter has temptations to melancholy.

PRIORESS. The Lord protect and keep you. You know how it displeases me to see the shadow of melancholy enter this house.

SISTER MARCELLA. [*Making a reverence.*] *Ay,* reverend Mother, pardon me and assign me some penance if I sin, but your daughter cannot help it.

PRIORESS. Who was thinking of sin? Go out into the garden and take a little sunshine, daughter; that is what you need.

SISTER MARCELLA. *Ay,* reverend Mother, you don't

know what you say! For when your daughter sees the
flowers in the garden, and the blue sky so bright above
them, and the sun so beautiful overhead, the temptation
comes upon her then to sigh more than ever. *Ay!*

PRIORESS. If that is the case, return to your seat and
let us pray that it may cease. But do not let me hear
you sigh again, for I do not wish to send you to the prison
to brighten your spirit with solitude and confinement.

SISTER MARCELLA. As your Reverence desires. [*Returning to her seat.*] *Ay,* my soul! [THE PRIORESS *raises
her eyes to heaven in resignation.*]

A NUN. *Ay,* Blessed Virgin!

ANOTHER. *Ay, Jesús!*

PRIORESS. [*Somewhat ruffled.*] What? Is this an
epidemic? Nothing is wanting now but that we should begin to sigh in chorus. Remember, it is with gladness and
thanksgiving that the Lord is to be served *"in hymnis et
canticis,"* for the second of the fruits of the Spirit is joy and
there is none higher but love, from which it springs. [*A
Pause.* SISTER MARÍA JESÚS *reopens the book, and without waiting for the signal from the* PRIORESS, *resumes reading.*]

SISTER MARÍA JESÚS. [*Reading.*] "I cannot resist the
shock of the horrible onrushing waves. They break over
me unceasingly; irresistibly they bear me down."

PRIORESS. Close the book, Sister María Jesús, for the
blessed father who wrote it, alas, he too was of a melancholy
turn of mind! [SISTER MARÍA JESÚS *closes the book, makes
a reverence and sits down to sew.* THE MOTHER VICARESS
*appears in the door on the left, accompanied solemnly by
two other nuns.*]

VICARESS. [*Greatly agitated.*] *Ave Maria Purissima!*

PRIORESS. Conceived without sin.

VICARESS. Have I permission, reverend Mother?

PRIORESS. Enter and speak. [*Looking at her.*] If I
am not mistaken, your Reverence is greatly disturbed.

VICARESS. You are not mistaken, reverend Mother. No, and I dare affirm it is not for a slight reason. Your Reverence will be judge if this is the time and place to confront with a charge of *ipso facto* a member of this community.

PRIORESS. Speak, if the knowledge of the fault in public will not in itself constitute a scandal and a cause of offense.

VICARESS. In the opinion of your handmaid all cause of scandal will be avoided by looking the offense straight in the face.

PRIORESS. Speak then.

VICARESS. [*Making a profound inclination.*] I obey. Reverend Mother, while making the round of my inspection of the cells with these two monitors, as your Reverence has been pleased to command . . . [*The two* MONITORS each make a reverence.] And coming to the cell of Sister Marcella . . . [*All the* NUNS *look at* SISTER MARCELLA, *who lowers her eyes.*] I found under the mattress of the bed—in itself a suspicious circumstance and sufficient to constitute a sin—an object which should never be found in the hands of a religious, an object which, to say nothing of the sin against the rule of holy poverty which the private possession and concealment of any property whatever must presuppose, is by its very nature a root of perdition and an origin and source of evil.

PRIORESS. Conclude, Mother, in God's name! For you keep us in suspense. What is this object?

VICARESS. Disclose it, sister. [*To one of the* MONITORS.]

> [*The* MONITOR *makes a reverence, and draws from her sleeve a piece of glass, covered on one side with quick-silver.*]

PRIORESS. A piece of looking-glass.

VICARESS. Exactly, a piece of looking-glass! [*Horrified silence on the part of the community.*]

PRIORESS. What has Sister Marcella to say to this?

SISTER MARCELLA. [*Leaving her place and kneeling before the* PRIORESS.] Mother, I confess my guilt and I beseech your pardon.

PRIORESS. Rise. [SISTER MARCELLA *rises.*] Unhappy woman! What was the use of this piece of glass?

VICARESS. To look at herself in it, and amuse herself with the sight of her beauty, thus offending her Maker with pride and vain glory, and the exhibition of her taste.

SISTER MARCELLA. [*Humbly.*] No, reverend Mother; no!

VICARESS. Or else to dress herself up and fix herself by it, and make faces and grimaces such as they do on the streets in these days. [*The* VICARESS, *who has taken the mirror, looks at herself in it for a moment, then turns it hurriedly away.*]

SISTER MARCELLA. No, reverend Mother.

PRIORESS. For what then?

SISTER MARCELLA. For nothing, reverend Mother.

PRIORESS. What? For nothing?

SISTER MARCELLA. Your daughter means for nothing evil. On the contrary . . .

VICARESS. H'a! Now I suppose we are going to hear that it is a virtue in a religious to have a glass!

SISTER MARCELLA. No, reverend Mother, it is not a virtue. But your Reverences know already that your Sister suffers from temptations to melancholy.

VICARESS. Yes, yes . . .

SISTER MARCELLA. And when they seize upon her too strongly, they put it into her head to climb trees and run along the tops of walls, and jump over the fences in the garden, and to throw herself into the water of the fountain, and since your Sister knows that, in a religious, these . . . these . . .

VICARESS. These extravagances.

SISTER MARCELLA. Are unbecoming, your Sister catches a sunbeam in the mirror and makes it dance among the leaves and across the ceiling of her cell, and over the walls

opposite, and so she consoles herself and imagines that it
is a butterfly or a bird, and can go wherever it pleaseth.

VICARESS.   It can, and stay there.

PRIORESS.   For this fault, Sister Marcella . . . [SISTER
MARCELLA *kneels.*] which, without being a grave one,
yet is more than a little, considered according to the con-
stitution of our rule, I assign you this penance.   Tonight,
before you retire, you are to repeat four times in your cell
the psalm *"Quam dilecta."* Rise, and return to your seat.
[SISTER MARCELLA *obeys, but before seating herself she
makes a reverence before each of the* NUNS.]   [*To the*
VICARESS.]   You may be seated.   [THE VICARESS *and the
two* MONITORS *seat themselves.*]   [*Three light knocks on
the door.   It is* TERESA *who says:*]

TERESA.   *Ave Maria Purissima!*

PRIORESS.   Conceived without sin.

TERESA.   May I come in?

PRIORESS.   Come in.   [TERESA *enters.   She is eighteen,
very pretty, very sunny and very gay, with nothing about
her to suggest the mystic or the religious.   She is dressed
simply in gray and wears a white apron.   She has a flower
in her hair, which is arranged modestly, and without an
excess of curls or ornament.*]   Where are you coming from
in such a hurry?   You are all out of breath.

TERESA.   [*Speaks always with the greatest simplicity,
without affectation or pretense of any sort.*]   From dressing the altar of the Virgin.

PRIORESS.   Did that put you out of breath?

TERESA.   No, Mother.   It's because I wanted it to be
all in white to-day, and there weren't white flowers enough
in the garden, so I had to climb up and cut some branches
off the acacia.

MISTRESS OF NOVICES.   Did you climb a tree?

TERESA.   Yes, I climbed two; there weren't enough
blossoms on one.

MISTRESS OF NOVICES.   *Jesús!*

VICARESS.   *Ave Maria!*

TERESA.   I wish you could see the view from the top of the big acacia! [SISTER MARCELLA'S *eyes open wide with envy.*]

VICARESS.   Child, you have put yourself beyond the pale of God's mercy!

SISTER JOANNA OF THE CROSS.   You might have fallen! It's too terrible to think of!

TERESA.   Fallen? No, Mother. Why, I've climbed it a hundred times!

PRIORESS.   Then you must not do it again.

MISTRESS OF NOVICES.   [*Regretfully.*]   It is too late to forbid her now.

PRIORESS.   [*Sorrowfully.*]   That is true.

SISTER INEZ.   It is the last day she will dress the altar.

SISTER JOANNA OF THE CROSS.   The very *last!*

TERESA.   Ah, Mothers! You mustn't talk like this. Don't be sad.

VICARESS.   No, we had better behave like you do, though it doesn't seem possible when you consider the day that it is, and you laughing and carrying on like one possessed!

PRIORESS.   The Mother is right. A little more feeling to-day, daughter, a manner more subdued, would not have been out of place.

TERESA.   You are right, reverend Mothers—you always are, in the holiness, which like a halo surrounds your reverend heads; but when a girl wants to laugh she wants to laugh, although, as Mother Anna St. Francis says, it may be the solemnest day of her life.

MISTRESS OF NOVICES.   It is a solemn day, a very solemn day. You are leaving this house in which you have passed eighteen years, without scarcely so much as taking thought how it was you came to be here. Tomorrow, you will be your own mistress, and you will have upon your conscience the responsibilities of a wife.

VICARESS.   Which believe me, are not light. Men are selfish, fickle . . .

TERESA.   [*Timidly.*]   Antonio is very good.

VICARESS. However good he may be, he is a man, and men are accustomed to command. They have been from the beginning of the world, and it has affected their character. And since you are very independent yourself, and like to have your own way . . .

TERESA. Yes, I have been spoiled I know; but you will see now how good I will be. It will come out all right.

SISTER JOANNA OF THE CROSS. Do you want to spoil the day for her?

TERESA. No, Mother—no; you won't spoil it, for I am very, very happy. You have all been so good to me!

VICARESS. Nonsense! No such thing.

TERESA. But it isn't nonsense. I know this is God's house, but you might have closed the doors to me, and you have flung them wide open, freely. I have lived here eighteen years and in all this time, to the very moment that I am leaving it, you have never once reminded me that I have lived here on your charity.

SISTER JOANNA OF THE CROSS. Don't say such things!

TERESA. Yes, I must say them. On your charity, on your alms—like a poor beggar and an outcast. I don't mind saying it nor thinking it, for I have been so happy here—yes, I am happy now—happier than the daughter of a king: for I love you all so much that I want to kiss even the walls and hug the trees, for even the walls and the trees have been kind to me. This has been the Convent of my Heart!

SISTER MARCELLA. It has been your home. If you had only been content always to remain in it!

PRIORESS. We must not talk like this. God moves in His own ways.

MISTRESS OF NOVICES. And in all of them His children may do His service.

VICARESS. The child was not born to be a religious. The things of the world appeal to her too strongly.

TERESA. It is true. The world appeals to me—poor me! It seems to me sometimes as if everybody loved me, as if everything was calling to me everywhere to come. I have been so happy in this house, and yet, all the time, I have been thinking how great the world was, how wonderful! Whenever I have gone out into the street, how my heart leaped.! I felt as if I were going to fly, it was so light! My brain was in a whirl. Then I was so glad to come back again into this house, it felt so good, as if you were all taking me up once more into your arms, as if I had fallen to sleep in them again and was warm, folded beneath the shelter of the everlasting wings.

VICARESS. The wings of your good angel, who stood waiting at the door—stood waiting till you came.

PRIORESS. Why should he have to wait? Her good angel always has gone with her, and surely there never has been a time when he has had to turn away his face. Am I right, daughter?

TERESA. You are, Mother. [Sincerely.]

SISTER JOANNA OF THE CROSS. They needn't have asked her that!

SISTER MARÍA JESÚS. [Rising.] Here are the bows for the corset covers. Do you want them pinned or sewed?

SISTER INEZ. Sewed, I say.

SISTER MARÍA JESÚS. Down the middle?

MISTRESS OF NOVICES. Of course, down the middle.

SISTER MARÍA JESÚS. The reason I asked was because in the pattern they are all fastened down the side.

MISTRESS OF NOVICES. [Bending over to examine the fashion plates with SISTER INEZ and SISTER MARÍA JESÚS.] Yes. Don't you see? She is right.

SISTER INEZ. That's funny! But they are pretty that way.

MISTRESS OF NOVICES. I say it's absurd.

SISTER MARÍA JESÚS. What do you think, Mother Crucifixion?

VICARESS. Don't ask me; I don't think. I neither understand nor wish to understand these things—pomp and vanity, artifices of the devil, who, they tell me, is very well acquainted with the dressmakers of Paris, and takes part in their designs and encourages their abbreviations. Take it away, take that paper out of my sight, for it never should have entered this holy house!

SISTER MARCELLA. *Ay,* but we have to know the fashions, Mother!

VICARESS. The fashions! The fashions! Go to hell and you will find the fashions! Any other place would be too far behind.

SISTER MARÍA JESÚS. But you don't want the child to be married, do you, in the dress of the year of the ark?

VICARESS. A pure heart and an upright spirit are what she should be married in, and if that is the case, no one is going to notice whether she has one bow more or less.

SISTER MARCELLA. They say men pay a great deal of attention to such things, Mother Crucifixion.

SISTER MARÍA JESÚS. And we must render unto Caesar the things which are Caesar's, and unto God the things which are God's.

VICARESS. So! We have philosophers, have we, in the house?

SISTER INEZ. Hand me the scissors, if you will. I want to cut off these ends.

SISTER JOANNA OF THE CROSS. I think now everything is ready to put in the trunk.

PRIORESS. Yes, for the carriage will be waiting. [TERESA *kneels on the floor beside the trunk. The* NUNS *hand her the various articles of the trousseau, which they remove from the benches and the table.*]

SISTER INEZ. Here are the chemises.

SISTER MARCELLA. And the lace petticoats.

SISTER JOANNA OF THE CROSS. Put them in the other tray, so they won't get wrinkled.

SISTER INEZ. Lord of Mercy! What a tuck!— What bungler ran this tuck?

MISTRESS OF NOVICES. You must not say anything against the sister who ran it, Sister; say it would look better if it were redampened and ironed.

TERESA. But it looks splendidly; really it does! Give it to me! Here—let me have them. This is too much trouble for you to take.

PRIORESS. Have you everything?

SISTER MARCELLA. The handkerchiefs?

SISTER JOANNA OF THE CROSS. The dressing-jackets?

VICARESS. Here is some edging that was left over, embroidered by hand. You had better put it in the trunk in case of accident.

MISTRESS OF NOVICES. And the patterns—you might need them.

SISTER INEZ. Here is a sachet, my child. It is filled with thyme and lavender and has lime peel in it. It will give a fresh scent to your clothes.

SISTER MARCELLA. She'll have real perfumes soon enough.

SISTER MARÍA JESÚS. Yes, expensive ones.

SISTER INEZ. They may be more expensive, but they won't be any better—I can tell you that; for these are plants that God has made, and they smell sweetly, and of a good conscience. I have them in all the presses in the sacristy, and it is a joy to smell them when you go up the steps to the altar.

TERESA. I think we have everything.

PRIORESS. Yes, everything. Now turn the key. Does it lock securely? [TERESA gets up.] And hang the key around your neck with the rosaries, for we have fastened it on a ribbon for you. Take care you don't lose it. The lock is an English one, and not every key will open it.

TERESA. Yes, Mother.

VICARESS. It will be a miracle if she has it tomorrow.

SISTER JOANNA OF THE CROSS. She will settle down soon under the responsibilities of a wife.

MISTRESS OF NOVICES. Well? Are you satisfied?

TERESA. Satisfied is too little, Mother. It does not express it. I don't deserve what you have done for me.

VICARESS. Yes, you do; you deserve it. And you might as well tell the truth as a falsehood. You have a good heart; you are a sensible girl. When you said what you did, you were thinking of your clothes; but you need have no scruples. Everything that you take away with you from this house, and more too, you have earned by your labor. That is the truth and you know it. Maybe we have taught you here how to sew and embroider, but you have worked for us in the convent, and outside of it. You owe us nothing. Besides, you had two hundred and fifty pesetas from the doctor to buy the material. Here . . . [*Producing a paper from under her scapular.*] is the account of the way they have been spent, so you can see for yourself and answer for it, since delicacy will not permit that we should be asked how it was used.

TERESA. [*Embarrassed and confused.*] What do you mean? Why, Mother Crucifixion!

VICARESS. That is all there is to it. You will find the account is correct. [TERESA *takes the paper and having folded it, puts it in her dress.*]

PRIORESS. [*To the* NUNS *who have been working.*] You may remove the table and gather up these things.

TERESA. No, Mother—let me do it. I will pick up everything. [*The* PRIORESS *makes a sign and all the* NUNS *rise and leave the room, except only herself, the* VICARESS, *the* MISTRESS OF NOVICES, *and* SISTER JOANNA OF THE CROSS.]

PRIORESS. [*To* TERESA.] What time do you go?

TERESA. My father is coming for me at five, but . . . Antonio has asked me . . . before I go . . . to say that he would like to see you all and thank you, and tell you how happy and grateful he is to you for the little girl you have brought up.

PRIORESS. We shall be very glad to see him.

VICARESS. Glad or not glad, no matter; it is our obligation. He cannot expect to carry her off like a thief in the night, and have no woman ask a question.

TERESA. I will call you when he comes. [*The* PRI-ORESS, *the* VICARESS *and the* MISTRESS OF NOVICES *go out.*]

[TERESA *and* SISTER JOANNA OF THE CROSS *remain behind picking up and arranging the papers, patterns and scraps that have been left on the seats or about the floor. They say nothing but presently* TERESA *throws herself on her knees before the* NUN.]

TERESA. Sister Joanna of the Cross!

SISTER JOANNA OF THE CROSS. What do you want, my child?

TERESA. Now that we are alone, bless me while there is no one here to see—no, not one—for you are my mother, more than all the rest!

SISTER JOANNA OF THE CROSS. Get up. [TERESA *gets up.*] Don't talk like that! We are all equal in God's house.

TERESA. But in my heart you are the first. You mustn't be angry at what I say. How can I help it? Is it my fault, though I have struggled against it all my life, that I have come to love you so?

SISTER JOANNA OF THE CROSS. Yes, you have struggled. You have been wilful . . . [*Then seeking at once to excuse her.*] But it was because you were strong and well. When a child is silent and keeps to herself in a corner, it is a sign that she is sick or thinking of some evil. But you . . .

TERESA. *Ay,* Mother! Where do you suppose that I came from?

SISTER JOANNA OF THE CROSS. From Heaven, my daughter, as all of us have come.

TERESA. Do you really think that we have all come from Heaven?

SISTER JOANNA OF THE CROSS. At least you have come from Heaven to me. You say that I am your mother more than the rest; I don't know—it may be. But I know that for years you have been all my happiness and joy.

TERESA. Mother!

SISTER JOANNA OF THE CROSS. I was so glad to hear you laugh and see you run about the cloisters! It was absurd, but I always felt—not now, for you are grown-up now—but for years I always felt as if you must be I, myself, scampering and playing. For I was just your age now, a little more or less, when you came into the Convent. And it seemed to me as if I was a child again and had just begun to live. You were so little, so busy—yes, you were—but I was busy too, if you only knew, before I entered here, at home in our house in the village. I was always singing and dancing, although we were very poor. My mother went out every day to wash in the river or to do housework—she had so many children!—and I was always carrying one about in my arms. And when I entered here, as I could do, thanks to some good ladies, who collected the money for my dowry—God reward them for it—although I had a real vocation, I was sorrowful and homesick thinking of my little brothers and sisters! How I used to cry in the dark corners, and I never dared to say a word! Then the Mother told me that if my melancholy didn't leave me she would be obliged to send me home. And then you came and I forgot everything! That is why I say you came to me from Heaven. And I don't want you to think I am angry, or ashamed—or that it has ever given me a moment's pain to have loved you.

TERESA. Is that the reason that you scold me so?

SISTER JOANNA OF THE CROSS. When have I ever scolded you?

TERESA. Oh, so many times! But no matter. I always tell Antonio, Sister Joanna of the Cross is my mother. She is my mother, my real mother! So now he always calls you mother whenever he speaks of you.

SISTER JOANNA OF THE CROSS. My daughter, will you be happy with him?

TERESA. Of course! I am sure I will. He is so good, he is so happy! He says he doesn't know where it is all his happiness comes from, because his father, who is dead now, was more mournful than a willow, and his mother, poor lady, whenever anything happened to her that was good, burst right out crying. How do you suppose it was she ever managed to have such a boy? It must be that sad mothers have happy children. How does it seem to you?

SISTER JOANNA OF THE CROSS. How do I know?

TERESA. It must be that way. The first boy I have is going to be—what is the solemnest thing in the world? No, the first is going to be an architect, like his father; but the second can be a missionary, and go to China if he wants to, and convert the heathen. Just think what it would be to have a son who was a saint! I shouldn't have to be so humble in heaven, then, should I? I should have influence. And here you are all the time, Sister Joanna of the Cross, praying for me and preparing miracles. So you see I have a good start already.

SISTER JOANNA OF THE CROSS. How you do love to talk!

TERESA. Isn't it foolish, Mother? Don't I? Listen! When you were little didn't you ever want to be a boy? I did. I used to cry because I thought then that I could have been anything I wanted to be—this, that, I didn't care what it was—Captain-General, Archbishop, yes, Pope, even! Or something else. It used to make me mad to think that because I was a girl I couldn't even be an acolyte. But now, since—well, since I love Antonio, and he loves me, I don't care; it doesn't make any difference any more, because if I am poor and know nothing, he is wise and strong; and if I am foolish and of no account, he is, oh, of so much worth! And if I have to stay behind at home and hide myself in the corner, he can go out into the world and mount, oh, so high—wherever a man can go—and instead of making me envious, it makes me so

happy! Ah, Sister Joanna of the Cross, when she truly
loves a man, how humble it makes a girl!

SISTER JOANNA OF THE CROSS. Do you really love him
so?

TERESA. More than life itself! And that is all too
little. Maybe it's a sin, but I can tell you. Do you believe that we will meet in Heaven the persons we have
loved on earth? Because if I don't meet him there and I
can't go on loving him always just the same as I do now,
no, more than I do now . . .

SISTER JOANNA OF THE CROSS. [Interrupting.]
Hush! Peace! You mustn't say such things. It is a
sin.

TERESA. *Ay,* sister Joanna of the Cross! How sweet
it is to be in love!

SISTER JOANNA OF THE CROSS. But he . . . he . . .
Does he love you too, so much?

TERESA. Yes, he loves me. How much, I don't know;
but it doesn't make any matter. What makes me happy
is that I love him. You needn't think that sometimes—
very seldom though—I haven't been afraid that perhaps
some day he might stop loving me. It used to make me
sad. But if I had ever thought that some day I could
stop loving him . . . No, it would be better to die first;
for then, what would be the good of life?

SISTER JOANNA OF THE CROSS. Ah, my child! To
continue in God's love!

TERESA. Do you know how I would like to spend my
life? All of it? Sitting on the ground at his feet, looking up into his eyes, just listening to him talk. You don't
know how he can talk. He knows everything—everything
that there is to know in the world, and he tells you such
things! The things that you always have known yourself,
in your heart, and you couldn't find out how to say them.
Even when he doesn't say anything, if he should be speaking some language which you didn't understand, it is wonderful . . . his voice . . . I don't know how to explain

it, but it is his voice—a voice that seems as if it had been talking to you ever since the day you were born! You don't hear it only with your ears, but with your whole body. It's like the air which you see and breathe and taste, and which smells so sweetly in the garden beneath the tree of paradise. Ah, Mother! The first day that he said to me "Teresa"—you see what a simple thing it was, my name, Teresa—why, it seemed to me as if nobody ever had called me by my name before, as if I never had heard it, and when he went away, I ran up and down the street saying to myself "Teresa, Teresa, Teresa!" under my breath, without knowing what I was doing, as if I walked on air!

SISTER JOANNA OF THE CROSS. You frighten me, my child.

TERESA. Do I? Why?

SISTER JOANNA OF THE CROSS. Because you love him so. For earthly love . . . I mean . . . it seems to me it is like a flower, that we find by the side of the road— a little brightness that God grants us to help us pass through life, for we are weak and frail; a drop of honey spread upon our bread each day, which we should receive gladly, but with trembling, and keeping our hearts whole, daughter, for it will surely pass away.

TERESA. It cannot pass away!

SISTER JOANNA OF THE CROSS. It may; and then what will be left to your soul, if you have set your all on this delight, and it has passed away?

TERESA. [Humbly.] You mustn't be angry with me, Mother. No! Look at me! It isn't wrong, I know. Loving him, I . . . he is so good, he is so good . . . and good, it cannot pass away!

SISTER JOANNA OF THE CROSS. Is he a good Christian?

TERESA. He is good, Sister.

SISTER JOANNA OF THE CROSS. But does he fear God?

TERESA. One day he said to me: "I love you because you know how to pray." Don't you see? And another time: "I feel a devotion toward you as toward some holy

thing." He! Devotion! To me! And whenever I think
of that, it seems to me as if I was just growing better, as
if all at once I was capable of everything there was to do
or suffer in the world—so as to have him always feel that
way!

SISTER JOANNA OF THE CROSS. I hear some one in the
parlor. Draw the curtains.

[TERESA, *pulling the cord, draws the curtains over
the windows, shutting off the light. The fore part of
the stage remains in shadow, but the outer parlor is
brightly illuminated. ANTONIO has entered and may
be seen through the crack where the curtains join.
He is twenty-five years of age, well-built, manly and
sensitive of feature. He remains alone and his foot-
steps may be heard on the boards as he paces nervously
up and down.*]

TERESA. [*In a low voice, going up to the* NUN.]
Yes. It is he.

SISTER JOANNA OF THE CROSS. [*Seizing her hand.*]
Ah! How tall he is!

TERESA. Yes, he is tall. Doesn't he look splendidly
though?

SISTER JOANNA OF THE CROSS. Yes, he does. Has he
golden hair?

TERESA. No, it's the light; his hair is dark brown, and
his eyes are between violet and blue. It's too bad you
can't see them. They are so beautiful! When he talks,
they sparkle.

SISTER JOANNA OF THE CROSS. How old is he?

TERESA. Just twenty-five.

[ANTONIO *crosses from one side to the other, and
continues to pace back and forth.*]

SISTER JOANNA OF THE CROSS. He seems to be of a
very active disposition.

TERESA. That is because he is impatient. Shall I speak
to him and tell him you are here?

SISTER JOANNA OF THE CROSS. [*Falling back.*] No!

TERESA. Why not? He loves you dearly. [*In a low voice, going up to the grille.*] Good afternoon, Antonio.

ANTONIO. [*Looking about from one side to the other.*] Teresa? Where are you?

TERESA. [*Laughing.*] Here, boy, here; behind the grille. It is easy to see you are not accustomed to calling on nuns.

ANTONIO. Can't you run back the curtain?

TERESA. No, because I am not alone. Can't you guess who is with me? My mother.

ANTONIO. Sister Joanna of the Cross?

TERESA. [*To the* NUN, *delighted because he has guessed it.*] There! Do you see? [*To* ANTONIO.] Sister Joanna of the Cross—exactly. We have been watching you through the grille, and she says that she thinks you are a very handsome young man.

SISTER JOANNA OF THE CROSS. Goodness gracious! You mustn't pay any attention to what she says.

TERESA. Don't be angry, Mother. I think so myself.

ANTONIO. You never told me that before.

TERESA. That is because in here, where you can't see me, I'm not so embarrassed to tell you. Listen! We have to send in word now that you are here; but I want you to tell my mother something first, for if you stand there like a blockhead without opening your mouth, I am going to be very much ashamed, after all the time I have spent in singing your praises.

ANTONIO. What do you want me to tell her?

TERESA. What you have in your heart.

ANTONIO. But I don't know whether it is proper to tell it to a religious, although it is in my heart, for I love her dearly.

TERESA. Ah! I tell her that a million times a day.

ANTONIO. Then let us tell her together two million; because I must say to you, Madam, that it is impossible to know Teresa and not to love you.

TERESA. What a treasure is this mother of mine!

SISTER JOANNA OF THE CROSS. For shame, my child!
[*Blushing, to* ANTONIO.]   I also have a great affection for
you, sir, for this child has been teaching me to love you.
She is a little blind perhaps, and trusting, for that is natural. She knows nothing of the world, and we—how
were we to teach her?   And now you are going to take her
far away; but don't take her heart away from us, sir, and
break ours, when we let her hand go.

ANTONIO. Madam, I swear to you now that I shall
always kneel in reverence before the tenderness and virtue
which you have planted in her soul.

TERESA. I told you that he was very good, Mother.

SISTER JOANNA OF THE CROSS. May God make you
both very happy. And may God remain with you, for
his handmaid must go now and seek the Mother.

ANTONIO. But you are coming back?

SISTER JOANNA OF THE CROSS. With the sisters . . .
Yes, I think so. Good-bye. I have been so happy to know
you.

[SISTER JOANNA OF THE CROSS *goes out, greatly
moved.* TERESA *remains standing by the grille until
the* NUN *has disappeared, without speaking a word.*]

ANTONIO. Now you can draw back the curtain.

TERESA. Yes, a little. [*She runs back the curtain a
little way.*]   But it won't do you any good, because you
won't be able to see me. Do you really like my mother?
Do you really? Why are you so silent? What are you
thinking about?

ANTONIO. I don't know; it is very strange. Since I
have come into this room, since I have heard your mother
speak, and have heard you, behind this grille, without
knowing for certain where you were in the dark, I have
been almost afraid to love you. But ah—how I do love
you!

TERESA. I like that better.

ANTONIO. Teresa!

TERESA. What is it?

ANTONIO. Will you never forget, will you carry with you always wherever you go, this peace and this calm?

TERESA. With you, Antonio?

ANTONIO. Yes, into the world, beyond these walls; for in the world we make so much useless noise. And you—I see it now—you are the mistress of peace and of calm.

TERESA. [*Laughing.*] I the mistress of calm? As if I hadn't been a little flyaway all my life, without an idea in my head! Mother Crucifixion says that since I was passed in on the wheel there hasn't been one moment in this house of what the rules call "profound calm." I know I don't talk much when I am with you—we have been together such a little while, and it has been all too short to listen to you; but you will see when I grow bolder and am not afraid. You will have to put cotton in your ears then. Ah, Antonio! Only think, we are going to have all our lives to be together and listen to each other talk and tell each other things—that is, all our lives for you to tell me things, because I . . . you will find out soon enough. Tell me really, truly, Antonio: aren't you going to be awfully ashamed to have such an ignorant wife?

ANTONIO. Ignorant or learned?

TERESA. I? Learned? In what?

ANTONIO. In a science which I did not know, and which you have taught to me.

TERESA. You are joking.

ANTONIO. I am in earnest. Until I met you, I knew nothing; I did not even know myself.

TERESA. Pshaw!

ANTONIO. You mustn't laugh. Did it ever seem to you, Teresa, that our soul was like a palace?

TERESA. Of course it is! It is like a castle. Santa Teresa says so: The soul is like a castle—the interior of a castle, all made of one diamond above and below. And it has seven courts, and in the last is stored a great treasure . . .

ANTONIO. Then in the innermost chamber of my soul

was stored the love I have for you, and if you had not
come and opened the door yourself, and helped me to find it,
I should have passed all my life in ignorance, without
knowing anything was there.

TERESA. Don't repeat such heresies!

ANTONIO. Is it a heresy—the love I bear for you?
No, it is a religion—the only one for me! My girl!
Seven courts, you say? Then with a great effort I had
passed into the first and I was running here and there
aimlessly, and you don't know what horrible things I found
—everywhere I stumbled on. They were my own traits.
I was cold, selfish, proud, without trust or faith, without
other ambitions than material desires—to pass through life
easily and well, to be the first in my own petty world, in-
capable of sacrifice, of abnegation, of compassion, of disinterested love.

TERESA. No! No! You were no such thing.

ANTONIO. But I lived as if I were! What difference
did it make? But then one day I heard your voice, and
summoned by you, I again searched through the castle, and
in the other courts I began to find—ah! under how
many cobwebs, all covered-up with dust—humility and devotion, warmth of heart, pity and faith in so many holy
things. And then I found my honor, self-respect and
sympathy with my fellow man, in which we live, Teresa,
for without it nothing else is life, and I began to be a man
when I first loved you. For in these things you are the
master, and I have learned them all from you!

TERESA. Hush! They are coming.

[TERESA *falls back from the grille, after first drawing
the curtains again. The* NUNS *in single file enter silently,
the youngest first, followed at last by the* MISTRESS OF
NOVICES, *the* VICARESS *and the* PRIORESS. *The* PRIORESS
seats herself in the arm-chair at the left of the grille; the
VICARESS *and the* MISTRESS OF NOVICES *in two other
chairs at the right. The remaining* NUNS *stand or are
seated round about.* TERESA *supports herself with her hand*

on the back of the PRIORESS'S *chair.* SISTER JOANNA OF THE CROSS *approaches her and takes her by the other hand. There is absolute silence as the* NUNS *enter and find their places. They look at each other with expectant attention, and some nod and smile among themselves. When they are seated, there follows an interval of further silence.*]

PRIORESS. *Ave Maria Purissima!* [ANTONIO, *somewhat embarrassed, and endeavoring vainly to penetrate the darkness behind the grille, does not answer. The* PRIORESS, *after waiting a moment, turns her head and smiles indulgently at the community.*] Good afternoon, young man.

ANTONIO. Good afternoon, Madam—or Madams—for behind the mystery of this screen, it is impossible for me to see whether I am speaking with one or with many. [*The* NUNS *smile quietly and discreetly.*]

PRIORESS. [*In a low voice.*] Run back the curtain, Sister Inez. [*The Sister runs back the curtain.*] You are speaking with the entire community, which takes great pleasure in knowing you.

ANTONIO. Ladies, the pleasure and the honor are mine, and they are much greater than you will be ready to imagine.

SISTER INEZ. Bless us! But isn't he a polite and polished talker?

SISTER TORNERA. Keep still! I want to hear what he has to say.

ANTONIO. For a long time I have desired greatly to visit you. Teresa knows it, and she must have told it to you.

PRIORESS. That is true. She has indeed. And we have greatly appreciated your desire.

ANTONIO. But the first time I was in this place it was Advent and the second it was Lent; and both times Teresa informed me that it was impossible for me to see you.

VICARESS. Clearly. In seasons of penitence we receive no visitors.

ANTONIO. But now it is May and past Easter time.

MISTRESS OF NOVICES. How well acquainted he is with the calendar! Surely you must be very devout, sir.

ANTONIO. I am, Madam—very; but chiefly in the worship of certain saints who as yet are not on the altars.

SISTER INEZ. What a nice compliment! Saints, did he say? [*Laughing.*] He *is* a polished talker.

ANTONIO. Ladies, after a hundred years they will be lighting candles to you, and invoking you in prayers, and in gratitude they will be bringing you thank offerings of crutches and wooden legs.

SISTER TORNERA. [*Laughing.*] Does he think we are going to be the patrons of rheumatism?

MISTRESS OF NOVICES. After a hundred years? You are giving us a century of Purgatory.

ANTONIO. No, Madam, by all that is holy! I am giving you a century of life, and entrance thereafter directly into the choir of seraphim.

PRIORESS. I fear you speak frivolously, Señor Don Antonio.

ANTONIO. Madam, I was never more earnest in my life. Whenever I think of death, you have no idea of the peace which enters my soul. I remember how many saintly white hands will be stretched down to me to help me into Paradise —for I suppose that you will be able to exercise a little influence on behalf of one of the family.

SISTER SAGRARIO. [*Laughing.*] One of the family?

VICARESS. Certainly. We are all God's children.

ANTONIO. But I shall be so in a double sense; first, in my own birthright, and then as your son-in-law, who are his brides.

VICARESS. Ah! It is not meet to jest about holy things.

ANTONIO. Madam, you are right. And you will pardon me all the inconsequences which I have said, for I swear to you that they have been nothing but nervousness and fear.

MISTRESS OF NOVICES. You are not afraid of us?

ANTONIO. I am, Madam, very—because of the respect

and admiration in which I hold you all. I came here more disturbed than I ever have been before in my whole life. I do not know whether I should thank you, or whether I should beg your pardon.

PRIORESS. Beg our pardon?

ANTONIO. Yes, because I fear that I am not worthy of the treasure which you are entrusting to me.

PRIORESS. We know already through the doctor that you are an honorable young man.

MISTRESS OF NOVICES. And the love which our daughter bears you is our guarantee. Surely the Lord would not permit His child, brought up in His fear, to throw herself away upon an evil man.

ANTONIO. I am not evil, no; but I am a man, and you, ladies, with all the great piety of your souls, have been nurturing a flower for the skies. When I first knew her, my heart whispered to me that I had met a saint. She was a miracle. When I first dared to speak to her, there came over me a fear and a trembling that were out of the course of nature; and when I told her that I loved her, my heart stopped, and bade me to fall on my knees, and now that I have come here to beg my happiness of you, I don't know what I can promise you in token of my gratitude, nor how I can give you thanks enough for the great honor which you do me.

VICARESS. It may be you are speaking more truly than you think, Señor Don Antonio.

MISTRESS OF NOVICES. Why, Mother!

VICARESS. No, let me speak. For he has said well. The girl is not one of those worldly creatures who take to their husbands a great store of physical beauty. That is certain. You cannot call her ugly, but it is the most that can be said. Nor does she bring with her any dower. She is poorer than the poor. But she carries in her heart a treasure, the only one which we have been able to give her, which is more priceless than silver or gold, and that is the fear of God. For this, sir, you must be answerable to us, and we ask you your word now, that you will always respect it in her and in her children, if you should have any, if it should be God's holy will.

ANTONIO.   Teresa shall always be the absolute mistress of her conscience and of my house, and my children shall ever be that which she desires.   I pledge my word.

PRIORESS.   You will never have reason to regret it, for she is a good and prudent girl.

VICARESS.   And not hypocritical, for, although, as you have said, we have nurtured her for the skies, we have never permitted ourselves to believe that she was to reach them through the cloister.

SISTER MARÍA JESÚS.   Do you mean to take her very far away?

ANTONIO.   Yes, Madam.   That is to say, there is no longer in the world either far or near.   We sail next week. I am going to America as the resident director of a firm of architects.

PRIORESS.   Yes, we know already.

ANTONIO.   That is the reason for this haste.   I do not wish to go alone.

SISTER TORNERA.   Aren't you afraid the child will be seasick?   They say you do get a terrible shaking-up upon the sea.

SISTER MARÍA JESÚS.   You must promise us to take good care of her.

SISTER INEZ.   If she gets overheated never let her drink cold water.   She is very pig-headed about that.

SISTER MARCELLA.   But you mustn't forget that she is accustomed to cold baths.

SISTER INEZ.   If she takes cold or gets a cough, make her drink a glass of hot milk with a teaspoonful of hot rum in it, with plenty of sugar, for that's the only thing that will make her sweat.

TERESA.   I think perhaps I had better attend to these matters myself, Sister.

SISTER INEZ.   Yes, you'd be a pretty one to attend to

them! Don't you mind what she says, Señor Don Antonio, for she is spoiled utterly. If you don't give her medicines and force the spoon down her throat, she might be dying for all you'd know, but she'd never ask for them herself.

PRIORESS. We had better not confuse him with too many recommendations. Surely he knows the more important precautions already.

ANTONIO. [*Smiling.*] Perhaps it would be better if you wrote them out for me on a piece of paper.

SISTER TORNERA. A good idea! [*Laughing.*] If we began where does he think we'd leave off?

SISTER SAGRARIO. How many days will you be on the ship?

ANTONIO. Two weeks.

SISTER MARCELLA. Mercy! What an age! Suppose there should be a storm?

MISTRESS OF NOVICES. It will be at least two weeks more before we can get letters back.

ANTONIO. We will telegraph when we arrive and we will send you a message from the middle of the ocean, so that you will hear from us the same day.

SISTER INEZ. Mother of God! Can they send messages now from the middle of the ocean? How do the words come?

TERESA. Flying through the air, like birds.

SISTER INEZ. What will men invent next? When your handmaid was in the world, they came by a wire, and yet it seemed the work of the devil.

ANTONIO. I should not advise you, Madam, to believe that the devil is ever very far away from these inventions.

SISTER INEZ. Whether he is or not, when the telegram comes it will be safest to sprinkle it with holy water.

PRIORESS. Ah, Sister Inez, you are so simple! Don't you see that the young man is only joking?

VICARESS. It is five o'clock—the hour we were to expect your father.

ANTONIO. I do not wish to molest you further.

PRIORESS. You do not molest us, but we must close the parlor at five.

ANTONIO. You will pardon me if I commit a terrible breach of etiquette, but I should like to ask you one favor before I go.

PRIORESS. If it is in our power to grant . . .

ANTONIO. Although, as it seems, you have run back a curtain, yet the mystery of this screen still remains a mystery to me, a poor sinner, inscrutable as before; and I should be sorry to go away without having seen you face to face. Is it too much to ask?

PRIORESS. For us this is a day of giving. Draw back the curtains, Teresa. [TERESA *draws back the curtain from one window, a* NUN *that from the other, lighting up the room.*]

ANTONIO. [*Bowing.*] Ladies! . . .

VICARESS. Well? How does the vision appear to you?

ANTONIO. I shall never forget it as long as I live.

PRIORESS. Then may God go with you, and may you live a thousand years. [*Taking* TERESA *by the hand.*] Here is her hand. See, we give her to you with a great love, and may you make her happy.

ANTONIO. I answer for her happiness with my life.

PRIORESS. And may God go with you.

MISTRESS OF NOVICES. Teresa will give you from us two scapularies, the remembrances of a nun. They are not worth anything, but they have lain beside the reliquary of our father, the blessed Saint Dominic. Keep them in memory of this day.

ANTONIO. I shall treasure them, ladies, from this hour. And I pray you, remember me always in your prayers.

VICARESS. And upon your part do not forget to pray with them from time to time, for although it lies within the province of everyone to help our souls along the way to heaven, yet we must take the first steps ourselves. And may God go with you.

ALL. God go with you.

ANTONIO. Ladies! . . . [*He retires and disappears.
A* NUN *draws the curtain over the grille. Then a moment's silence. Some of the* NUNS *sigh and say:*]

NUNS. Ah, Lord! Good Lord! May it be God's
holy will! [*The bell by the door rings twice.*]

VICARESS. I thought so—your father.

[TERESA *stands in the midst of the group of* NUNS,
*bewildered, looking from one to the other, greatly
moved.* SISTER TORNERA *goes to open the door.*]

PRIORESS. Ask him to come in.

[*The* DOCTOR *enters on the arm of* SISTER TORNERA.
He is now very old, but neither decrepit nor cast down.]

DOCTOR. Good afternoon, ladies; good afternoon,
daughter.

TERESA. [*Kissing his hand.*] Good afternoon, father.

DOCTOR. The whole assembly—the parting, eh? Well,
did you see the young man? [*The* NUNS *do not answer.*]
A fine fellow, isn't he? He is waiting outside. We have
an hour in the coach before we arrive at the station, so
you had better get ready now, daughter. [TERESA *goes
out with* SISTER JOANNA OF THE CROSS.] Ah! The
trunk? Good! Carry it to the door. The boys outside
will take care of it. [*Two* NUNS *lift the trunk and carry
it out by the door on the right.*] There, that is done.
[*He seats himself in the* PRIORESS's *chair.*] Well, how are
we to-day?

PRIORESS. You see, Doctor.

MISTRESS OF NOVICES. Who would ever have believed
it eighteen years ago?

DOCTOR. Eighteen years? We are growing old, Mother.
We are growing old.

PRIORESS. That is not the worst of it.

SISTER INEZ. How old are you now, Doctor?

DOCTOR. Seventy-eight, Sister.

SISTER INEZ. No one would ever think it.

DOCTOR. [*Attempting a witticism so as to cheer up the*
NUNS.] That is because I am preserved in sanctity, like

a fly in thick syrup. [*But none of the* NUNS *laugh.*]
A little mournful to-day, eh?

SISTER MARCELLA. What else did you expect?

SISTER SAGRARIO. She is not even going to be married
in our chapel.

DOCTOR. No, his mother is old and sick, and naturally
she wants him to be with her, so they must be married
in her house.

PRIORESS. Naturally. Poor woman! [*A pause.*]

MISTRESS OF NOVICES. She is going so far away!

DOCTOR. But she will come back, Mother. She will
come back.

PRIORESS. She knows nothing of the world.

DOCTOR. There is no cause to be alarmed. He is an
honorable man.

VICARESS. Yes, he seems to be one. [TERESA *and*
SISTER JOANNA OF THE CROSS *re-enter. It is plain that they
have both been crying.* TERESA, *wearing a mantilla, and
with her coat on, carries a shawl over her arm for use as a
wrap on the voyage. She stops in the middle of the room
and stands still, not daring to say good-bye.*]

DOCTOR. Well? Are we ready now?

TERESA. Yes . . . Now . . .

DOCTOR. Then say good-bye. It is late. We must be
going, daughter.

PRIORESS. Yes, you must not delay.

TERESA. [*Throwing herself on her knees before the*
PRIORESS *and kissing her scapular.*] Mother!

PRIORESS. Rise, my daughter, rise.

TERESA. Bless me, Mother! Bless me!

PRIORESS. May God bless you; so. Rise. [*As* TERESA
rises, the NUN *embraces her.*]

TERESA. Mother! I don't know what to say to you
. . . I don't know how to leave you . . . but you must
forgive me all the wrong I have ever done in all these
years. I have been foolish, wilful. I have made so much
trouble for you all. You must forgive me. I would like

to do something great, something splendid for you all.
But—but may God reward you! May God reward you!
God reward you! [*She bursts into tears.*]

PRIORESS. My daughter, come! You must not cry.
You must not allow yourself to be afflicted so.

TERESA. I am not afflicted, Mother; but . . . it's . . .
Mother, I can never forget you! You must pray for me,
pray for me! And you must never forget me!

PRIORESS. Ah, no, my child! Never! We will pray
God to help you, and to be with you, and you must pray
to Him for guidance and for counsel always, whenever
you are troubled or perplexed in anything. For the liberty which they enjoy in the world is like a sword in the
hands of a child, and life at best is hard, and bitter often-
times.

MISTRESS OF NOVICES. Be thankful that your heart is
well steeled to resist all the temptations that may come.
Is it not, my daughter?

TERESA. It is, Mother.

PRIORESS. Will you promise always to be reverent and
good?

TERESA. Yes! Yes, Mother!

VICARESS. Remember that your obligation is greater
than that of others, because you have come forth from
God's own house.

TERESA. Yes! Yes, Mother!

PRIORESS. Remember all the blessings He has showered
upon you from the cradle; remember that your whole life
has been as a miracle, that you have lived here as few have
ever lived, that you have been brought up as few have ever
been brought up, like the Holy Virgin herself, in the very
temple of the Lord.

MISTRESS OF NOVICES. As He was to the Evangelist,
so God has been to you a father and a mother, more than
to any other living thing.

PRIORESS. Remember that you are the rose of His
garden and the grain of incense upon His altar.

TERESA. Yes! Mother, yes! I will! . . . I will remember all . . . all . . . all . . .

MISTRESS OF NOVICES. And do not forget each day to make an examination of your soul.

TERESA. No, Mother.

SISTER JOANNA OF THE CROSS. And write often.

TERESA. Yes, Mother.

DOCTOR. It is time to go, Teresa.

TERESA. [Throwing herself suddenly into his arms.] Oh, father! Promise me never to leave them! Never abandon them!

DOCTOR. Child of my heart! Ah, may they never abandon me!—for this is my house. For more than forty years I have been coming here day by day, hour by hour, and now there is nobody within these walls who is older than I. I have no children. I have had my loves—yes, a moment's flame—but it was so long ago! I have forgotten them. And these Sisters, who have been mothers to you, have been daughters to me; and now, when I come, they no longer even cover their faces before me. Why should they? It seems to me as if I had seen them born. And in this house [Greatly moved.] I should like to die, so that they might close my eyes, and say a prayer for me when life itself has closed!

MISTRESS OF NOVICES. Who is thinking of dying, Doctor?

PRIORESS. It is time to go.

TERESA. [Looking from one to the other.] Aren't you going to embrace me? [The NUNS, after hesitating and glancing a moment doubtfully at the MOTHER PRIORESS, embrace TERESA in turn, in perfect silence. Only SISTER JOANNA OF THE CROSS, taking her into her arms, says:]

SISTER JOANNA OF THE CROSS. My child!

PRIORESS. May you find what you seek in the world, daughter, for so we hope and so we pray to God. But if it should not be so, remember, this is your Convent.

TERESA. Thanks . . . thanks . . . [*Sobbing.*]

DOCTOR. Come, daughter, come . . . [*The* DOCTOR *and* TERESA *go to the door, but* TERESA *turns when she reaches the threshold and embraces* SISTER JOANNA OF THE CROSS, *passionately. Then she disappears.* SISTER JOANNA OF THE CROSS *rests her head against the grille, her back to the others, and weeps silently. A pause. The bells of the coach are heard outside as it drives away.*]

MISTRESS OF NOVICES. They are going now. [*The chapel bell rings summoning the* NUNS *to choir.*]

PRIORESS. The summons to the choir.

MISTRESS OF NOVICES. Come, Sisters! Let us go there.

[*All make ready to go out sadly. The* VICARESS, *sensing the situation, to her mind demoralizing, feels it to be her duty to provide a remedy. She, too, is greatly moved, but making a supreme effort to control herself, says in a voice which she in vain endeavors to make appear calm, but which is choked in utterance by tears:*]

VICARESS. One moment. I have observed of late . . . that some . . . in the prayer . . . have not been marking sufficiently the pauses in the middle of the lines, while on the other hand, they drag out the last words interminably. Be careful of this, for your Reverences know that the beauty of the office lies in rightly marking the pauses, and in avoiding undue emphasis on the end of the phrase. Let us go there. [*The* NUNS *file out slowly.* SISTER JOANNA OF THE CROSS, *unnoticed, remains alone. With a cry, she falls upon her knees beside an empty chair.*]

CURTAIN

THE LOVER

COMEDY IN ONE ACT

TEATRO DE LÁ COMEDIA, MADRID
1913

ARTS LEAGUE OF SERVICE, MANCHESTER
1924

FORTUNE THEATRE, LONDON
1926

CHARACTERS

THE QUEEN.
THE LOVER.
THE LADY IN WAITING.

THE LOVER

Salon in a Royal Palace. Although of extreme richness, the furnishings preserve an atmosphere of simplicity.

The stage is empty when the curtain rises. Loud shouts and cries are heard outside, as if an accident were taking place. Then various noises follow, clamor and confusion. After a moment THE QUEEN *enters, followed by* THE LADY IN WAITING.

THE QUEEN *is a beautiful woman, gowned in faultless taste. She is about forty years of age. Her hair is very dark, except for a solitary white lock which appears almost directly above the middle of her forehead; but this she does not attempt to conceal by any artifice. She enters in full regalia, as if attired for some court ceremony. From her shoulders hangs the royal mantle.*

THE LADY IN WAITING *is about sixty years of age, rather nobly plain. She also is in full court dress.*

THE QUEEN. [*As she leaves* THE LADY IN WAITING, *who attempts to support her.*] No, let me be, I am not hurt. . . . It is nothing.

LADY IN WAITING. Has Your Majesty suffered no injury?

THE QUEEN. None, I assure you.

LADY IN WAITING. But the shock, the fright—be seated, Your Majesty. [*She assists her to remove the Court Mantle.*] Your Majesty must rest. At least drink a glass of water.

THE QUEEN. [*Seating herself in an arm-chair.*] You may bring the water, but I will have nothing in it. Let it be pure as God made it.

[THE LADY IN WAITING *brings the water from a table which stands near by.*]

77

LADY IN WAITING. But, Your Majesty, it is cold; Your Majesty is overheated—

THE QUEEN. Give me the glass. [*She takes it from the* LADY IN WAITING.] You are trembling all over.

LADY IN WAITING. Ah, Your Majesty, you have no idea how frightened I was, how frightened we all were, when the horses reared in the traces! Your Majesty can imagine . . . the overturn, the coach shattered into pieces, Your Majesty thrown upon the ground!

THE QUEEN. [*Smiling.*] Fortunately there was somebody waiting to receive me. How fortunate that that man [*Laughing.*]—my knight-errant—was so near!

LADY IN WAITING. [*Displeased.*] Certainly, Your Majesty.

THE QUEEN. [*Looking at her for a moment, then laughing.*] We shall have to award him the Grand Cross. Are you frowning?

LADY IN WAITING. Your Majesty!

THE QUEEN. But what is the matter? What is on your mind?

LADY IN WAITING. Your Majesty, that man was unmannerly and impertinent. Your Majesty will not be displeased, but his deportment was horribly incorrect. To catch Your Majesty in his arms without permission!

THE QUEEN. Yes, if he had allowed me to break my neck, his conduct would have been more correct. In that case he would not have committed a breach of etiquette. No, indeed! It is not every day that a woman, even if she is a queen, is in peril of her life, and has the experience of being saved from death in a gallant's arms.

LADY IN WAITING. Your Majesty amuses herself.

THE QUEEN. Perhaps I do, but not unkindly. Poor fellow! However, you may malign him as much as you like.

LADY IN WAITING. Your Majesty, I do not malign him when I suggest that it is incorrect and impertinent for this person to follow Your Majesty wherever you go.

THE QUEEN. [*Laughing.*] Like my shadow!

LADY IN WAITING. Like a rude, ill-bred fellow who is ignorant of decency and of the requirements of etiquette. Your Majesty never leaves the Palace but that he is standing on the pavement opposite. You cannot go to church, or to the theatre, or visit the parks, or attend any public ceremony but that he is there in the front row, yes, or nearer than the front row, as he was to-day.

THE QUEEN. Fortunately for me.

LADY IN WAITING. Your Majesty, loyal vassals were not wanting to fly to Your Majesty's assistance.

THE QUEEN. [*Gently.*] Yes, so I saw when the horses reared. Half a dozen dukes began to run, but what with etiquette which kept them at a safe distance and rheumatism which would not permit them to run, my royal person was in grave danger. [*Laughing.*] Indeed, if it had not been for him—

LADY IN WAITING. Skulking in a bramble bush, like a lover in comic opera!

THE QUEEN. Love is no respecter of hiding places. It is foolish to laugh at hidden lovers, even in comic opera. Besides, what you say was a bramble bush appeared to me to be a laurel, and men take as naturally to laurels nowadays as they did in the time of Petrarch. Some of the leaves have even clung to my robe. [*Picking off two or three.*] Almost enough to weave a crown for my lover.

LADY IN WAITING. Your Majesty surely does not imply that that man is in love?

THE QUEEN. Why not? Don't you think so?

LADY IN WAITING. He is utterly deficient, lacking. How do we know? Perhaps he may be . . .

THE QUEEN. An anarchist? But how stupid! In the twenty years he has followed me, he never yet has found an opportunity . . .

LADY IN WAITING. [*Horrified.*] Your Majesty!

THE QUEEN. [*Laughing.*] Of showing disrespect.

LADY IN WAITING. Does Your Majesty consider that this extraordinary persecution shows no disrespect?

THE QUEEN. But what has become of him? Where is he?

LADY IN WAITING. He has been detained.

THE QUEEN. Where? For what reason?

LADY IN WAITING. For having introduced himself without permission into the Palace Gardens.

THE QUEEN. To save the life of his Queen! The end justifies the means.

LADY IN WAITING. Your Majesty, he could scarcely have been advised beforehand that Your Majesty's coach was to be overturned, and at that particular spot in the Palace Gardens.

THE QUEEN. Then you do not believe in presentiments?

LADY IN WAITING. Your Majesty, I am too old for such things.

THE QUEEN. [*With a note of melancholy in her voice.*] So am I—for such things.

LADY IN WAITING. Your Majesty!

THE QUEEN. No, we both know how old I am, and so does the world. Decreeing her age is not one of the prerogatives of a queen. [*Taking up a hand-glass, she gazes into it attentively.*] Horrible, is it not?

LADY IN WAITING. Your Majesty is marvellously young.

THE QUEEN. Even so, marvels do not last long. Whenever I look into the mirror I am aghast at the wrinkles which I shall find there very soon. I know, too, where they will come. [*Indicating her eyes and mouth.*] They show already when I laugh. Ah, when she is twenty, how carelessly a woman laughs! [*Putting down the mirror.*] When I laugh, I cover my face with my fan. When I am forty, I shall have all the Palace mirrors broken. [*She recites simply.*]

"When forty winters shall besiege thy brow"

You recall Shakespeare's sonnet?—

"When forty winters shall besiege thy brow
And dig deep trenches in thy beauty's field,
Thy youth's proud livery, so gazed-on now,
Will be a tatter'd weed, of small worth held;
Then being ask'd where all thy beauty lies,
Where all the treasure of thy lusty days,
To say, within thy own deep-sunken eyes,
Were an ill-eating shame and thriftless praise.
How much more praise deserved thy beauty's use,
If thou couldst answer 'This fair child of mine
Shall sum my count and make my old excuse,'
Proving his beauty by succession thine!
This were to be new made when thou art old,
And feel thy blood warm when thou feel'st it cold."

[*Sighing.*] I have never had a child!

LADY IN WAITING. Your Majesty! [*Affectionately but disapprovingly.*] Your Majesty has no right to consider such a thing.

THE QUEEN. No, of course not. Ah! [*Smiling again.*] Do you suppose he could be a poet?

LADY IN WAITING. Why a poet?

THE QUEEN. Why not? In any case we shall soon know.

LADY IN WAITING. We shall? How?

THE QUEEN. I shall ask, and learn his answer.

LADY IN WAITING. Surely Your Majesty does not intend—

THE QUEEN. To receive him? Precisely.

LADY IN WAITING. But Your Majesty, he is nobody.

THE QUEEN. In that case we shall become acquainted more easily. I shall offer him my thanks.

LADY IN WAITING. Your Majesty's Government will thank him officially.

THE QUEEN. But he has saved me personally, and I shall thank him personally. I will receive him now.

LADY IN WAITING. Your Majesty!

THE QUEEN.   If there is nothing else that you wish to suggest . . .

LADY IN WAITING.   Unless Your Majesty has changed her mind?

THE QUEEN.   No, do not be alarmed.   There is nothing to fear.— Ah! And I will receive him alone.

LADY IN WAITING.   As Your Majesty commands. [*She goes out.*]

   [THE QUEEN *again takes the mirror and gazes into it fixedly. With a woman's instinct, she rearranges her hair; then laughs at herself and lays the mirror down again.*]

THE QUEEN.
"When forty winters shall besiege thy brow" . . .

[THE LADY IN WAITING *and* THE LOVER *appear in the doorway. He is forty years of age, neither well nor badly dressed. He wears a black sack suit, his beard is pointed, his hair somewhat long and slightly touched with gray. He comes forward greatly agitated.* THE LADY IN WAITING *retires.*]

THE LOVER.   Your Majesty!

THE QUEEN.   No, come in.

THE LOVER.   [*Advancing a step, then making a reverence.*]   Your Majesty!

THE QUEEN.   Come nearer.

THE LOVER.   Your Majesty!

THE QUEEN.   I have sent for you to offer my thanks.

THE LOVER.   I do not deserve them.   Your Majesty will command.

THE QUEEN.   It was a happy chance that brought you into the garden.

THE LOVER.   Yes, Your Majesty, yes.

THE QUEEN.   And I am deeply grateful to you.

THE LOVER.   No, Your Majesty, no.

THE QUEEN.   But I am.   Indeed I am!

THE LOVER.   Your Majesty will decide.

THE QUEEN.   But how is it that you were able to gain admission to the Gardens?

THE LOVER.   Very simply.

THE QUEEN.   In spite of my guards?

THE LOVER.   Your Majesty, it was not the fault of your guards.   I climbed the wall at the rear by the plane trees, out of sight of the guards.

THE QUEEN.   In broad daylight?

THE LOVER.   No, Your Majesty, last night. Your Majesty must not be alarmed—

THE QUEEN.   But the wall is very high there.   You might have injured yourself.

THE LOVER.   No, Your Majesty, I am used to it.

THE QUEEN.   Used to it?

THE LOVER.   Yes, Your Majesty, on Saturdays.   The factory shuts down over Sunday, so I am not obliged to work.   I have plenty of time; I can sleep where I like.

THE QUEEN.   Do you spend the night in the open air, in the garden?

THE LOVER.   It is very pleasant in the summer time.

THE QUEEN.   Do you mean that in winter?—

THE LOVER.   Just the same; yes, Your Majesty. [*She makes a gesture of astonishment.*]   Only when it freezes, I go into the house with the orang-outang.   Your Majesty keeps him now on the further side of the parterre. Don't be alarmed, Your Majesty; we are great friends. He is very fond of tarts and roast chestnuts, so you see there is no danger.

THE QUEEN.   Great Heaven! Is it possible?   Are you in your right mind?

THE LOVER.   Yes, Your Majesty.

THE QUEEN.   But, my good man, what is the object of exposing yourself in mid-winter in this fashion, in such singular company?

THE LOVER.   Your Majesty . . . really . . . I don't know whether or not I ought to tell you.

THE QUEEN.   But you must!

THE LOVER. Your Majesty, every night before you retire, and when you get up in the morning, Your Majesty
comes out upon the terrace before your apartments. In
the evening, you look up at the stars; in the morning, you
feed the white doves.

THE QUEEN. Yes, I do, poor things! I like to toss
them a few handfuls of corn.

THE LOVER. [*Interrupting.*] Indian corn.

THE QUEEN. How do you know?

THE LOVER. The wind usually carries some grains off
the terrace.

THE QUEEN. Do you pick them up?

THE LOVER. Yes, Your Majesty, when I can, which
is not often. The paths are swept every morning, so when
night comes, they are no longer there.

THE QUEEN. What? Do you keep them?

THE LOVER. Yes, Your Majesty. I have a collection
of souvenirs:—the grains of corn; a feather from Your
Majesty's hat, which blew out one day while you were
driving; a piece of fur from one of Your Majesty's boas,
which you wore at the last Carnival—it caught in the rail-
ing as Your Majesty left the stand; a coin Your Majesty
threw from your coach to a little beggar boy in the street;
a tortoise-shell hairpin which fell into the garden one morning
along with the corn; a pair of gloves; two of Your Majesty's
slippers—I purchased them from a maid of one of the
Ladies of the Wardrobe—and I don't know what else!
You see, it is a little museum. An Englishman offered me
a thousand pounds sterling for it.

THE QUEEN. [*Interested.*] What did you do?

THE LOVER. Your Majesty, the heart is not for sale.

THE QUEEN. You must be rich.

THE LOVER. No, Your Majesty, I was—that is to say,
rich enough; I made a good living. But now, I am poor.

THE QUEEN. Have you lost your money?

THE LOVER. Yes, Your Majesty. But we will not
speak of that; it is of no interest to Your Majesty.

THE QUEEN. But it is. It interests me very much. May I ask . . . ?

THE LOVER. How I lost my money? Yes, Your Majesty, it is not a secret. Even if it were, since it is Your Majesty . . . I spent it upon railway tickets, sea-voyages, rooms in hotels. Your Majesty is such a great traveller!

THE QUEEN. Were you following me? [*He nods his head in assent.*] But this is incredible.

THE LOVER. No, Your Majesty, no. Travelling is very expensive. As long as Your Majesty remained in Europe, it was not so bad; but when you made a voyage to India and another to the Fair at Chicago, and immediately after, a pilgrimage to the Holy Land—

THE QUEEN. Did you follow me even as far as India?

THE LOVER. Yes, Your Majesty. Your Majesty will remember that the voyage was undertaken on account of your health. Your Majesty may not know it, but the doctors agreed that it was a question of life and death. It was necessary for you to have a change of climate. Thanks be to God, Your Majesty recovered, but you might have died on the journey. Your Majesty will understand that under the circumstances it was impossible for me to remain in Europe.

THE QUEEN. Impossible!

THE LOVER. [*Ingenuously.*] Absolutely.

THE QUEEN. But I cannot consent to have you spend your fortune like this.

THE LOVER. Your Majesty, do not give it another thought. It was not exactly a gold mine. A few thousands, that was all—the factory which I had the honor to mention to Your Majesty: "The Unrivalled, Makers of Butter and Cheese"—purveyers to Your Majesty, yes, indeed! It was mine, now it belongs to another. That is all.

THE QUEEN. But you . . . ?

THE LOVER. I am assistant bookkeeper now; I check up the accounts.

THE QUEEN. That must pay you very little.

THE LOVER. Pshaw! Nothing to speak of. It is a humble position. Believe me, Your Majesty, I am capable of much more than that. If not proprietor, I might still have been manager, or foreman at least, only—

THE QUEEN. Only?

THE LOVER. Only . . . Your Majesty will not be displeased, but I must keep my time free. The fact is . . . well, I have taken this position because it gives me a living and—[*Looking down at his clothes*]—and enough to appear respectable, because it requires only two hours a day, from half past nine until half past eleven in the morning, precisely the hours at which Your Majesty confers with your Ministers. Your Majesty will understand . . ´.

THE QUEEN. [*Laughing.*] Certainly! At that same hour we are both at the office.

THE LOVER. No, no, Your Majesty! Your Majesty misinterprets my meaning. I never presumed to think . . . the fact is . . . well, between those hours my mind is more free; I am able to work without distraction, to apply myself. I am sure that Your Majesty is not upon the streets.

THE QUEEN. How long do you expect to continue this life?

THE LOVER. As long as I am able, Your Majesty, and Your Majesty does not prevent. Your Majesty is not offended at what I have said?

THE QUEEN. Offended? No! But . . . you must be very unhappy.

THE LOVER. No, Your Majesty, very happy. *Very* happy! That is, not as happy as I was, because now, when Your Majesty leaves Court, I am not always able to travel. Rascally coin! But, fortunately, now Your Majesty travels less. It will not do to ask too much of fortune. Your Majesty, after what happened this morning, I . . . I am repaid for everything which I have suffered in the world. Your Majesty cannot imagine how happy it makes me that . . . that is, Your Majesty cannot imagine how glad I am that this incident . . . although I would have given my life to have prevented it . . . I mean . . . Your Majesty understands what I mean.

THE QUEEN. Yes, yes, I do. Do not distress yourself. I, too, am glad that it was you—

THE LOVER. Your Majesty!

THE QUEEN. Because . . . I have noticed your face for so many years, I have seen you for so long a time.

THE LOVER. Your Majesty has noticed me?

THE QUEEN. Naturally.

THE LOVER. Probably Your Majesty thought that I was a photographer for one of the illustrated papers?

THE QUEEN. I thought that you were a poet.

THE LOVER. No, Your Majesty! No! Never!

THE QUEEN. Have you never written verses?

THE LOVER. [*Disappointed.*] Does Your Majesty like verses?

THE QUEEN. Yes, I am very fond of them.

THE LOVER. Goodness gracious! No, Your Majesty, no! Never! Never! [*Brightening.*] But I know by heart almost all the verses which have been published about Your Majesty—birthday verses, verses celebrating your victories, your works of charity, and so on, and so on. There are so many of them! Your Majesty of course knows them, too?

THE QUEEN. Not those verses. [*Smiling.*]

THE LOVER. God bless us!

THE QUEEN. But you must not be troubled. One may be a poet, and yet not write verses.

THE LOVER. Does Your Majesty think so?

THE QUEEN. Certainly, we may write poetry or we may live it. [*Deeply affected.*] And devotion and self-denial, illusion and dreaming, the sacrifice of one's life to an ideal,

an impossibility—these things are also true poetry, great
poetry, are they not?

THE LOVER. [*Not understanding.*] No doubt, Your
Majesty, no doubt. Of course, since Your Majesty says
so.

THE QUEEN. And you are a great poet of life.

THE LOVER. Your Majesty says so.

THE QUEEN. And I—because you are—in memory of
this day, of this event, which also is an extraordinary one
in my life—I am going to give you a present to add to that
collection which you tell me of, and I hardly know—because of your delicacy, your sacrifices, really—will you
accept this remembrance from me? [*She offers him a
jewel which she wears upon her breast.*]

THE LOVER. No, no, Your Majesty! No! By no
means! Really. Not that jewel! No, no!

THE QUEEN. But why not?

THE LOVER. Because a jewel is—a jewel. That is,
it has value—in itself; and—no, Your Majesty! No, no!

THE QUEEN. I did not wish to give offense.

THE LOVER. No, Your Majesty, no! It is not that.
It is . . . the way I feel. A caprice! If your Majesty
would deign to give me some reminder, something personal,
perhaps, of no value.

THE QUEEN. As you wish.

THE LOVER. If you would let me have that mirror,
Your Majesty, after looking into it, once. [THE QUEEN
looks into the mirror and then hands it to the Lover.]
There . . . Your Majesty! Thanks! Your Majesty will
permit me to kiss your hand? [*He kisses it.*] Thanks,
thanks, Your Majesty! Believe me, Your Majesty—
[*Deeply moved.*] This is the happiest day of my life.

THE QUEEN. I, too, am greatly obliged to you, and
I wish to ask you a favor. If at any time you desire anything, anything which it is within my power to grant, you
will do me a great kindness by coming to me.

THE LOVER. [*Hesitating, wishing to ask something.*]
Your Majesty!

THE QUEEN. Now . . . Tell me truly, is there nothing that you wish?

THE LOVER. Your Majesty! Since Your Majesty has been so kind . . . If Your Majesty would exert your influence with the Minister of the Interior to have him grant me a pass over the railways of the Kingdom.

THE QUEEN. You shall have it this very day. Is there nothing else? What is your name?

THE LOVER. Matthew, Your Majesty. Matthew Brown, Your Majesty's humble servant.

THE QUEEN. [*Repeating the words so as to fix them in her memory.*] Matthew Brown. You shall have it this afternoon. Now, you may retire. [*She strikes a small silver bell.*] And many thanks yet again. [*To the* LADY IN WAITING, *who enters.*] Let this gentleman be escorted to his home, and a note be made of his address. [*She bows, dismissing him.*]

THE LOVER. Your Majesty! . . . [*Bowing very low, he is about to disappear, but as he reaches the door, he turns and says:*] It need not be first class. [*Goes out.*]

THE QUEEN. [*Disturbed, pacing up and down the room, without knowing whether to laugh or to cry:*] Matthew Brown! Matthew Brown! [*To* THE LADY IN WAITING, *who re-enters.*] Has he gone?

LADY IN WAITING. Yes, Your Majesty. But Your Majesty is unwell! Has this man given offense? He has been impertinent—

THE QUEEN. No! No! On the contrary. Poor fellow!

LADY IN WAITING. Was he a poet?

THE QUEEN. A poet? No. That is—yes, in his way. Imagine—but how can you imagine? My God! This poor man has given his life for me, for to him his cheese factory was his life. Four centuries ago he would have

fought under my banners, he would have conquered a kingdom for my sake, he would have discovered a new world
and have laid it at my feet, and now—now, to see me
feed corn to the doves, he sleeps in a cage with the orang-
outang! And his name is Matthew Brown—Matthew
Brown, the Lover! The poet was right:—We have been
born too late into a world which has grown too old!

CURTAIN

LOVE MAGIC

COMEDY IN ONE ACT AND TWO SCENES

SALÓN NACIONAL, MADRID
1908

WALDORF-ASTORIA, NEW YORK
1918

CHARACTERS

THE PROLOGUE.
PIERROT.
COLUMBINE, *Pierrot's Wife.*
PIERRETTE, *Maid and Confidant of Columbine.*
POLICHINELLE, *An Old Magician.*
HARLEQUIN.
A LITTLE GIRL.

LOVE MAGIC

THE PROLOGUE. Rum-a-tum-tum! Ladies and gentle-men! Although I am a marionette, I am the Prologue. And invested with so high a dignity, permit me to announce the subject of the comedy which is about to be presented, and to address you in eulogy of the personages who are to appear in it. Ladies and gentlemen! Inevitably it treats of love. Love! Love! I wish, ladies and gentle-men, I were a poet at this moment so that I might present to you in a nosegay of the sweetest smelling syllables a pane-gyric of that dear misfortune, that delightful pain, that fatal passion, that enchantment, that irresistible effluence of the stars, that fierce consuming of the soul, that death-dealing microbe—or whatever it is that you may decide this delicious inquietude to be, which, through all the cen-turies, men and women have agreed to call love. You would listen amazed, if I were such a poet, to the crackling and scintillation of my metaphors; you would admire and marvel at the unstable, shifting winds, the soft, unfolding flowers, the broad expanse of heaven, the silver fountains, the caverns, the eagles, the sun rays and the moonbeams, and all the twinkling stars which I should make dance before you upon the rope of my imagination to embellish my discourse. You would twiddle your thumbs with de-light, ladies and gentlemen, listening to my discourse, if I were a poet; but I have already told you that I am not one; I am only a marionette and the Prologue. I see you smile. Smile, then, but don't disdain me. To be these two things at one and the same time one must amount to something. Marionette! I see you laugh. Joy sparkles in all your eyes. Do you suppose that it is a small thing to have a name the very mention of which is enough to

95

make people laugh? And do you suppose it is nothing, when you have it, to be able to live up to it throughout the ages and to uphold such a reputation with a dignity which, after all, is purely ridiculous? And we have upheld it, yes we have, ladies and gentlemen, splendidly, like kings and princes. Our little bodies are our witnesses. To win applause they disjoint themselves, twist and turn and bend backward, throw off their arms and heads into the air, or lose a leg in a high prance to get it back again in a pirouette. See! We palpitate from head to foot, every inch of us, as if our bodies were all hearts. And yet, ladies and gentlemen, beyond a doubt we have no hearts. What should we need of them when we vibrate and fly from one thing to another so continuously without them?

A LITTLE GIRL. But, Mr. Prologue, how can marionettes love if they have no hearts?

THE PROLOGUE. I did not say that they could love, my dear young lady.

LITTLE GIRL. Didn't you say, Mr. Prologue, that your comedy was about love?

PROLOGUE. That is exactly it. It is about love, but it is a comedy.

LITTLE GIRL. Oh!

PROLOGUE. But do not be sad, beautiful black eyes, for our comedy will be incomparably played. All the love in the world could never discover lover's sighs anywhere which would be like those of Columbine.

LITTLE GIRL. Good! Good! Are you going to tell us about Columbine?

PROLOGUE. Why not? Know then that she is white, but not pale, because in each of her cheeks every instant a rose is about to be born. She has painted her lips with the red of poppies, and one day when she sat down to dream, looking out over a meadow, two violets sprang up and jumped into her eyes. Since then nobody has been able to tell whether her glances were fragrance or light, and out of this sweet confusion, as out of all beautiful confusions, a harmony springs, which we call music. And so the look of Columbine is a song. Merely listening to her sing and hearing her laugh, men have gone mad. So her mind is like a wonderful bird-cage, filled with nightingales, which, like all captive nightingales, feed upon hearts —upon her heart. That is why Columbine is unfaithful to Pierrot, sometimes—to feed her heart. For Pierrot, who is a marionette and a puppet as she is, refuses her the heart's meat on which, as I have told you, the nightingales feed.

LITTLE GIRL. Good! Good! Now tell us about Pierrot.

PROLOGUE. What shall I tell you about Pierrot? His mind is like a sunbeam which has fallen into a globe of crystal and clear water, and all the colors are there in it, except one, which is constancy. You see today he imagines he is a philosopher, but out of his philosophy roses spring, so that our comedy which begins with a sigh, ends with an embrace, or, rather, with two embraces, because Harlequin, after he has sung his song so earnestly, and to such utter disdain, consoles himself for love by loving, and for the kisses which he cannot get, by those the girls will give. For this is the proper way all love songs should end. Try and sing them, gentlemen, you will always find some ear that is willing to hear. And you, beautiful ladies, listen to the song of love while it is floating in the air and catch it on the wing, for you will find that it is tame and it thrives in captivity. Ask Pierrette if the kisses have not turned to honey which she has taken in when they had lost their way and had nowhere else to go. Now, ladies and gentlemen, I can only add that wisdom is about to appear upon the stage of our farce, but the triumph of folly will oblige him soon to break his wand. [*The curtain rises.*] The comedy begins. This is the garden—I forgot to tell you that the stage represents a garden. Open your ears, for the foun-

tain begins to play, open your eyes for the roses are bursting into bloom.

[*The* PROLOGUE *retires.*]

SCENE I

In PIERROT'S *garden. There is an arbor with
rustic benches at the right. It is spring. Trees and
bushes droop their boughs, laden heavily with flowers,
perfuming all the air. The breezes sing with the
voices of birds, and the sky smiles bright with sunshine.*

COLUMBINE, *seated within the arbor, whose foliage
conceals her almost completely, seems wrapped in melancholy thought.* PIERROT *walks up and down at the
rear, musing, and gazing contemplatively from the sky
to the ground and from the ground to the sky, ling-
ering lovingly before the flowering trees and talking
to the flowers.*

PIERROT. [*Declaiming.*] O Nature! Mother without
beginning and without ending, beyond the touch of time!
What can I do to merit all thy gifts? Roses of fire!
How can I ever hope to know the mystery which is flaming
at your hearts? Lilies! How can I penetrate the secrets
of your petals of white snow? Thanks, thanks, O Beauty,
thanks, for thou hast rent thy veil before mine eyes!
And in comtemplation of thy treasures I must end my
life.

COLUMBINE. Ah! Woe is me!

PIERROT. [*Disappearing, lost in the depths of the
garden.*] Thanks, thanks, a thousand thanks! I value my
vision and my poet's dreams above all the splendors and
above all the loves of earth and heaven.

COLUMBINE. Ah! Woe is me!

[PIERRETTE *enters, accompanied by* POLICHINELLE.]

PIERRETTE. Enter, Signor Polichinelle, quickly; for now Signor Pierrot is wrapped in his meditations. He will not discover that you are here. Enter . . .

POLICHINELLE. Did you say that your mistress had sent for me?

PIERRETTE. Oh, how eagerly, Signor Mage! Could I but make you understand how wretched the poor child has been! Does it not pierce the very soul to look at her? She spends all the day and the night-time sighing, she is fading away so fast. That divine form of hers is not what it once was, alas!

POLICHINELLE. Alas!

PIERRETTE. How oblivious men are to such things, Signor Mage!

POLICHINELLE. Not all men.

PIERRETTE. My lady is like the driven snows of heaven to her spouse. [*Turning toward the back with a menacing gesture.*] Ah, Signor Pierrot! Signor Pierrot!

POLICHINELLE. Hush! I think Columbine has discovered us.

COLUMBINE. [*Coming out of the arbor and advancing in tears toward* POLICHINELLE.] Ah, Signor Magician! How impatiently I have awaited your arrival!

POLICHINELLE. [*Bowing.*] Signora Columbine!

COLUMBINE. Bring chairs, Pierrette.—Ah! Woe is me!

POLICHINELLE. Do not sigh, lady.

COLUMBINE. I am so unhappy!

POLICHINELLE. I congratulate you—

COLUMBINE. Upon being unhappy?

POLICHINELLE. No; upon finding that your beauty has not faded so fast as I had been led to suppose. Of course, I had heard from Pierrette—

PIERRETTE. [*Returning with the chairs.*] What do you know about such things, you old dotard? Nonsense! I suppose a woman's beauty is like an article of religion in your eyes—there is no more to it than seeing and believing.

COLUMBINE.   Leave us, Pierrette!

PIERRETTE.   [*Before retiring, she looks toward the rear, where it is to be supposed that she sees* PIERROT.]   There he is now.   Look at him!—bending over the roses, and, I dare say, composing verses in their praise.   I would hand him a bunch of roses if he had the honor to be my spouse! Ah, Signor Pierrot!   Unhappiest of men!   Don't you know that you are not the only poet in the world; that there are others who compose as beautiful verses as you do, and to better purpose? . . . [*The notes of a cithern are heard in the distance.*]   Didn't I tell you?   It is the good Harlequin.

HARLEQUIN.   [*Singing.*]

> White roses are her forehead,
> The waving grain her hair,
> The stars her eyes;
> Alabaster pure her shoulder,
> And the beauties that enfold her
> The starry skies.

> Who would not be of the roses,
> Or the grain that is her hair?
> Her starry eyes?
> Or her neck of alabaster,
> Serf and slave where she is master—
> Her deep heart's sighs?

[*The words are heard afar off, linked with a haunting melody.* PIERRETTE *listens, entranced, emphasizing them with gestures of approval.* COLUMBINE *rises indignantly, the first stanza scarcely concluded, and presently addresses* PIERRETTE.]

COLUMBINE.   Pierrette!

PIERRETTE. Lady!

COLUMBINE. Didn't I command you to send that impertinent fellow away? His music is displeasing, to my ear.

PIERRETTE. In compliance with your command, I shut the gate in his face, and the body of your lover remains outside in the alley, sore distressed. But his spirit—woe is me!—is an immaterial thing, and who can deprive Signor Harlequin of the consolation of sending it after you wherever you may be, on the wings of his songs?

COLUMBINE. Go and tell him that he offends me with his music.

PIERRETTE. I would not be too severe with him, if I were you. What harm can it do just to hear?

COLUMBINE. [*Indignantly.*] Pierrette!

PIERRETTE. [*As she turns to go.*] All, all are blindly in love with the impossible: my lady with her husband, Harlequin with my lady, and with me, nobody—which, alas, is only too possible!

[COLUMBINE *sinks again into her chair and sighs wearily.*]

POLICHINELLE. [*Greatly perplexed.*] But will you be kind enough to explain to me what the matter is? What is the meaning of these tears, these songs of Harlequin's, this inexplicable discontent upon the part of your maid? Why all this mystery? I am distracted—I shall go out of my head.

COLUMBINE. Ah, Signor Polichinelle, love is the most mysterious thing in the world!

POLICHINELLE. I should be sorry to have you think so. Love is a natural function; it is simple, perfectly simple. The difficulty is that we complicate it with spiritual distinctions. Ah! That is where the trouble begins. Nature is never willing to have man improve upon her processes.

COLUMBINE. The fact is—

POLICHINELLE. That is precisely the fact.

COLUMBINE. The fact is that my husband does not love me.

POLICHINELLE. What do you say? What is that? Pierrot is deceiving you?

COLUMBINE. He is not even deceiving me. Oh, if only once he would deceive me! Then, at least, I might be thankful that he had had the grace to consider me, to make some effort to preserve my ideals.

POLICHINELLE. But your rival?

COLUMBINE. My rival, Signor Mage, is Nature. [POLICHINELLE *is dumbfounded.*] Yes, Pierrot is a poet —the more miserable he! He adores the carmine in the roses, but he disdains it upon my lips. He worships the azure of the overarching sky, but he cannot see it in the teardrop which glistens in my eye. He drinks sweet perfumes on the breezes, but he will not quaff them from the zephyrs which are wafted from my mouth. . . . Ah! Woe is me! Woe is me!

POLICHINELLE. Pierrot a poet? You are right. Poetry in marriage is entirely out of place. It is an intruder, an interloper, like anything else which we do not expect. But these songs of Harlequin's?

COLUMBINE. They are another complication, Signor Mage. My misfortune, thanks to the little pains which my husband takes to deceive me, has become known to all men, and Harlequin has had the audacity to presume to console me for it. He wishes me to follow the old adage which says that "Love is cured by love," he . . .

POLICHINELLE. What is it that he wishes you to do?

COLUMBINE. Have no fear, I shall not follow his advice.

POLICHINELLE. You are right. For this notion that love can be cured by love is sheer nonsense. Believe me, there is no cure for anything on earth, outside of science. You can trust me for that, Signora. I am a wise old man.

COLUMBINE. That is the reason I have sent for you.

POLICHINELLE. You have done well, my daughter. [*He meditates.*] You say that your husband has deserted you, he has abandoned and is tired of you, he writes verses —all of these are bad signs, very bad. However, fortunately—

COLUMBINE. Is there no remedy?

POLICHINELLE. One—one which is well-nigh infallible. [*He draws a crystal phial from the recesses of his robe.*] Take this phial. In it has been brewed a philter, compounded by magic art out of the essence of your tears.

COLUMBINE. But what shall I do with this philter?

POLICHINELLE. Whenever Pierrot is pensive and absorbed, wrapt in his poetic ecstasy, let but one drop from this phial, and poesy—adieu!

COLUMBINE. I do not understand.

POLINCHINELLE. Listen. For example, you say that Pierrot is enraptured with the azure of the skies. Spill but one drop, let fall but one tear, and the sky will be covered with thick clouds in his sight.

COLUMBINE. I understand.

POLICHINELLE. So, little by little, hour by hour, he will become disenchanted with all natural beauty, and he will turn again to yours.

COLUMBINE. Which also is natural, believe me, Signor Mage.

POLICHINELLE. I believe you—ah, too well! Adieu!

COLUMBINE. How can I ever thank you?

POLICHINELLE. Do not thank me too much, or your gratitude will overcome my wisdom, and lay it prostrate in the dust. Signora! . . .

[*He bows and retires.*]

COLUMBINE. I am saved. [*Calling.*] Pierrette! Pierrette! [PIERRETTE *enters.*] Come and rejoice with me.

PIERRETTE. [*Disappointed.*] Do you mean—that is to say—Has the Sage found a remedy? Then—

[*Endeavoring to conceal a note which she is carrying in her hand.*]

COLUMBINE. What is that? What paper are you trying to conceal? [*She seizes it.*] A letter from Harlequin! Is this the way that you obey my commands?

PIERRETTE. I gave your message to Signor Harlequin, and he was cast down into the uttermost depths when he heard that his song had given you pain; and so, to prove that he intended no offense, he has written out the verses on this piece of paper, which he begged me to put into your hands; but if you do not wish it——

COLUMBINE. No, no, let me see. Surely I ought to read what they are. It is my duty to make an example of him—a horrible example! [*She runs her eye over the paper.*] Words and phrases of fire, fire shall put out your fire!

PIERRETTE. My lord!—my lady.

COLUMBINE. Spirit of God, aid me now!

[PIERROT *enters. He carries a bunch of purple roses in his hand. As he advances, he gazes lovingly from flower to flower, and begins meditatively to recite the verses which he has composed in their praise.*]

PIERROT.

> Purple petals, rich in hue,
> God has shed his blood for you—

[COLUMBINE *lets the first drop fall from the phial.*]

PIERROT. [*Crying out.*] Ay!

COLUMBINE. [*Running up to him.*] What is the matter?

PIERROT. A thorn pierced my hand.

COLUMBINE. My love, leave the roses, for they are full of thorns. [*She takes the flowers from* PIERROT'S *hands and dashes them violently upon the ground. They leave a purple trail behind them as they pass through the air, and then fall, their stems bare.* PIERROT *watches them fall and sighs heavily.* COLUMBINE *flings herself into his arms.*] What are you thinking of? What is on your mind? Don't you know that my love is a flower that can never be stripped bare?

SCENE II

PIERROT'S *garden in autumn. There are no more flowers in it—only a few pallid roses and some hardy chrysanthemums. At the back glows the red of the setting sun. Above, little white clouds are driven fitfully across the sky, while at intervals gusts of wind shake the trees and scatter the dry leaves upon the ground, or rustle them about in restless golden whorls.*

COLUMBINE and POLICHINELLE are seated in the garden. COLUMBINE is even more melancholy than in the first scene.

POLICHINELLE. But it is clearly impossible! Do you say that my remedy produced no effect?

COLUMBINE. A most marvelous effect.

POLICHINELLE. Frankly, then, I do not understand.

COLUMBINE. The remedy was worse than the disease. Pierrot has ceased to be a poet, but he has become a philosopher.

POLICHINELLE. A philosopher?

COLUMBINE. Yes, so much the more miserable he! Your philter was too efficacious. For days now there has been no sky without clouds for Pierrot, no rose without a thorn, no pleasure without loathing and disgust. Even the perfume of the flowers gives him pain, so that I, too, have almost begun to pity him.

POLICHINELLE. But have you manifested your pity with tenderness and affection?

COLUMBINE. As affectionately as I was able; but alas! when my husband, disillusioned with the perfidies and imperfections of Nature, turned to hate and despise them, he took it into his head that my beauty, also, was a natural thing, and it has been impossible to disabuse him of it. You can imagine the consequence. My lips seem to him like roses, my eyes like the sea or the sky, my hair like the sunbeams; and not only that, but Pierrot has discovered in various parts of my person all the blots, scars, stains, blemishes, tempests and storm-clouds that afflict the universe or offend the sense of beauty. I am worse off than I was before, Signor Mage. [*A pause ensues.*] Have you no new remedy to prescribe for this new evil?

POLICHINELLE. It will be difficult, Signora Columbine. It seems that the spirit of your husband is obdurate to love. If you could only learn to forget, to resign yourself—

COLUMBINE. Is that all your boasted science can do? Know then that I do not wish to resign myself; I wish to love. I am looking for a cure, not for consolation.

POLICHINELLE. Do not be angry with me, lady. The problem is stubborn and involved. But I shall study it in my laboratory, and I swear to you that I will never emerge from it so long as I shall live, unless I have found an infallible medicine. [*He goes out.*]

COLUMBINE. Science and wisdom hear!

[PIERRETTE *enters.*]

PIERRETTE. Wisdom? I should like to know what wisdom has got to do with love? What does that old impostor know about it anyway? At his age!

COLUMBINE. Age is a guarantee of knowledge.

PIERRETTE. Not to me. It may be in some things, but in affairs of the heart practice makes more perfect than learning. In love, experience is the key which opens hearts; if it is not used, it rusts. And I do not need to ask you how long it must be since Signor Polichinelle has used his key.

COLUMBINE. Will you always destroy my illusions, Pierrette?

PIERRETTE. Yes, because one reality is worth a thousand illusions. Signor Harlequin—

COLUMBINE. Do not talk to me about Harlequin!

PIERRETTE. Signor Harlequin is a reality. Believe me, my lady, there is no illusion about him. I know, and I can answer for it. Besides, you must be convinced by this time that all the drugs of the sorcerers are of no avail to win back the heart of Signor Pierrot.

COLUMBINE. Alas! So I am. Woe is me!

PIERRETTE. So that you will never find a remedy through the aid of science?

COLUMBINE. I fear it.

PIERRETTE. Leave it to me, then, and let me put my plan into execution.

COLUMBINE. What plan? What is it that you wish to do?

PIERRETTE. You will soon see. Without any other science than experience, which I have picked up on my way through the world, I shall save you. The first thing to do is to receive Harlequin.

COLUMBINE. Pierrette!

PIERRETTE. Though it be only to undeceive him. One angry word from your lips would have a thousand times more effect than a thousand sermons from mine, which, to tell the truth, were not made for sermons.—But in any case, he is here.

[HARLEQUIN *enters and throws himself at* COLUMBINE'S *feet.*]

HARLEQUIN. Queen of my soul, sun of my spirit, magnet and pole of my desire!

COLUMBINE. What is this? Rise!—Pierrette, is this the way that you obey my commands?

PIERRETTE. Pardon, lady, but it is too much for you to expect me to stand forever between the fire and the wall. You don't know to what dangers I have been exposed, contending continually against the ardors of Signor Harlequin!

HARLEQUIN. My lady, in turn I beseech you to pardon

Pierrette. It was not her negligence, but my audacity, which caused this wrong, if wrong it be.

COLUMBINE. How?

HARLEQUIN. Does the heart overwhelmed in darkness sin because it desires the light?

COLUMBINE. Desire is one thing, performance is another.

HARLEQUIN. Columbine, in the minds of lovers desire is performance. The desires of Love are mandates, peremptory as the laws of life!

COLUMBINE. You blaspheme, Signor Harlequin. Certainly, to love like this is a crime.

HARLEQUIN. What matter so long as it is love? Do not shrink and draw away from me! Move closer, lady. At least listen to my tale of woe. Grant me this solace—

COLUMBINE. Will you promise to go away then immediately, if I do?

HARLEQUIN. If you ask me to.

COLUMBINE. And will you promise never to come back?

HARLEQUIN. If you are not convinced by my arguments.

COLUMBINE. You may talk.

HARLEQUIN. Thanks.

[*He kisses her hand.*]

COLUMBINE. I said talk.

HARLEQUIN. My lady, that was the irrepressible cry of my soul.

COLUMBINE. You have a soul that has been most rudely brought up.

PIERRETTE. [*To* COLUMBINE.] Good! Lead him on.

HARLEQUIN. Pardon, lady, for my soul and for me. We have both hungered through so many ages for a sight of this glory, that now when we find ourselves in your presence, my soul and I, face to face, it is small wonder that we forget our ill-fortune, and become boys again, and throw to the winds all sense of proper restraint.

COLUMBINE. Which my dignity cannot excuse, Signor Harlequin.

HARLEQUIN. But your love and your sympathy ought to excuse it.

COLUMBINE. Do you presume to talk to me of ought?

HARLEQUIN. Ought there not to be many oughts between you and me, Columbine, oughts and never an ought not?

COLUMBINE. Between you and me?—You?

HARLEQUIN. Yes, Columbine, me; me—and you. For I am wretched for your sake!

COLUMBINE. It is not for my sake.

HARLEQUIN. It may not be through your fault.

COLUMBINE. I like that better.

HARLEQUIN. But it is the same to me; my misery is the same, because I love you, Columbine, I love you, I love you so much that when I love you all I can, I hate myself—unhappy that I am!—because I cannot love you more. I love you, I love you, I love you!

[*Each time that he says "I love you," he kisses her hands passionately.*]

COLUMBINE. [*Defending herself a little, but not displeased at heart.*] Not so loud, Signor Harlequin! Not so loud—there may be an echo in the garden.

[*They wander off at the rear, pursuing the debate, and disappear.*]

PIERRETTE. I should never have believed it possible that the grief of my mistress would have been so difficult to console.—Ah, me!

[PIERROT *enters. He carries a book in his hand. He reads and meditates.*]

PIERROT. To think that even in the dewdrops—the radiant tears of morning—there is a world of monsters, a contending universe of pain! To know that the smiling verdure of the fields is but the mask of foul decay, the immortal beauty which we love, the veil and dull similitude of death!

> [*He paces back and forth, absorbed in his meditations.*]

PIERRETTE. [*Approaching him, sympathetically.*] Signor Pierrot—

PIERROT. Who speaks to me? Ah! Is it you? [*Angrily.*] Why are you smiling? Why are you so happy?

PIERRETTE. Signor, life is beautiful.

PIERROT. Do you know what you bear within? A skeleton, a void, nothing! [*A pause follows.*] Where is your lady?

PIERRETTE. She was here a moment since, so wretched over your philosophy. She was in tears. But now she is consoling herself—that is to say, she has company. Signor Harlequin—

PIERROT. Harlequin?

PIERRETTE. A most extraordinary young man, proud, handsome, amorous—

PIERROT. What is that?

PIERRETTE. And an excellent poet. My lady could not possibly have chosen better company.

PIERROT. What do you say? Why do you tell me these things?

PIERRETTTE. Because they are true.

PIERROT. What makes you look at me like this?

PIERRETTE. I was counting sadly the wrinkles which philosophy has dug in your brow.

PIERROT. Tell Columbine that I wish to see her.

PIERRETTE. Do you think it will be wise to interrupt them now?

PIERROT. Is she so intent upon that visit?

PIERRETTE. Look and see. There they are . . . [PIERROT *retires and peers through the shrubbery.*] Do you see anything?

PIERROT. That Harlequin is a fool.

PIERRETTE. Oh, no, he is not! Why, all the while one is with him, he has such winning ways. [COLUMBINE *laughs.*] My lady laughs. Poor lady! It is so long since I have heard her laugh. Ah! Look!—I wondered what they were doing. That was a happy stroke of Signor Harlequin's. But what is the matter? [PIERROT *starts to run and rushes headlong off the stage like one possessed.*] Where are you going? Ah, ha, ha, ha! See him run! Ha, ha, ha! A jealous man is always ridiculous! There he is now. He is furious . . . My lady pleads for mercy. And Signor Harlequin—he effaces himself—he fades modestly out of sight . . . I am sorry for that man!

> [*The sound of rude voices is heard in the garden; shortly afterward* HARLEQUIN *emerges from the trees. He comes forward with a dejected, disappointed air, and hurries rapidly across the stage.*]

PIERRETTE. [*Detaining him.*] What is the matter, Signor Harlequin? Was not my lady willing to be consoled?

HARLEQUIN. Your lady is a model of conjugal fidelity.

PIERRETTE. Who told you to go wandering in other people's gardens, exploring hearts which have masters? Better stick to the highways and the byways, Signor Rover, and to fields which are virgin.

HARLEQUIN. Do you know any?

PIERRETTE. That is a reflection upon me. What do you mean, Signor Harlequin?

HARLEQUIN. I mean any disposed to receive me?

PIERRETTE. Why, Signor Harlequin! I—What do you want me to say? I am a young and inexperienced girl, but I am sure that there must be someone—perhaps not so very far away. You know what the song says: "When least you expect it"—And I never expected it. Don't look at me like that . . .

> [*A pause ensues.* PIERRETTE'S *eyes become eloquent in the silence of her lips, and pronounce a significant discourse.*]

HARLEQUIN. [*With sudden resolution.*] Could you love me, Pierrette?

PIERRETTE. Ha, ha, ha! Do you think I win my victories through other people's arms?

HARLEQUIN. Don't be cruel!

PIERRETTE. My lady is much more beautiful than I.

HARLEQUIN. Illusion! The beauty of woman is all one great store, one vast and perfect body, of which every woman is but an individual part. Your lady is beautiful, you are as beautiful as she—both different parts of the same great beauty.

PIERRETTE. But, I wonder, just what part of this great beauty that you tell me of, am I?

HARLEQUIN. From what I feel, you must be very near the heart! [*They embrace.*]

[PIERROT *and* COLUMBINE *re-enter and advance into the garden. They also are locked in an embrace, and gaze steadfastly into each other's eyes, full of happiness.*]

COLUMBINE. Swear to me that you are telling me the truth, Pierrot.

PIERROT. I swear it. The fear of losing you has revealed to me the truth that your love was the soul of my life. Your words are the most beautiful of poems, and your embraces the most enduring of philosophies.

POLICHINELLE. [*Entering precipitately with a phial in his hand.*] Signora, here is the philter, the love magic, the true, the infallible medicine!

[*All laugh gaily, and* PIERRETTE *carries her impertinence so far as to mimic the magician with many a comic grimace.* POLICHINELLE *stares at them in amazement. The phial which he carries in his hands explodes with a loud report, and the Elixir of Love is scattered upon the ground.*]

PIERRETTE. It was about time to explode it.

POLICHINELLE. What is this I see?

PIERRETTE. What you see, Signor Mage, is simply this:

that science is superfluous when it comes to affairs of the heart. There all wisdom is vain, and all philters are colored water. For love is cured by love, and disdain by jealousy; so it has been since the beginning of the world, and so it will be until the world has ceased to be. Spells and conjurations are of very little use. The love that has fallen asleep through excess of good fortune is not be awakened again without the menace of another love which is more passionate, and which burns like youth's fire. That is all there is to it. My master was asleep because my lady loved him too much, and he has waked at the fear that she might cease to love him so. Don't you see?

POLICHINELLE. Hum—what I see. But—[*Pointing at* HARLEQUIN.] Wasn't this gentleman also in love?

PIERRETTE. Head over heels; you can surely see it.

POLICHINELLE. [*Protesting.*] But not with you.

PIERRETTE. Ha, ha, ha! He thought not himself, but he soon found his mistake, through my assistance—and the force of circumstances.

POLICHINELLE. Hum!

HARLEQUIN. Although I am a young man, Signor Polichinelle, and a poet, I too have my philosophy. And in the first chapter, there is this maxim: "He who refuses to console himself for the kisses which he cannot get, by those the girls will give, is mad entirely."

[*The sorcerer, scandalized, takes to his heels, covering his ears with his hands, then throwing his arms into the air, brandishing them wildly. Soft, sweet music sounds, and the two pairs of lovers begin a slow and stately dance.*]

CURTAIN

POOR JOHN

COMEDY IN ONE ACT

TEATRO LARA, MADRID
1912

PACIFIC GROVE, CALIFORNIA
1920

THEATRE, LONDON
1928

CHARACTERS

MARIANA, *aged 20*
JOHN, *aged 22*
ANTONIO, *aged 23*
MAMÁ INÉS, *aged 66*
MAMÁ PEPA, *aged 70*
DON CARLOS, *aged 48*
TWO FACTORY HANDS
TWO MAIDS

POOR JOHN

A formal garden en parterre. A number of wicker arm chairs, rocking chairs and a chaise longue, all of which are plentifully provided with cretonne cushions, are set out in the shade of a sturdy walnut tree. Two tables stand near by, one containing a tray with fruit and breakfast service, the other, boxes of candy, flowers, and a bundle of lace tied with ribbon. There are flowers also on the chaise longue.
MAMÁ PEPA *and* MAMÁ INÉS *are seated together.* MAMÁ INÉS *is sewing.* MAMÁ PEPA *has been reading, and removes her spectacles, wipes them with her handkerchief, and puts them on again.*

MAMÁ PEPA. It is going to rain this afternoon.

MAMÁ INÉS. Nothing of the sort! What makes you think it is going to rain?

MAMÁ PEPA. Don't you see that cloud coming up?

MAMÁ INÉS. Yes, it is wind.

MAMÁ PEPA. I say it is rain. My leg tells me so.

MAMÁ INÉS. Well, my arm tells me that we shall have fine weather for the rest of the week.

MAMÁ PEPA. God help us both! [*The factory whistle blows.*] There goes the whistle. The factory clock must be fast today.

MAMÁ INÉS. Nothing of the sort. How can it be fast when it was eight o'clock ten minutes ago?

MAMÁ PEPA. Did your arm tell you that?

MAMÁ INÉS. No, the sun told me. It is around on the second stone in the gallery floor already.

MARIANA. [*Speaking outside.*] Good-bye, good-bye! Thank you, thank you all so much . . . [*Laughing.*] Of course! Thanks awfully just the same. Good-bye, good-

119

bye! [*She enters carrying a bouquet of roses in one hand.*]
I believe they all love me. Everybody seemed so happy
as they went away. Perhaps they really do love me,
too; exerything in this world cannot be put on. [*She
goes over to the table.*] Roses, lilies, carnations . . .
Gracious! And chocolates! [*Taking one.*] I must save
a few, though, for John. Poor boy, he has such a sweet
tooth—just like me! Our tastes are the same in everything. [*The old ladies cough.* MARIANA *looks up, but
pays no attention.*] Isn't it too lovely to be twenty and
have so many presents? [*The whistle blows again.*] The
second whistle! It sounds more like a ship's siren than
it does like a factory whistle. I should like to go on a long,
long voyage.

MAMÁ PEPA. Yes, and get sea-sick.

MARIANA. What of it? I should go ashore on some
islands which are nowhere on the map, and discover them,
and civilize the natives—that is, not altogether, because
then they would have to wear trousers and gloves and
top-hats. Men are never so ugly as when they are all
dressed up.

MAMÁ INÉS. You don't know what you are talking
about.

MARIANA. Mamá Pepa and Mamá Inés, you two dear
old grandmothers, I am so happy! But, oh, how I do long
to be so much happier!

MAMÁ PEPA. It would make no difference to you.

MARIANA. Yes, it would; that is, it seems to me it
would make a great deal of difference. I am happy now
because the sun shines and I am twenty, and there is nothing the matter with me, I thank God for that. Everything seems to be so simple and easy, so much a matter of
course. But happiness must be something a great deal
more—it must be more inside of you, don't you know?
It must be something awfully solemn. No, not exactly
solemn either. I mean . . . Anyway, sometimes a girl
feels so happy that she would just love to cry.

MAMÁ PEPA. Mercy on us! What is wrong with the child?

MARIANA. You will find out when the time comes— if the time ever does come.

MAMÁ INÉS. She is out of her head.

MARIANA. My two dear, old respectable grandmothers, do you really think that the time ever will come? Do you really? Or are you just perfectly certain that it will not?

MAMÁ PEPA. Think what time will come?

MARIANA. The time that every girl is longing for, without having any idea what it is?

MAMÁ INÉS. My dear, you will find out soon enough for yourself that everything in life is either unpleasant, or else it comes too late.

MARIANA. God bless us!

MAMÁ PEPA. Pay no attention to what she says; it all depends upon the point of view. When the night is darkest, God sends the morning. Don't allow yourself to brood and mope. However bad things may be, they might be worse, or else we should not be here to see them. A chicken may be light-hearted and yet have a stone in its gizzard.

MARIANA. Do you know what the factory girls say? That I ought to pray for a sweetheart every day, because it's high time for me to have one.

MAMÁ INÉS. What would you do with a sweetheart at your age?

MAMÁ PEPA. She could get married, like everybody else.

MARIANA. Of course! And then I could have lots of children. I mean to have ten at least, all boys, hard workers, strong, clever, fearless, brave, so that they can travel all over the world doing great and splendid things, and build roads and factories and houses and schools, and make laws and conduct revolutions. They will be strong as castles, every one of them. I believe that ten real men would prove the salvation of any country. [*Discovering her father,* Don Carlos, *who enters.*] Father, how many ministers have we in the Spanish cabinet?

Don Carlos. Such as they are, I believe there are eight.

Mariana. Then I shall have two over. One can be a poet and the other a philosopher. And a grateful country will erect a statue to my memory!

Don Carlos. What is all this nonsense?

Mariana. Congratulate me. This is my birthday. I am of age—I am twenty. [*Submitting to an embrace.*] Aha! Are you sorry? You seem sad. [*Sympathetically.*] I know . . . it is mother.

Mamá Pepa. Carlos, she looks more like my poor daughter every day.

Don Carlos. Yes, she does.

Mamá Inés. Nothing of the sort! She is the living image of her father.

Don Carlos. Omitting all his faults, let us hope.

Mamá Inés. There are no faults to omit. I don't say so because he is my son, but I wish you could have seen him when he was twenty-five.

Mamá Pepa. I wish you could have seen my daughter when she was eighteen.

Mariana. Well, all you have to do is to look at me. How dreadfully embarrassing it is to be such a beautiful girl!

Mamá Pepa. Thank Heaven, she is good-natured.

Mamá Inés. Yes, it is a family trait.

Mamá Pepa. Naturally.

Mariana. [*To her father.*] Do look at all my presents! The flowers are from the factory hands, the candies from the girls at the sewing-school, and the Sunday School children sent me this piece of lace. The cross is from Mamá Pepa, and the rosary from Mamá Inés, with real coral beads, so you see I have two really good grandmothers, as far as one can judge from their presents. What are you going to give me?

DON CARLOS. Whatever you like. [*Taking out his pocket-book.*]

MARIANA. No, don't give me any money; I have more than I know what to do with. We started the sewing-school to help the poor girls along, but now we are all making our fortunes. I had nothing myself, yet we can scarcely keep up with the orders. The preserves that Mamá Inés and I put up are a success, too, though we only began because it was such a pity to throw the fruit away. We have had inquiries, even, from a shop in Madrid.

DON CARLOS. Name anything you wish.

MARIANA. I would if I dared. There is one thing— yes, I am going to ask for it. Now don't you say no! Promise not to be angry. It . . . it . . . it isn't for myself, but it is just the same, you know; it's for John.

DON CARLOS. For John?

[*Both old ladies cough.* MARIANA *turns and glares at them.*]

MARIANA. Yes, it's for John . . . that is, not exactly for him either, it's for his father. Don't you see? I told you that I didn't want money, but now that I come to think of it, it is money. At least it is something very like it.

DON CARLOS. Well, is it or is it not?

MARIANA. Don't be cross. No, it isn't money. Only I want you to go surety for them so that they won't lose their house.

DON CARLOS. Do you expect me to guarantee all the old Marquis's bad debts?

MARIANA. Why, papa!

DON CARLOS. Do you realize what it means to stand sponsor for a man of that character?

MARIANA. All they have left is the house, and now they are going to lose that for a miserable trifle which they borrowed of that skinflint. John's mother is sick, too, and John is worried about her. Poor John! I know that to be responsible for them—that is, for John's father—I suppose though he can't help it; it's the way he is made. I tell you what to do. You buy the mortgage, and then they can owe the money to you. You will never put them out, so everybody will be satisfied.

DON CARLOS. You have strange ideas of business.

MARIANA. It isn't business, it's a birthday present. I am twenty—think of it, twenty! What wouldn't you give to be twenty again? And you are, don't you see, because I am, and whatever I am, is yours. Besides, I promise never to do it again. [*Embracing him.*] Oh, haven't I a rich and stingy father! Do say yes! Look me in the eye and say yes! Say yes!

DON CARLOS. Very well, to please you. [*Smiling.*] But I don't want to hear any more about it. When John comes, send him to me, and we will talk it over; I shall have nothing to do with his father. Only I want you to understand that it is casting pearls before swine; they will be worse off by the end of the month. However, to please you—

MARIANA. Thanks, thanks, oh thanks!

DON CARLOS. Do not thank me, for I am doing it against my will. Enough for the present!

MARIANA. Where are you going?

DON CARLOS. Back to the factory.

MARIANA. How you do love to see people work! Remember, be home on the stroke of twelve, because Mamá Inés has promised us all sorts of good things, and if the rice is spoiled, we shall be lost. It will be a lovely surprise, too, for poor John!

[DON CARLOS *goes out.*]

MAMÁ PEPA. [*Scornfully.*] Poor John!

MAMÁ INÉS. Some day we are going to get sick of poor John.

MARIANA. Do you think so?

MAMÁ INÉS. Before long we shall have him in the soup.

MARIANA. Nonsense!

MAMÁ PEPA. Mamá Inés is right, my dear. I do not approve myself of a young lady of twenty keeping company with a young gentleman of twenty-two. He follows you wherever you go.

MAMÁ INÉS. I see nothing to object to in that. She and John were brought up together, almost like brother and sister. There is no harm in their going about. What I do not like is having the child take an interest in him which is improper.

MAMÁ PEPA. I see nothing improper in that. It is the duty of those who have plenty to be generous with those who have not. What I am afraid of is that she may encourage him to expect something else.

MAMÁ INÉS. Nothing of the sort. He is as modest as a mallow and as good as God's bread.

MAMÁ PEPA. He may be as good for all I know, but he is a man, and men —

MAMÁ INÉS. Do you think you can tell me anything about men, Mamá Pepa?

MAMÁ PEPA. Probably not. You know it all already.

MAMÁ INÉS. What am I to understand by that remark?

MARIANA. Come, come, don't be angry, you two dear grandmothers! What if John is good? Well, so much the better for him. What if I do love him? He loves me as much, at the very least. We have always been together, so nobody is surprised; it has become a habit. I help him whenever I can because I am rich and he is poor. Besides, everybody has somebody to look out for; you have me, and I have John. So I say God help us all! Here he comes as calm and placid as can be.

MAMÁ INÉS. If he is coming, I am going. There is plenty to be done in the kitchen, and it behooves us all to roll up our sleeves.

MAMÁ PEPA. In that case, I had better run and feed the canaries.

[MAMÁ INÉS *and* MAMÁ PEPA *go out.*]

MARIANA. [*Laughing.*] Enter the ogre. Poor John!

[JOHN *appears. He is a young man of winning personality, distinguished in manner and faultless in dress,
but evidently depressed and greatly cast down.*]

JOHN. May I . . . ?

MARIANA. Come in.

JOHN. [*Advancing.*] What were you laughing at?

MARIANA. My grandmothers are jealous of you.

JOHN. Your grandmothers hate the sight of me.

MARIANA. Mamá Inés says that you are as good as
God's bread.

JOHN. A polite way of intimating that a man is a fool.

MARIANA. Why do you look at me?

JOHN. You are entirely too lovely for this hour in the
morning.

MARIANA. I am not as lovely as I was, for I am aging
very rapidly. Don't you notice it?

JOHN. You?

MARIANA. Do you notice anything unusual in my face?
Don't I seem serious? I am a year older at least than I
was yesterday.

JOHN. A year older than you were yesterday?

MARIANA. Exactly. I was nineteen yesterday and I
am twenty today.

JOHN. Well, I *am* a fool!

MARIANA. [*Laughing.*] I accept your congratulations.

JOHN. I am a blockhead, an idiot not to remember!

MARIANA. [*Laughs.*]

JOHN. Don't laugh. Why didn't you tell me yesterday?

MARIANA. So as to be able to remind you that you
had forgotten today—as usual, of course.

JOHN. Mariana, you are not fair with me.

MARIANA. Of course not! But look at all the bonbons
I have saved for you. Help yourself. Besides, I have good
news. How is your mother?

JOHN. What do you expect? Her cough is worse, she
is exhausted. Then, by some accident, she heard about the

house, although we intended to keep it from her. So now
she has something else to worry over. She says that if we
are compelled to give it up, it will kill her; she will die.
That is all there is about it.

MARIANA. How does your father feel?

JOHN. Father says he will shoot himself.

MARIANA. He never will.

JOHN. I know, but mother believes him. Whatever
he says, she takes literally. Mariana, we have lost our
home. This is not living. I don't know what I should do
if it were not for you. If it were not—

MARIANA. If it were not?

JOHN. If it were not for you, *I* might be the one who
shot my-self.

MARIANA. You certainly are a brave man!

JOHN. How can you expect a man to be brave when
he meets with nothing in life but misfortune? Everything
has gone wrong with me since the day I was born. Whatever I put my hand to fails utterly. You know it better
than I do. I was brought up to be rich, and I am poor.
I studied law, and I can not string three words together.
A man must be strong in that profession, he must have
vigor of body and mind, yet I am all out of breath if I
walk up a hill; I have not the heart to crush even a fly. To
save the little that remains to us after the folly of my
father, I need to be unscrupulous and bold, yet my mother,
God bless her, has taught me to be good, good, always good,
like God's bread, as you have just heard from your grand-
mother.

MARIANA. [*Laughs.*]

JOHN. Yes, laugh. I have a letter which I wish you
would translate into English. You can help me. It will
only be time wasted, but never mind. It is to some lord
who is visiting the province in search of antiques—fabulous
creatures, are they not? He might stop in at our house and
offer us a handful of duros for the silver which still remains in the chapel.

MARIANA. Do you mean to tell me that you would sell the chapel silver?

JOHN. Yes, and the genealogical tree that hangs in the drawing-room. I have an idea that it might be worth a few pesetas.

MARIANA. Why, it would be like selling your name!

JOHN. My name? We would sell our souls, if Satan had not abandoned the practise of buying them.

MARIANA. Hush, you heretic!

JOHN. But I weary you with my troubles.

MARIANA. No, I was only thinking what a strange thing life is. Why is it that some people always have good luck, while others are always down? Everything always turns out well with me.

JOHN. [*Earnestly.*] Because you deserve it.

MARIANA. Nobody deserves anything, because nobody chooses his disposition, or the place in life he is going to fill.

JOHN. Now you are the one who is talking heresy.

MARIANA. Then I am sorry, for it is the truth. What have I ever done to deserve anything? I have simply lived and have been happy, and that is the way I go on. I thank God again and again for all my happiness whenever I remember how good He has been to me, but most of the time I forget even that. I do not believe that I have had one sorrow since the day I was born—I mean one real sorrow, that was my own. When my mother died, I was too young. Of course, I am sorry for other people who are unhappy, but all the while I am happy myself. I have never been ill. I never had any trouble with my lessons, like most children. Nobody ever found fault with me, and whatever I do prospers. Yet all the while, I hear people complain. The times are hard, they say. So I suppose my good luck, which seems to me the most natural thing in the world, is nothing short of miraculous, and I begin to ask myself when I think it over: "Why is it, good God, why is it?"

JOHN. Accept it and do not think it over.

MARIANA. Sometimes I am terribly provoked with you.

JOHN. Why?

MARIANA. Because you are so meek. Whatever happens, you resign yourself and submit to it; you ask no questions. I believe that you walk through the world with your eyes shut, and that is why you bump your head against stone walls all the time.

JOHN. Please don't be angry with me. I cannot bear it.

[*He covers his face with his hands.*]

MARIANA. Does your head ache?

JOHN. A little.

MARIANA. [*Drawing near.*] You look pale. Have some coffee?

JOHN. No, I have drunk too much already.

MARIANA. Last night? I knew it. You sat up reading. How late was it before you went to bed?

JOHN. It was morning. Don't be angry with me. You were awake yourself.

MARIANA. I? Goodness gracious!

JOHN. There was a light burning in your room all night.

MARIANA. [*Laughing.*] Because I fell asleep so quickly that I didn't have time to put it out. What did you think? I rode to Robledo yesterday to see my cousins, and we played tennis, I don't know how long, and then we went rowing, so I was tired out when I came home. I am ashamed to tell you, but I never went to bed at all. I knelt down by the bed to say my prayers, and when I came to, it was morning. I fell asleep with the first *Pater Noster.*

JOHN. You must feel ill today.

MARIANA. Don't you believe it! My eyes were a little heavy at first, but a cold shower, and no one could ever have suspected it.

JOHN. You are a cold shower, my dear girl, from head to heels, and a draught of health, outside and inside sunshine and morning. I envy you, and how I love you!

MARIANA. How you say it! Come, we had better write that letter. You might dictate it in Spanish, although it will be a waste of time, now that I think of it. I told you that I had good news for you, and you haven't even asked me what it was. However, I remembered my own birthday, so I asked father for a present. You could never guess what he gave me—the mortgage!

JOHN. [*Not comprehending.*] The mortgage?

MARIANA. Yes, yours—your mortgage. Don't you remember? The mortgage which is held by that man who threatened to foreclose and sell your house. My father is going to pay it off, whatever it is, and then you can owe it to him, just as you did to the other man, only father won't foreclose, so you can stay on and live in the house forever. [*Greatly affected.*] And you won't have to sell the silver or the family tree either!

JOHN. Mariana!

MARIANA. Hurry and see father and you can fix everything.

JOHN. [*Choking.*] Mariana!

MARIANA. Won't your mother be happy?

JOHN. Mariana! [*Seizing both her hands.*] You are the best woman in the world. Nobody else would ever have dreamed of such a thing. Thank you, thank you! I can never thank you enough. Oh, Mariana, how it humiliates me, and how it makes me happy! Because it is charity, I know that it is charity, but blessed be the charity of your hands, of your heart, because it is yours, and blessed, too, be you yourself, a hundred thousand times! [*Passionately.*] You are my life, my soul! The only reason for my existence!

MARIANA. [*Greatly surprised.*] John!

JOHN. Yes, the only one. Didn't you know? The

only one! But of course you did. Say yes, you did, my
own!

MARIANA. No, John, no.

JOHN. Yes, Mariana.

MARIANA. But, then—

JOHN. Yes, I love you, I adore you, I am mad over
you, head over heels in love with you, lost irretriev-
ably!

MARIANA. Don't say that!

JOHN. I have loved you all my life.

MARIANA. No, no!

JOHN. Didn't you know it?

MARIANA. I don't want to know it.

JOHN. Why not?

MARIANA. Because it is ridiculous—no, not exactly
ridiculous, but it is a pity; I am awfully sorry.

JOHN. Do you mean that you do not love me?

MARIANA. [*Somewhat more composed.*] No. Forgive
me, John. I do love you. I love you very much, very, very
much more than I love my father, more than I do my grandmothers, but then—I don't love you.

JOHN. Mariana!

MARIANA. I love you more than anybody else in the
world, but not like that—not like that. [*She begins to
cry.*]

JOHN. Don't cry; you will break my heart. Do—do
you love someone else?

MARIANA. No, nobody. Honestly, I don't love anybody.

JOHN. Then—

MARIANA. But I shall some day—I am going to love
somebody.

JOHN. Whom?

MARIANA. I don't know. Whoever it is, somebody—
not anybody, somebody.

JOHN. But why not me, Mariana?

MARIANA. Because I can't. I tell you, because I love

you so. I don't want you to say that I have deceived you.

JOHN. You must have a very poor opinion of me.

MARIANA. A poor opinion of you? You are the best man in the world.

JOHN. Must you say that, too?

MARIANA. It is true.

JOHN. It only makes it worse.

MARIANA. John, John! Lift up your head. Look at me, John!

JOHN. Is it possible? Can it be?

MARIANA. Why, did you think that I—

JOHN. I don't know. When I thought of it, it did seem incredible, with this miserable luck of mine, but I felt that you were so close to me, that you were so entirely my own—or that I was yours, I don't know which—and you were so good to me, so kind, so much the woman! All the happiness I have ever known in my life until now, has sprung from you—it may have been only a little, now and then, in small things, trifles, help, advice. It was presumptuous of me, Mariana, but I am so accustomed to relying upon you, that I imagined that the treasure was all mine. Besides, I love you so—I mean I need you so. Why should you not be all goodness, Mariana, and take me like a little child into your life, like a toy that you play with, or a dog of which you are fond? But let me be yours, all yours, because I love you! If you could love me only a little, I should be satisfied.

MARIANA. A little is not enough. To be husband and wife, if that is what you mean, we should have to love each other a great deal and in a different way.

JOHN. How?

MARIANA. I love you tremendously, you and everything that is yours, because it is yours—your mother, your house, yes, and your father, or, because—well, I would give my life to help you. If anybody said anything against you, I should knock him down. To save your family, I would starve. Even your name, your title which will

be yours very soon, seem to me so noble, so dignified—
I don't know how to explain it, but I just don't want
to marry you, because—because—you must not be angry,
but I think I am cleverer than you are.

JOHN. You are a great deal cleverer than I.

MARIANA. No, I don't mean exactly cleverer; I am
quicker than you are.

JOHN. No, you are cleverer and you are braver than
I. Besides you are good and beautiful. I am nothing but
a poor devil, an unlucky fellow!

MARIANA. No, you are not. You know a great deal
more than I do. You know all about books and all about
art. You are a handsomer man than I am a woman. I
am crude. My hands are red and yours are white. Then,
you are so fastidious, you have such good taste. If it
had not been for you, I am sure that I should always
have dressed like a gay masquerader. You amount to a
great deal more than I do; there is more to you.

JOHN. Yet, although there is so much to me, I am
not your ideal.

MARIANA. No, I have no ideal. Don't think that I
am so romantic.

JOHN. Well, enough of this talk! What sort of man
do you want for a husband?

MARIANA. I don't know. Wait and see. You always
lean on me when we walk out into the country—I always
have to help you up the hills. Well, the man who is my
husband will run up the hills and carry me along in his
arms.

JOHN. I will do my best.

MARIANA. Hills are symbolic of so many things!

JOHN. Ah, me!

MARIANA. I simply cannot bear to make you unhappy
—but I suppose I must; there is no escape. I should never
dream of asking you to carry me; I feel that I was born
to take care of you. When your head aches, I always
wish it was mine. You are older than I am, but it seems

to me that you must be a great deal younger; I feel as if you were my child.

JOHN. Don't say that.

MARIANA. Why not?

JOHN. Because all this love of yours, which you say you feel, which is so great, so deep, is nothing but contempt —loathing and contempt.

MARIANA. No, it is not!

JOHN. Or pity, I don't know which is worse.

[*A brief pause.*]

MARIANA. Oh, but I am so angry!

JOHN. Why?

MARIANA. To think that another woman hasn't done this to you, and then I could have consoled you afterward!

JOHN. No, Mariana, if another woman had made me suffer as you have because I loved her as I love you, even you could not have consoled me.

MARIANA. It would have been the first time. [*Drawing nearer to him.*] Don't be foolish, John; think it over, and control yourself. You don't love me as much as you think you do. If you had really been mad over me, you would have told me so before; you could never have remained silent through all these years.

JOHN. [*Tenderly.*] Don't talk nonsense.

MARIANA. Only you didn't know where else to turn to find one misfortune more. Now you can say that you have been unlucky even in love. How could two people love each other who have lived together all their lives like brother and sister? Love must come from outside, all of a sudden, from somewhere else—what is the matter? Don't you feel well? Are you ill? John, for Heaven's sake, don't take it like this! I'll have to say yes, if you do, out of pity, and then both of us will be unhappy—yes, both! John! John!

JOHN. [*Rising.*] Never mind. It is over now. You are right, your children ought not to carry the poison of a degenerate blood in their veins, they must not be born to the curse of a decaying, a contaminated race. You splendid woman, you are right to refuse a hand that is bloodless and cold.

MARIANA. How can you talk like that?

JOHN. Enough! Leave me—yes, I mean it. Then, you can come back. Leave me alone a moment, until I can collect myself, until I can persuade myself that today is to be again like yesterday—that nothing has taken place between us.

[*She retires slowly, looking back at him as she goes. When she reaches the top of the steps, she pauses, hesitating, before entering the house.*]

MARIANA. I am so sorry! Poor John! [*Stamping her foot.*] But it is not my fault. What a pity!

[*She disappears into the house.* JOHN *remains alone, seated, attempting to compose himself. A bell rings at the garden gate, but no one answers it. After a moment, it rings again. Presently,* ANTONIO *pushes the gate open and advances into the garden. He looks about, but discovers no one.*]

ANTONIO. Goodness gracious! The house must be enchanted.

[*Falling back a little, better to look up at the façade, he collides with the chair which is occupied by* JOHN. JOHN *turns sharply in great annoyance.*]

JOHN. Eh? What is this?

ANTONIO. I beg your pardon. [*Recognizing* JOHN.] John!

JOHN. [*Staring at him for a moment in return.*] Antonio!

ANTONIO. The very man!

JOHN. What are you doing here?

ANTONIO. Come, come! Embrace me!

JOHN. But where did you drop from?

ANTONIO. From your house. Where did you think?

JOHN. From my house? I thought you were in America.

ANTONIO. So I was, but you know a man can return from America—although it seems incredible.

JOHN. But what are you doing here? Have you lost anything?

ANTONIO. Nothing to speak of, my son; my heart, that is all. And I have a presentiment that if I can find it here, I shall encounter eternal happiness as well. I stopped off to have a look at you by the way—pardon my insistence on my own affairs—I thought, perhaps, you might introduce me; I did not wish to enter paradise unannounced. Your friend is charming, my boy! And charming does not express it. She is beautiful, she is glorious, she is irresistable, she is unique! One woman among ten thousand! By the way, I don't suppose you happen to be engaged?

JOHN. Engaged? What makes you say that? Explain yourself. Don't talk like an ass.

ANTONIO. Are you always so good natured when you wake up from a nap?

JOHN. A nap?

ANTONIO. You were asleep when I came in—now don't deny it. I rang the bell, I can't say how often. Then I called, I don't know how many times. Lucky devil!

JOHN. I?

ANTONIO. Yes, to be able to sleep in immediate proximity to this marvel of the ages. But you are used to it —it is force of habit. O, Mariana, Mariana!

JOHN. What business have you with Mariana?

ANTONIO. None, unfortunately, up to the present. I am mad over her.

JOHN. Absurd!

ANTONIO. Do you suppose that all men are like you— incombustible? I saw her yesterday for the first time— now don't you laugh—and I cannot live another hour without her. How do you manage not to fall in love? You have lived near her all your life.

JOHN. Well, perhaps that may be the reason. How can two people love each other who have lived together like brother and sister ever since they were children? Love must come from the outside, all of a sudden, from somewhere else—

ANTONIO. Like lightning! That's a fact. That is the way it was with me. Didn't you notice when I came in that I had been struck by it? How can a man fall in love, my boy, in twenty-four hours—no, in less—in a night, lying awake, dreaming of her? She hasn't another sweetheart, has she? Pardon the question; it interests me . . .

JOHN. No, none, whatever, but she is going to have one.

ANTONIO. Who?

JOHN. [*With exceeding ill grace, annoyed.*] How do I know?—somebody, anybody.

ANTONIO. Is that so? You seem to be pretty well acquainted, you are great friends, of course. What sort of person—you don't mind my asking these questions in confidence—what sort of person does she seem to prefer? If it is not too much trouble—

JOHN. No indeed! Don't consider me, anyhow. What do you care?

ANTONIO. I knew you were a friend of mine.

JOHN. As you say.

ANTONIO. This ideal which she has formed in her mind —does it happen to present any resemblance to me? For if it does—

JOHN. Her ideal? Could you run up a hill with her in your arms?

ANTONIO. And jump over the moon with her in them, and then back again, and run up to the top a second time without stopping to take breath!

JOHN. Well, that is just her ideal of a man. Good-bye and good luck!

[*He goes out.*]

ANTONIO. John! Where are you going? One moment! Wait! What shall I do without you? I must be introduced. [*The garden gate slams, causing the bell to ring violently.*] What is the matter with him? Is it possible that they can be engaged? No, or he would have said so, or else have knocked me over the head. I wonder—

[MARIANA *appears at the top of the steps.*]

MARIANA. John, John! Where are you?

ANTONIO. He is not here, señorita, but I am—if I can be of service—

MARIANA. Oh! [*She comes down the steps.*] How do you do?

ANTONIO. Pleasant morning, isn't it? Fine! Yes, indeed!

MARIANA. Do you wish anything?

ANTONIO. Nothing. [*Continuing, as she makes a gesture of surprise.*] Nothing, now that I have seen you.

MARIANA. [*Laughing.*] Oh!

ANTONIO. Don't you believe me?

MARIANA. Naturally.

ANTONIO. But how can you take it so calmly?

MARIANA. Surely you did not expect me to be greatly surprised?

ANTONIO. Of course not; you are accustomed to it.

MARIANA. To what?

ANTONIO. To admiration which is fervent.

MARIANA. Nobody has ever killed himself for my sake.

ANTONIO. You do not know me.

MARIANA. I remember—aren't you the man who passed on horseback yesterday afternoon, as I was standing at my cousin's gate?

ANTONIO. *Si, señora,* I am the man.

MARIANA. Were you on the beach afterward when we finished playing tennis?

ANTONIO. And after that I was on the float when you got out of the boat. Yes, indeed, I was there—at your service.

MARIANA.   You are a stranger here?

ANTONIO.   No, I was born here.

MARIANA.   Then why did you stop at the gate to ask me the way?

ANTONIO.   I was anxious to learn whether your voice was as sweet as your face.

MARIANA.   I never saw you until yesterday.

ANTONIO.   I have been five years in America, and home again only two weeks.

MARIANA.   Where did you keep yourself before you went to America?

ANTONIO.   You have often seen me, although, perhaps, you may not remember it.

MARIANA.   I wonder—yes.   No!   What is your name?

ANTONIO.   Antonio Losada.

MARIANA.   Are you Antonio Losada?   With that moustache?

ANTONIO.   Yes, indeed.   America is a wonderful country for hair.

MARIANA.   [*Laughing.*]   But then, of course, you know John?

ANTONIO.   Of course!   We went to school together with the *Escolapios,* and we were suspended together at the University—that is, the first time.

MARIANA.   I remember.   In Roman Law?

ANTONIO.   No, Canon Law.

MARIANA.   But that wasn't the first time.

ANTONIO.   Right again!   You remember better than I do.

MARIANA.   Poor John!

ANTONIO.   Poor John!

MARIANA.   What makes you say "Poor John"?

ANTONIO.   You said it first.

MARIANA.   I was not thinking.   Poor John!

ANTONIO.   Perhaps if you could forget him a little, and sympathize with me—

MARIANA.   Oh!   Are you in trouble?

ANTONIO. Terrible trouble.

MARIANA. Nobody would ever suspect it from your face.

ANTONIO. No, it is more deeply seated; there is nothing the matter with my face.

MARIANA. I hope it is not your heart.

ANTONIO. It might be, for all you know.

MARIANA. Has it pained you very long?

ANTONIO. Since the beginning of the world.

MARIANA. That is a very long time.

ANTONIO. And not one day less. When God made up his mind to create the universe, he jotted down in his note-book that I was predestined, after centuries and centuries had passed, to suffer torment because of two beautiful black eyes which I am gazing into now.

MARIANA. Very likely. Can't you ever be serious?

ANTONIO. Very. Will you marry me?

MARIANA. *Ave Maria!* God bless us! You frighten me out of my wits.

ANTONIO. Am I as unattractive as that?

MARIANA. [*Looking at him.*] No, I do not object to your looks.

ANTONIO. Thanks.

MARIANA. Thanks for what? Besides, looks are of no importance anyway.

ANTONIO. Certainly not. Would you mind telling me what is of importance?

MARIANA. Have you a cough?

ANTONIO. No, I never cough.

MARIANA. Are you subject to headaches?

ANTONIO. Yes, I had a headache once when I was a boy. Another boy cracked me on the head with a stone.

MARIANA. Oh, then you must be quarrelsome?

ANTONIO. I am; fairly so—when I can't get what I want.

MARIANA. What you want, or what you ought to get?

ANTONIO. Will you tell me the difference?

MARIANA. Don't you know?

ANTONIO. No. Neither do you.

MARIANA. I?

ANTONIO. You always get what you want; I can see it in your face.

MARIANA. Then you must be clairvoyant.

ANTONIO. Love sees at a distance; it penetrates.

MARIANA. Not at all. Love is blind.

ANTONIO. That was in the old days; but now it has been operated upon, and we have removed the cataracts.

MARIANA. Only imagine the sights that that poor boy must see!

ANTONIO. Some of them very nice, no doubt, beginning with you.

MARIANA. But where will he leave off?

ANTONIO. With you, too. After encircling the globe and seeing everything, he will come back to you.

MARIANA. After encircling the globe?

ANTONIO. What do you say? Shall we go along?

MARIANA. I warn you that he would find me an extremely disagreeable traveling companion.

ANTONIO. In what way?

MARIANA. I should expect too much of him.

ANTONIO. Expect it of me, then, and you will not be disappointed.

MARIANA. Never?

ANTONIO. Never.

MARIANA. Suppose that what I have set my heart on proves difficult to get?

ANTONIO. I will get it.

MARIANA. But suppose it does not exist?

ANTONIO. I will invent it.

MARIANA. Suppose that it costs you your life to obtain it?

ANTONIO. I shall give up my life, and then come straight back to life again, for you may be perfectly certain that I shall never leave the world as long as it contains you.

MARIANA. Not even if I marry some one else?

ANTONIO. John?

MARIANA. No, I shall never marry John, but the man who marries me must take care of him and protect him, for I shall always have him around. You are not laughing at John?

ANTONIO. By no means.

MARIANA. Because it is not safe to laugh at him. Wherever I go, he is coming along. Whatever I have, I mean to share it with him; my house shall be his house, and whenever he calls, I shall rush to his side.

ANTONIO. Yet the man complains of his fate!

MARIANA. He is a privileged person. Besides, I don't want you to be jealous. You must not be ridiculous. John is John.

ANTONIO. From this hour forth evermore. Anything else?

MARIANA. If I marry—

ANTONIO. If you marry!

MARIANA. I must have ten children, all boys.

ANTONIO. [*As a matter of course.*] Anything else?

MARIANA. I thought perhaps that might be enough.

ANTONIO. Why not add a couple of girls while we are about it, if it is not inconvenient, so that the breed of valiant women shall not become extinct?

MARIANA. Are you laughing at me?

ANTONIO. No, only I think we had better hurry. We are wasting valuable time.

MARIANA. I don't know. What are you doing?

ANTONIO. Loving you madly, passionately. I have been doing nothing else since yesterday, at eight o'clock in the morning.

MARIANA. I mean, what are you doing for a living?

ANTONIO. Why not do anything that happens along? Don't you think that with courage and a little luck, pretty nearly anything would do?

MARIANA. Yes, but—

ANTONIO. In America, my dear, I did a little of everything; I grew tobacco, I canned meat, I raised cane.

MARIANA. How perfectly dreadful! I am sure you must have thrown your money away.

ANTONIO. Dreadful? It was fine! I made lots of it.

MARIANA. You must be very rich, then.

ANTONIO. No, I enjoyed life as I went along. I shall be rich, however, when I marry you.

MARIANA. Do you plan to turn miser at my expense, when it is your duty to support me?

ANTONIO. Not miser, precisely; although we shall need to be economical if we are to provide for the boys.

MARIANA. [*Laughing.*] When do you expect to return to America?

ANTONIO. I expect to return—when, I don't know. As I shall not sail without you, perhaps I shall remain ashore.

MARIANA. I hope you don't think that I am afraid of the water?

ANTONIO. You? No, indeed! But John might be sea-sick.

MARIANA. [*Laughing.*] You are a real man. [*Holding out her hand.*]

ANTONIO. [*Kissing it.*] And you are an angel!

MARIANA. So you think now.

ANTONIO. Yes . . . I'll see you later.

[*Shouts and confusion outside.*]

VOICES. No, no! Here—not that way!

MARIANA. What has happened?

[MAMÁ INÉS *and* MAMÁ PEPA *rush in from the gallery, greatly agitated, followed by two servants.* DON CARLOS *and a group of factory hands enter simultaneously at the garden gate. They carry* JOHN *in their arms, covering him up with a poncho which conceals him from view almost completely. They lay him down upon the chaise longue, where* MARIANA *and the other women surround him. Meanwhile the dialogue proceeds with great rapidity, almost all speaking at the same time.*]

DON CARLOS. This way! This way! In here. . . .

MAMÁ INÉS. John!

MAMÁ PEPA. John!

MARIANA. Why, John!

MAMÁ INÉS. God bless us! An accident?

MARIANA. John! John! Can't you speak? Look at me! What have you done? What is the matter? Can't you answer?

DON CARLOS. He is unconscious, my dear. He is not able to talk.

MAMÁ INÉS. Mercy on us! A terrible calamity!

MAMÁ PEPA. He was a fine young man.

A MAID. Oh, he was lovely!

SECOND MAID. He was so handsome!

DON CARLOS. Ladies, he is not dead yet.

MAMÁ INÉS. But he is going to die.

MAMÁ PEPA. Nothing of the sort, unless his time has come—which may be now.

FIRST MAID. He has opened his eyes.

MAMÁ INÉS. Quick! Run for a cup of hot broth.

ANTONIO. I should suggest a nip of cognac.

MAMÁ INÉS Give him a warm punch.

MARIANA. [*At the table.*] Yes, strike a match.

MAMÁ PEPA. [*To one of the maids.*] Bring some rum.

MAMÁ INÉS. But how did it happen? Why don't you tell us?

FIRST FACTORY HAND. It was nothing much. He was walking up along the edge of the cliff, and he toppled over into the sea. That's all.

SECOND FACTORY HAND. He didn't fall, I tell you; I saw him jump.

Mamá Pepa and Mamá Inés. God have mercy on our souls!

First Factory Hand. I tell you I saw him topple off the edge of the cliff.

Second Factory Hand. I tell you I saw him jump. How could he fall when the track there is wide enough for a team?

First Factory Hand. He got dizzy.

Mariana. Yes, but who pulled him out of the water?

First Factory Hand. Nobody, because he fell plop into Little John's boat, which was tied up there below the rock, waiting to catch lobsters.

Mamá Pepa. Praise God and bless His Holy Name!

Mamá Inés. If he isn't drowned, then what on earth is the matter with him?

First Factory Hand. He fell fifty feet, lady, which is plenty to give a man a bit of shock.

First Maid. [*Entering.*] The punch!

Mariana. Give it to me. [*She goes up to* John *and forces the punch into his mouth.*] Drink this! Here, more, more. Do you feel very badly? [John *coughs.*] He coughs—naturally, after the wetting.

John. [*Faintly.*] No, I didn't get wet. The water splashed into the boat; it tipped a little when I came down, that was all. I am all right now, thanks; don't worry. Forgive me—

Mamá Inés. You did give us a nice fright!

Don Carlos. Everybody pass into the house and take something. [*To* Mamá Pepa.] See what you can do.

Mamá Pepa. Come with me.

First Factory Hand. [*To* John.] All right, son. Glad it wasn't any worse.

Second Factory Hand. Better luck next time.

[*All pass into the house except* Mariana, Antonio *and* John.]

Mariana. [*In a low voice.*] Did—did you really commit suicide?

JOHN. Yes, really. And even then I had bad luck.

MARIANA. A nice way to celebrate my birthday, making it as unpleasant for me as you can!

JOHN. I am sorry, but the temptation to leave this scurvy world was too strong.

MARIANA. Promise never to do it again!

JOHN. What good would it do if I did?

ANTONIO. [*Advancing sympathetically.*] Well, well, man! What was the trouble?

MARIANA. Nothing. He was walking along the edge of the cliff, and grew dizzy.

JOHN. [*To* ANTONIO.] What! You here yet?

ANTONIO. Yes, indeed! No sooner were you out of the way, than she appeared, so I—

MARIANA. Exactly. I appeared, so he—

JOHN. Say no more! It was foreordained.

MARIANA. Yes, he dropped from the clouds, as it were.

JOHN. [*Forcing a smile.*] When—when is the happy day?

ANTONIO. Whenever she fixes the date.

MARIANA. Oh, there is no hurry.

ANTONIO. No hurry?

MARIANA. We have so much to do before we sail.

JOHN. Sail?

MARIANA. Yes, Antonio feels that we must return to America.

ANTONIO. But you are coming along.

JOHN. I?

ANTONIO. Yes. You are to be godfather to the first of our ten. We are planning to christen him John.

MARIANA. That is if, as we hope—

JOHN. No, no, never! Impossible! . . .

MARIANA. What makes you think so?

JOHN. Because if he inherits my luck with my name, the poor wretch will not be able even to drown. Besides, when things go wrong with him, I don't want to hear you saying forever: "Poor John!"

MARIANA. No, and we ought not to say it to you either. [*Moving away unconsciously.*] Poor John!

ANTONIO. Poor John!

CURTAIN

MADAME PEPITA

COMEDY IN THREE ACTS

TEATRO DE LÁ COMEDIA, MADRID
1912

THE PLAYHOUSE, OXFORD
1924

TO RICARDO LEON

CHARACTERS

Madame Pepita, *aged 38.*
Catalina, *aged 17.*
Galatea, *aged 25*
Carmen, *aged 28.*
Cristina, *aged 16.*
A Sewing Girl, *aged 20.*
Don Guillermo, *aged 40.*
Alberto, *aged 22.*
Don Luis, *aged 55.*
Augusto, *aged 25.*
Andrés, *aged 30.*

ACT I

Reception salon in the establishment of MADAME PEPITA, *a fashionable dressmaker. The room is elabo.·ately fitted out with gold furniture. upholstered in silk, but too elaborate for good taste. In the centre and at the right, small tables strewn with fashion magazines, colored plates of French and Viennese models and samples of materials such as wholesale houses supply to dressmakers. A large three panelled mirror, in front of a pier glass reaching to the floor, points to the fact that, on busy days, the salon is pressed into service as a fitting room also. One or two smart hats hang about on high stands; almost in the centre of the stage is a dress-form, on which is draped an elaborate evening gown.*

At the rise of the curtain, CARMEN, *one of* MADAME PEPITA'S *fitters, is kneeling before the form, pinning a design of flowers and foliage on the gown. She pauses every now and then to compare the result with the fashion plate which she takes from the floor at her side, in order to examine it more closely.* CRISTINA *stands near by. handing her pins from a small box, besides flowers and buds from a large carton which is placed on a chair.*

CARMEN, *a smart looking young person of the type employed in the better dressmaking establishments of Madrid, wears a black frock set off with a small white apron. Her shoes are neat and her hair and general appearance faultlessly correct.*

CRISTINA, *an apprentice, still in short skirts, is well-groomed and smart. Both girls speak with the easy sophistication of the capital, but without marked vulgarity.*

CARMEN. Give me a pin, a rose, a bud . . . quick!

153

CRISTINA.   You're not in any hurry, are you?

CARMEN.   Well, you'll see what will happen if the Snapdragon appears upon the scene, and this dress isn't finished.

> [CATALINA, *a girl of seventeen, enters, innocent and attractive in appearance. She is horribly dressed, and her hair is done frightfully. Although her clothes are well cut and of good material, her skirt is on crooked and dips down on one side, her blouse gapes where it fastens, and her apron, which is made of lace and batiste of excellent quality, is decorated with a huge ink spot. Her skirt is neither long nor short, while her hair hangs loose, except for a large bow tied where it does the least good. In moments of abstraction, she bites her nails furiously. In one hand she carries a book. Her conversation is that of a spoiled child who is aware of her importance as daughter of the head of the establishment.*]

CATALINA.   [*Entering, overhearing* CARMEN'S *last words.*]   See here, you needn't call my mother the Snapdragon.   She has a name, like everybody else.

CARMEN.   Dearie, you're a sweet ghost—you always appear when you're not wanted.

CATALINA.   Whether I'm wanted or not, is none of your business.

CARMEN.   Excuse me, dearie.

CATALINA.   [*Walking over and seating herself in an armchair.*]   You needn't excuse yourself, but be a little careful what you say; I'm here.   [*Cuddling herself down into the chair like a cat.*]   And I'm not as silly as you think.

> [*She opens the book and begins to read to herself, evidently with great difficulty.*]

CARMEN.   [*Under her breath.*]   Little Miss-Know-It-All is not as silly as you think.

CATALINA.   [*Turning quickly.*]   See   here!   You

needn't call me Little-Miss-Know-It-All. I've got a name, like everybody else.

CARMEN. What you've got is a consumptive's quick ear.

CATALINA. [*Much offended.*] Consumptive yourself.

CRISTINA. [*Intervening.*] Ah, now, don't be cross. It was only a joke.

CATALINA. [*Immediately appeased.*] That's all right, but be a little careful with your jokes. My name is Catalina, I'll have you know, and my mother is not the Snapdragon, she's the Señora, the head of this establishment.

CARMEN. [*Maliciously.*] The madam.

CATALINA. No, sir, not the madam—Madame Pepita, which is very different. [*Insisting.*] Madame Pepita, Madame Pepita!

CARMEN. We heard you, dearie. [*Maliciously.*] Well, then, if Madame Pepita comes in and this trimming isn't finished, [*Emphasizing every word.*] *the head of this establishment* is going to create a disturbance that will make a hurricane seem tame.

CATALINA. And quite right, too, because you're lazy things, all of you.

CARMEN. Wise talk, eh, from the pet of the house?

CRISTINA. Why don't you turn in and help?

CATALINA. [*Scornfully.*] I? You've got cheek. [*Turning her back, she begins to read again, applying herself laboriously, pronouncing each syllable as children do when they learn.*] "The hu-man bod-y con-sists of three parts: head, trunk, and ex-trem-i-ties," [*Repeating, without looking at the book*] "The human body consists of three . . ."

    [*A bell rings at the entrance, which is at the head of the stairs.*]

CARMEN. [*To* CRISTINA.] Look and see who is coming. The doorbell rang.

CRISTINA. [*Glancing toward the door upon the right.*] It's the boy from the silk shop.

[ALBERTO *appears in the doorway. He is a youth of twenty-two, unusually well-educated, of good family, whom reverses have obliged to seek employment as clerk in "La Sultana," silk, lace and haberdashery shop. He dresses plainly but respectably, and displays the excessive timidity of a person who feels himself above his position. He is delivering a number of large boxes containing laces.*]

ALBERTO. [*Hesitating before he enters.*] May I? With your permission . . . I beg your pardon . . . [*The two girls do not answer, as they are busy laughing.*] Good morning. . . .

CATALINA. [*Raising her eyes from her book, instantly attracted by the young man. As the scene progresses, little by little her attitude alters from sympathy to admiration. The actress should mark the transition simply and ingenuously, as the girl's innocence does not permit her to realize its significance.*] Good morning. Did you wish anything?

ALBERTO. [*Advancing a few steps, smiling timidly.*] Here are the laces from "La Sultana," so that you may select what is required.

CARMEN. Very well, you may leave them and return a little later.

ALBERTO. [*Timidly.*] But . . . pardon me. The proprietor wishes me to bring back what you do not desire. When all the laces are here, and ladies call at the shop, naturally we have nothing to show.

CARMEN. Well, madame has a fitting at present; she has no time to make selections now.

CRISTINA. The idea! You wouldn't refuse to oblige a lady, would you, just because your employer tells you to?

ALBERTO. No, indeed! I shall retire, then, with your permission, and return later.

[*Backing awkwardly toward the door, in his embarrassment he collides with a chair, which, in falling, carries with it a table loaded with fashion plates, both crashing down together.* Greatly disconcerted, ALBERTO *attempts to gather up the scattered papers, becomes entangled, proceeds to extricate himself, finally almost falling in his turn. The two girls burst out laughing, while* CATALINA *rushes toward him with a cry.*]

CATALINA. [*Hurrying to* ALBERTO.] Oh! Did you hurt yourself?

ALBERTO. [*Smiling, in spite of his confusion, but looking askance at the two girls, who are still laughing.*] No, señorita. Thank you very much.

CATALINA. Won't you let me get you a glass of cold water?

ALBERTO. Oh, no, señorita! It is quite unnecessary.
[*The girls continue to laugh.*]

CATALINA. [*Turning to the girls.*] I don't see what you are laughing at.

CARMEN. Can't we laugh if we feel like it?

CATALINA. Not when there's nothing to laugh at.

ALBERTO. Never mind, señorita, they are laughing at me. When a man trips, it invariably amuses the ladies, I suppose it seems only natural.

CRISTINA. Yes, we can't teach you anything.

CATALINA. [*To* ALBERTO, *confidentially.*] They're stupid things, both of them.

ALBERTO. [*Gratefully.*] You are an angel, señorita.

CATALINA. [*Drawing away, half shyly, half surprised.*] Am I?

[*During this episode, the girls have returned to their task of trimming the gown.* CARMEN, *kneeling on the floor, leans backward better to sense the effect, and presently makes a gesture of dissatisfaction.*]

CARMEN. This can't be right.

CRISTINA. I don't think so, either. It's too broad; there's too much of it.

CARMEN. [*Rising and taking the sketch in her hand.*]

Well, it is exactly like the drawing, and that is awfully smart. I don't know what it is.

ALBERTO. [*Interrupting.*] Pardon me—[*Snatching the sketch from* CARMEN, *who looks up, astonished.*] The lines of this model were designed for the ideal woman, a woman with a figure built on Gothic lines. [*His self-assurance now offers a striking contrast to his former embarrassment.*]

ALL. What?

ALBERTO. [*Smiling, looking from one to the other, as if making a demonstration in mathematics.*] I mean to say that she has very long legs.

CARMEN. Say, now!

ALBERTO. I am sure of it. [*Estimating the height of the plate with his eye, and measuring it off with one finger, as painters do.*] One, two, three. . . . We have exactly eight heads.

CRISTINA. Eight heads?

ALBERTO. [*Smiling pleasantly.*] Yes, señorita, that is, in total height; and the lady for whom you are making this gown must be only— [*Glancing at the dress-form.*] Let me see. One . . . two . . . three . . . we may give her five and a half. [*With perfect assurance.*]

CRISTINA. Five and a half? Heads?

CARMEN. [*Sarcastically.*] Five and a half heads ought to seem a lot to you.

ALBERTO. [*Intensely serious.*] No, not at all. Five and a half are not nearly enough. The ideally proportioned figure has a total height of seven heads—that is the Greek type in all its purity and elegance. French and Viennese models always exaggerate somewhat, but Spanish women, particularly here in Madrid, are rather Romanesque in contour, like—like you, señorita. [*To* CRISTINA.]

CARMEN. [*Laughs.*]

CRISTINA. [*Offended.*] Like me?

ALBERTO. Don't be offended. I mean wide and thick. So, when we attempt to adapt the ideal lines of the model to the shapes which we actually see, the result is ridiculous. [*Waxing eloquent, as he studies the garment.*] Three parallel rows of trimming on a short skirt? Horrible! And the pity of it is that just as long as women neglect to study the divine mysteries of line, they will continue to go about looking as if their worst enemies had designed their clothes. It breaks a man's heart to go out for a walk and meet masterpieces of the Creator transformed into monstrosities by the sacrilegious, criminal hands of tailors and dressmakers.

CRISTINA. [*Laughs.*]

CARMEN. [*Half amused, half angry.*] What was that about tailors and dressmakers?

ALBERTO. [*Recollecting himself, his customary timidity returning as he realizes what he has said.*] Please excuse me. I wasn't thinking of you.

CATALINA. [*Who has been listening in openmouthed admiration.*] But who are you? How do you know so much?

ALBERTO. I am nobody, señorita; I amount to nothing. Only I draw a little, I sketch, and I hope to become a painter, some day. In the meantime, I am working in "La Sultana," silk, lace and haberdashery shop. I shall retire, now, with your permission, ladies. . . .

[*Goes out. A moment of astonished silence follows.*]

CARMEN. [*Laughing.*] What do you think of that?

CRISTINA. He's a scream.

CATALINA. [*Earnestly.*] I don't see what makes you call him a scream. I think he's awfully nice and attractive.

CARMEN. Ahem! Attractive and everything else. So Don Simplicity has turned your head, has he?

CATALINA. [*Almost in tears.*] I don't see what makes you call him Don Simplicity. He's got a name, like everybody else.

CARMEN. But we don't know his name.

CRISTINA. Yes, we do; it's Alberto.

CATALINA. [*To herself.*] Alberto? What a nice name! [MADAME PEPITA *is heard talking outside.*] Oh, here comes mamma!

CARMEN. [*Resuming work precipitately.*] Good-bye my wages! [*To* CRISTINA.] Give me another pin.

MADAME PEPITA. [*Outside.*] Yes, yes! I tell you, yes!

A SEWING GIRL. [*Outside.*] But, *Madame*—

[MADAME PEPITA *enters. She is still a fine looking woman. Her tailored suit is strictly in the môde, and her coiffure arranged with extreme care. She carries an elaborately trimmed sleeve in one hand, talking and gesticulating immoderately as she enters, evidently in great annoyance. At the same time, she is careful to maintain a noticeable affectation of refinement. The Sewing Girl follows deferentially.*]

MADAME PEPITA. There is no "but" about it. I tell you the sleeve is a botch, and a botch it is. You'll rip it this very minute, and baste it over again and say nothing, and if that doesn't suit you, you can go. The idea of a little monkey like you presuming to differ with me in a matter of taste!

SEWING GIRL. But I didn't say anything.

MADAME PEPITA. So much the better! Here, take your sleeve. [*Throws it at the girl, who catches it.*] The thing's a nightmare—it's about as *chic* as you are. To think I pay this girl six pesetas a week!

SEWING GIRL. [*Between her teeth, as she goes out.*] Any one who stands you ought to be paid six hundred.

CATALINA. [*Going up to* MADAME PEPITA.] Mamma, do you hear what she says? She says any one who stands you ought to be paid six hundred.

MADAME PEPITA. [*Brusquely.*] Is that your business?

CATALINA. [*Completely cowed.*] Oh!

MADAME PEPITA. [*Approaching* CARMEN *and* CRIS-

tina.] What are you doing? Wasting time—as usual? Why aren't you in the workroom?

CARMEN. We were finishing this gown for exhibition.

MADAME PEPITA. [*Examining the model through her lorgnette, which is attached to an extravagantly bejewelled chain.*] And a sweet exhibition it is!

CARMEN. Don't you like it?

MADAME PEPITA. It might do for the patron saint of your village, which is in the back country—way back, if one is to judge by the taste.

CARMEN. I was born in Madrid, the same as you.

MADAME PEPITA. Then, my dear, your taste is bad naturally.

CARMEN. It's an exact copy of the model as you ordered. Won't you look?

    [*Hands her the sketch.* MADAME PEPITA *examines the gown and the model alternately through her lorgnette.*]

CATALINA. [*Breaking in, eagerly, perfectly sure of herself.*] But the model was designed for a woman built on Gothic lines.

MADAME PEPITA. [*Looking at her daughter, alarmed.*] What's that?

CATALINA. [*Positively.*] Of course! And the lady who ordered this is Romanesque.

MADAME PEPITA. What are you talking about?

CATALINA. Yes, Romanesque. She has only seven heads, and to be true to type, with perfect proportion, you must have. . . . [*Stops to think.*] Oh, a great many more—I don't know just how many; and if you put three rows of trimming on a short skirt, why, the woman who wears it will go around looking like a Greek monstrosity whose worst enemy has made her clothes. There! Just see if I'm not right. [*Breaks off suddenly.*]

MADAME PEPITA. [*Alarmed.*] Child, have you a temperature? Come here, let me see.

CATALINA. No, mamma!

CARMEN *and* CRISTINA. [*Laugh.*]

MADAME PEPITA. [*Angrily.*] What are you laughing at?

CRISTINA. [*Intimidated.*] Nothing, *Madame.*

CARMEN. We just heard all that rigmarole from the boy from "La Sultana."

MADAME PEPITA. Has the boy from "La Sultana" been here?

CARMEN. With the laces.

MADAME PEPITA. The same boy?

CARMEN. No, another one, *Madame.*

MADAME PEPITA. Did you tell him that he was no good and that the proprietor is a cheat and an extortioner?

CARMEN. [*Smiling.*] No, *Madame.*

MADAME PEPITA. You missed a fine opportunity. I'll tell him when I see him.

CATALINA. [*Aroused.*] No, don't you do it, mamma.

MADAME PEPITA. [*Brusquely.*] Is that your business?

CATALINA. [*Moving off, suppressed.*] Oh!

CARMEN. [*Pointing to the dress-form.*] What shall we do with this?

MADAME PEPITA. Take it to pieces and pin it together all over again. But not here. People will be coming soon, and the whole place is a mess. Carry it into the workroom—I'll be there in a minute. Get out of my sight!

CARMEN. [*With her tongue in her cheek.*] Yes, *Madame.* [*Picking up the form with* CRISTINA'S *help and carrying it out, muttering between her teeth as she does so.*] With the greatest of pleasure.

CATALINA. [*Approaching her mother.*] Mamma, she says "With the greatest of pleasure."

MADAME PEPITA. [*Brusquely.*] Is that your business?

CATALINA. [*Intimidated.*] Oh!

MADAME PEPITA. What are you doing here? Idling?

CATALINA. No, Mamma, I am studying.

MADAME PEPITA. Is that so? Let me see that book. Is it a novel?

CATALINA. [*Protesting.*] No, mamma, it's a book Don Guillermo lent me—don't you know? The gentleman on the floor above. It is, really—if you want to see it. [*Giving her the book.*]

MADAME PEPITA. [*Turning the pages.*] Heavens and earth! What's this? A skeleton?

CATALINA. [*As pleased as a child.*] Yes, mamma. It's a book that tells how many bones we have and how we are made, inside and out.

MADAME PEPITA. Eh?

CATALINA. [*Continuing.*] And what everything inside us is for. [*Reciting.*] "The human body consists of three parts: head, trunk"—

MADAME PEPITA. [*Interrupting, scandalized.*] Hush, hush! That's immoral! Throw the book away this minute. Such things are only for men to know. No decent woman has any occasion to study her insides.

CATALINA. [*Innocently.*] Oh, yes, mamma, she has. Don Guillermo says that women are just the ones who ought to know, so that when they grow up and become mothers, they can nurse their own children, as God intended.

MADAME PEPITA. [*Sincerely shocked.*] The man's a satyr!

CATALINA. [*Innocently.*] Oh, no, mamma, you mustn't say that! He writes articles for the papers, and he's a member of the Academy.

MADAME PEPITA. [*Softening, as if by magic.*] A member of the Academy! Who told you so?

CATALINA. The janitor's wife. She saw it on his letters, and it's on the papers, too, that come to him from the printers: Don Guillermo de Armendáriz y Ochoa, of the Royal Academy of Fine Arts, yes, mamma. Besides, he's awfully nice and awfully sweet to me, and he has his rooms all stuffed full of big pieces of stone and statues

that haven't any heads, and whenever he meets me on the
stairs he always stops to talk to me, and he's told me he'll
lend me books so that I can learn something, because he
thinks it's a great pity that I am such a big girl and such
an ignoramus, and he asked why didn't you send me to
school when I was little, and I told him that you didn't
want me to associate with common children, and he says
that it is better to be common than to be ignorant, and
that's true, isn't it, mamma?

MADAME PEPITA. [*Abstracted, impressed.*] A member of the Academy?

CATALINA. [*Enthusiastically.*] Yes, mamma. And the
other day he had his picture in the *Nuevo Mundo* with the
King and Queen.

MADAME PEPITA. With the King?

CATALINA. Yes, mamma, at the opening of the picture
exhibition; he was there to receive them and explain everything, so that they could tell which were the good pictures
and which were the bad ones. You can see them all here
for yourself. [*Producing a copy of the Nuevo Mundo,
which is concealed among the fashion plates.*] He has
medals all over, and wears a sash.

MADAME PEPITA. [*Impressed.*] Probably the Order
of Carlos III, or maybe he's María Luisa. [*Mollified,
gazing at the photograph.*] How attractive a man does
look when he's decorated!

[*The doorbell rings, after which* CARMEN'S *voice
is heard outside.*]

CARMEN. [*Outside.*] Yes, Señor Conde. Will the
Conde step in? I'll tell *Madame.* [*Appearing in the door-
way, and discovering* MADAME PEPITA.] Oh, here is
Madame Pepita! *Madame,* the Conde de la Vega de
Lezo.

MADAME PEPITA. [*Suddenly becoming sweeter than
honey.*] Conde! Come in, come right in. [*Giving her
daughter a hasty push.*] Go and dress yourself! Don't
stand there in the middle of the room—you're a sight.

CATALINA. [*Cowed.*] Oh! [*Runs out, escaping by one door as the* CONDE *enters by the other.*]

[DON LUIS DE LARA, CONDE DE LA VEGA DE LEZO, *though but fifty-five, is in appearance much older, love, wine and other excesses having undermined his health prematurely. Nevertheless, he still affects the airs and graces of the beau, which contrast lamentably with the general decay of his person. He dresses with undue pretense to fashion, carrying himself gallantly in the grand style, although his gestures and poses are marred for the most part by his premature senility. He wabbles and totters and bends forward unexpectedly, which causes him the keenest annoyance. Kissing the girl who opens the door as he enters, he appears to be dispensing a favor. The girl receives the salute with ill-concealed disgust, wiping her face with her apron as soon as the* CONDE'S *back is turned. Then she goes out.*]

DON LUIS. My dearest Pepita!

MADAME PEPITA. I was afraid the Conde had forgotten us. It is three months since we have seen you.

DON LUIS. Oh, my dear, I have been traveling—troubles and worries without number! I have not been well.

MADAME PEPITA. The Conde has been ill?

DON LUIS. Yes, mental anguish, moral suffering; that is all. Society is in bad case, Pepita; the aristocracy has degenerated. Money is replacing blue blood nowadays, and it is prejudiced against the nobility. Poverty devours our vellum riches. We are nobodies.

MADAME PEPITA. Oh, don't say that, Conde! Money cannot purchase blue blood.

DON LUIS. [*Sighing.*] No, blue blood cannot be bought, nor sold either, for that matter.

MADAME PEPITA. Be seated, Conde.

DON LUIS. Ah, Pepita, who would believe that your dear, departed mother had lived in our house, that she had acted as maid to my departed wife?

MADAME PEPITA. [*Unduly affected.*]   Your poor wife!

DON LUIS.   Yes, you were born in our house, brought up under the protection of my wing. [*Looking about the room.*]   But, today, you travel the road to riches, while I. . . .

MADAME PEPITA. [*Countering promptly.*]   Conde, I have troubles of my own.   Believe me!

DON LUIS.   Come, come, don't tell me you'll ever hang for want of a couple of thousand pesetas.

MADAME PEPITA.   Conde, what put that idea in your head?   A dressmaker invests her entire capital in clothes. These gowns cost me a fortune, and just as soon as the style changes, nobody will look at them.   Then, I have to pay wages to no end of girls, and, finally, there are the customers.   They grow meaner and meaner every day. Even the actresses and the demi-mondaines, who only a little while ago never dreamed of questioning the price of anything, would you believe it—nowadays the way they scrutinize their bills is something shameful.   They know what everything, down to a yard of satin, costs.   Why, Conde, I had a lady here the other day, the wife of a cabinet minister—I'd rather not mention her name—who insisted upon supplying her own trimming for a court costume.   Fancy!   Trimming!   To me!   [*Greatly outraged.*] What next, I wonder?   She said the lace was antique, it had a history.   I thought to myself, it's antique all right. As for the history, there's plenty of that that's not so antique, in which your husband figures conspicuously.

DON LUIS.   It is the way of the world, Pepita.

MADAME PEPITA.   Dressmaking is not what it used to be, Conde.

DON LUIS.   Come, come, you have land at Escorial, which is money assured.   Everybody knows you have property.

MADAME PEPITA.   What good is a little property when you haven't the money to build?

DON LUIS.   Your daughter will be one of the finest matches in Spain.

MADAME PEPITA. [*Flattered.*] Oh, Conde, how can you say that?

DON LUIS. I have a soft spot in my heart for you, Pepita.

MADAME PEPITA. Thank you, Conde.

DON LUIS. You are an exceptional woman, enterprising, systematic, who has exquisite taste.

[*At each additional flattery,* MADAME PEPITA *swells with pride, blushing with excess of emotion.*] I express my admiration freely whenever I can find the opportunity.

MADAME PEPITA. I am more than grateful, Conde.

DON LUIS. Today, I have come with a purpose.

MADAME PEPITA. Conde!

DON LUIS. A lady will arrive shortly—naturally, at my suggestion—who wishes to order some clothes.

MADAME PEPITA. A relative of the Conde's?

DON LUIS. [*With a superior air.*] No, she is not of my world, socially. Rather, I should say, of the artist class. Her name is Galatea—a stage name, of course. You must have heard of her—something quite out of the ordinary—high class vaudeville, don't you know? Living pictures.

MADAME PEPITA. Oh, yes! Of course!

DON LUIS. Stunning creature! Exquisite! She has been in despair in Madrid over the problem of clothes. She can find nothing appropriate. [*With a deprecatory gesture.*] Finally, I said to her: Why not see Madame Pepita?

MADAME PEPITA. I am overwhelmed, Conde!

DON LUIS. So now she is coming to you. The difficulty is—at least, I assume it is—she treats me like a father, or even more so. Although she is fond of me, there are some subjects we never discuss. However, I am convinced that somewhere, in the background, there must be somebody who pays the bills. Tragic, is it not? But, obviously, that is not our affair.

Madame Peptia. [*Innocently.*] Certainly not, as long as they are paid.

Don Luis. Naturally, that is understood. I might suggest that in fixing the price. . . .

Madame Pepita. [*Quickly.*] The Conde knows that my prices are not exorbitant. As the lady is a friend of his . . .

Don Luis. No, no, that is not it exactly. Permit yourself, for once, the luxury of a few hundred pesetas more or less. Suppose we say a thousand more.

[Madame Pepita *responds with a gesture of astonishment.*]

Times are hard. I could use seven hundred and fifty myself . . . [*Quickly.*] which you may set aside for me when the bill is paid, unless of course, you care to advance them, if it is not inconvenient.

Madame Pepita. [*Disconcerted.*] But, Conde—

Don Luis. [*Affecting depression, pacing up and down the room.*] Sad, Pepita, is it not? Democracy has reduced us to this. A Conde de la Vega de Lezo accepting commissions upon clothes! Think of it! I shed tears.

Madame Pepita. [*Capitulating.*] Don't feel too badly, Conde. If there is anything I can do. . . .

Don Luis. [*Simulating feeling.*] Thanks, Pepita. [*Embracing her.*] I accept it because your heart is pure gold. But it demeans me.

Madame Pepita. Not at all, Conde.

[*The door bell rings.* Galatea's *voice is heard.*]

Galatea. [*Outside.*] Is Madame Pepita in?

Don Luis. Here she is; I recognize her voice. [*Transported.*] Ah, her voice! [*Advancing to the door.*] This way, Galatea. [*Hurrying forward to offer his hand.*]

[Galatea, *a woman of twenty-five, displays an extremely smart street costume, somewhat over-elaborate, but nevertheless in good taste. Her manners and speech are vulgar, contrasting with her appearance, and*

*indicating that she has been brought up among the least
sensitive of the lower classes.*]

GALATEA. [*To the* CONDE.]   So you're here, are you?

DON LUIS. [*Obsequious and infatuated, losing all his
grand manner at once.*]   Yes, I am here, as you see—
whispering naughty things about you.   I am interested in
whatever you do.

GALATEA. Well, I'll have to credit you one for getting
up early, and it was cold this morning, too.

DON LUIS. I am capable of any sacrifice for your sake.

GALATEA. The sacrifice will come later, but remember
I don't count asthmatic attacks any sacrifice.

DON LUIS. Asthmatic attacks?   A great joke!

GALATEA. Is this the Madame Pepita you talk so much
about?

MADAME PEPITA. Yes, indeed.   At your service.

GALATEA. [*As affable with* MADAME PEPITA *as she is
abrupt with the* CONDE.]   I am charmed.

MADAME PEPITA. The pleasure is mine.   The Conde
informs me that you are very particular in the matter of
clothes.

GALATEA. Usually, I think clothes so commonplace.

MADAME PEPITA. I am sure that we have something
which will appeal to your tastes.

GALATEA. I suppose you're frightfully expensive?

MADAME PEPITA. Quality is always expensive.   However, I do not believe that we shall differ over the price.

DON LUIS. You may have absolute confidence in Pepita.
Although not nobly born, she holds herself high.

[*Whenever the* CONDE *speaks,* GALATEA *stares at
him contemptuously, looking him over from head to
foot, but he simulates entire obliviousness.*]

MADAME PEPITA. You embarrass me, Conde.   [*To*
GALATEA.]   Have you any ideas, or would you prefer to
look over some of our models first, so as to see what we
have?

GALATEA. Yes, perhaps you might show me something.

MADAME PEPITA. If Madame will step into the other room. . . .

GALATEA. I am anxious to see your display.

DON LUIS. [*Unable to resist.*] Quite right. Step this way!

GALATEA. No, trot along; you're excused. Dressmakers despise nothing so much as men who hang about fitting rooms.

MADAME PEPITA. Oh, no indeed! If it is any pleasure to the Conde. . . .

GALATEA. Well, if you don't mind, I do. That settles it.

DON LUIS. [*Visibly disappointed.*] Always clever and coy!

GALATEA. Yes, it's the way I'm made.

DON LUIS. I must be off, then. I have business of my own to attend to. Does your motor happen to be at the door, by any chance?

GALATEA. What do you want of my motor?

DON LUIS. [*Smiling.*] Nothing of your motor, but I should like permission from you to ride in it, as far as my house.

GALATEA. [*After a moment's hesitation.*] Very well, if you send it right back. Mind that you don't smoke and get my cushions all smelling of tobacco, because, when I'm alone, I don't care to be reminded that there are such things as men in the world. [*Fanning the air with her handkerchief.*] Ouf!

DON LUIS. *Au revoir,* Pepita. Good-bye. By the way, attend to that little matter as soon as possible; the need is urgent.

MADAME PEPITA. I shan't forget, Conde.

[*The* CONDE *goes out.*]

GALATEA. [*As he disappears, utterly indifferent as to whether he overhears or not.*] Silly ass! Side-splitting, isn't he? And he thinks he's a sport!

MADAME PEPITA. [*Alarmed, fearing the* CONDE *may*

hear.] Oh, but the Conde is so distinguished! He is just in his prime.

GALATEA. Yes, prime for a mummy in a museum. My God, I've no use for antiques, not even when they're gold lined! Men oughtn't to be allowed after they are twenty. These hang-overs disgust me. [*Sighs.*]

[MADAME PEPITA *lifts the curtain at the door leading to the fitting room, and ushers* GALATEA *out. For a moment the stage is empty. Then the bell rings, and* CARMEN *enters with* AUGUSTO.]

[AUGUSTO *is a young man of twenty-five, whose sole preoccupation is the care and adornment of his person. He is dressed in an ultra-fashionable, light colored morning suit, which is slightly effeminate in effect. His shirt, tie, shoes—in short all the articles of his attire—blend in a harmony of delicate hues. He sports a velour hat, whose soft, wide brim, turned up on one side and down on the other, rivals the meticulous lure of the coquette. His blond hair billows above his brow in sweeping waves, one or two of which break gracefully over his forehead. His moustache is equally exquisite, yet, in spite of his preciosity and affected speech, there is something about his person which is undeniably attractive.*]

CARMEN. [*Obsequiously.*] Do step in, Señor Vizconde, and be seated. I will deliver the message.—My God, how sweet that man smells!

AUGUSTO. [*Deigning to accept the proffered chair, but without sitting down.*] Thanks awfully.

CARMEN. Did the Vizconde meet his father, the Conde, on the stairs?

AUGUSTO. Meet my father? No.

CARMEN. [*Seeking a pretext to prolong the conversation.*] The Conde left a moment ago. . . .

AUGUSTO. Did he? Tell Madame Pepita that I am here—that is, if she is disengaged.

CARMEN. Certainly. If the Vizconde has a moment to

spare . . . *Madame* is with a customer, an actress. Perhaps you have heard the name? Galatea.

AUGUSTO. [*Quickly.*] Galatea? When did she arrive?

CARMEN. Half an hour ago, Vizconde. She is selecting models with *Madame.*

AUGUSTO. Let me see her at once.

CARMEN. Galatea?

AUGUSTO. No, Madame Pepita.

CARMEN. Yes, Vizconde.

AUGUSTO· Do not tell her I am here, but say it is urgent. Remember, not one word to Galatea.

CARMEN. No, Vizconde. She will be with you directly.—Holy Mother! What beautiful nails! [*Goes out examining her own.*]

AUGUSTO. [*Smiling fatuously.*] It cannot be helped. Ah, I wonder what they see?

> [*He looks at himself in the three-panelled mirror, then in the pier glass, then in a hand mirror which lies upon the table, adjusting some detail of his suit, tie or hair at each. Pulling a chain, to which a small bottle of perfume is attached, from his trousers pocket, he pours a few drops upon his handkerchief. Then, he takes a small comb from a case and deftly fluffs the waves of his hair. Then, he twists the ends of his moustache between his thumb and forefinger, makes the circuit of the mirrors again, and, finally, selecting a slender Egyptian cigarette from an incredible case, lights it with a patent lighter before sitting himself down to smoke, seated midway between the two mirrors, from which point of vantage he is able to survey himself upon all sides at once. He is interrupted in this agreeable occupation by* MADAME PEPITA, *who enters hurriedly, followed by* CARMEN.]

MADAME PEPITA. [*To* CARMEN.] But why all this mystery? Will you tell me who wants to see me? What is the matter with you, anyhow?

Augusto. [*Remaining seated, without deigning to remove his eyes from the mirror.*] Pepita, it is I.

Madame Pepita. Vizconde!

[Augusto *directs a killing glance at* Carmen, *who responds with a look of admiration.*]

Carmen. [*As she goes out.*] When he looks at you, it's divine!

Augusto. [*Twirling his moustache complacently, without taking his eyes from the glass.*] Yes, Pepita, it is I. Don't call me Vizconde, call me what you used to when you lived with us.

Madame Pepita. [*Ravished.*] Oh, Señorito Augusto!

Augusto. [*Still more condescendingly.*] Or just plain Augusto.

Madame Pepita. Señorito Augusto! The very idea!

Augusto. You witnessed my entrance into the world, Pepita.

Madame Pepita. How long ago it seems! [*About to cry.*] Your poor mother!

Augusto. [*Abstracted, still preoccupied with himself.*] Yes, my poor mother! Such is life; some die, others are born. Which is which?

Madame Pepita. Who knows, Vizconde?

Augusto. No doubt you wonder how it is I come to be up so early?

Madame Pepita. The Vizconde knows he is welcome at any hour.

Augusto. It may surprise you, but I have come, my dear, to ask a favor.

Madame Pepita. Oh, Vizconde!

Augusto. Pepita, times are hard. Although my habits may be. . . . [*Lowering his eyes.*] The pace today is a trifle rapid. A man of my age with my advantages. . . . [*Gazing at himself from head to foot.*] Well, I must resign myself. [*Smiles.*] Love is expensive. And women have become so dreadfully prosaic. I am madly in love with a woman—why conceal it? You know her—Galatea?

MADAME PEPITA. Galatea? Who . . . ?

AUGUSTO. Precisely. [*Smiles.*] Who is looking over your models. Hence the need of secrecy: I do not wish her to see me. [MADAME PEPITA *moves over and closes the door.*] Thank you so much. She is a regal creature. [*Turning to admire himself again in an ecstasy of self-satisfaction.*] Although I say it myself, she has exquisite taste.

MADAME PEPITA. Well, she is certainly hard to please.

AUGUSTO. But she is crazy about me. I am sorry for the poor girl. She is in despair over the question of clothes; you know what models are in Madrid. Finally, I said to her: Why not see Madame Pepita?

MADAME PEPITA. Oh, Vizconde!

AUGUSTO. It will be worth your while—and so I dropped in myself. Money is no object in this case. When you make out the bill. . . .

MADAME PEPITA. Oh, Vizconde! Since you are to pay the bill. . . .

AUGUSTO. No, Pepita, no; not exactly. Unfortunately, I shall not pay.

MADAME PEPITA. Eh?

AUGUSTO. I adore her, she adores me, but there are complications. In fact, I suspect that somewhere, in the background, there is some despicable creature who does pay. [*Sighing.*] Some miserable old reprobate—at least so I gather from her maid, Carmelina, an adorable blonde —[*Lowering his eyes*] who conceals nothing from me.

MADAME PEPITA. [*Sincerely alarmed.*] You don't tell me . . . ?

AUGUSTO. Permit yourself a little liberty when you make out the bill—I mean as to price. [*With an endearing pat.*] And we'll split the difference. How is that?

MADAME PEPITA. But, Vizconde—

AUGUSTO. [*Growing more and more affectionate.*] Nonsense. Let the other chap do the worrying. Ah,

Pepita, you are just like my poor, dear mother. [*Becoming sentimental.*] She was fond of you.

MADAME PEPITA. [*Overcome, preparing to cry.*] Yes, your poor mother.

AUGUSTO. But enough of that! Charge her fifteen hundred pesetas.

CATALINA. [*Entering suddenly, without noticing* AUGUSTO.] Mamma, I am going out to the corner to buy some note paper. Gregoria has asked me to write to her young man.

MADAME PEPITA. What on earth is the matter with you? Don't you know how to address a gentleman?

CATALINA. [*Frightened.*] Oh!

MADAME PEPITA. Here is the Vizconde.

CATALINA. Yes . . . I didn't see him first.

MADAME PEPITA. Well, what else have you to say for yourself?

CATALINA. [*Offering her hand to* AUGUSTO, *who takes it gingerly.*] How do you do?

MADAME PEPITA. Say how do you do, Vizconde?

AUGUSTO. [*Condescendingly.*] Oh, never mind!

CATALINA. [*Firmly.*] I'm sure I don't care.

AUGUSTO. [*Insinuatingly.*] Is this . . . original young lady your daughter?

MADAME PEPITA. Yes, Vizconde, my daughter and my punishment.

AUGUSTO. Very well, then we understand each other. You needn't bother to see me out. [*Smiling.*] The girls will be waiting at the door.

[*Retires, accompanied by* MADAME PEPITA, *who returns immediately.*]

CATALINA. [*As he disappears.*] Conceited puppy.

[*She has changed her dress, but is still ungroomed and untidy, as before.*]

MADAME PEPITA. [*Re-entering.*] Are you still here?

CATALINA. [*Intimidated.*] I was looking for my book.

MADAME PEPITA. Haven't I told you a hundred times

not to come in when I have people here, without first
dressing yourself properly?

Catalina. [*Inspecting herself in the mirror.*] But I
am dressed properly.

Madame Pepita. [*Surveying her from head to foot.*]
For what?

Catalina. [*With sincere conviction.*] I have on a new
skirt and a clean waist.

Madame Pepita. And then you've taken a turn with
them on in the coal bin! Come here! [*Pushing her this
way and that, as she fixes her dress.*] Aren't you ashamed
to be seventeen and not be able to put your skirt on
straight yet?

Catalina. Ouch! You hurt.

Madame Pepita. [*Still pushing her around.*] It will
do you good.

Catalina. Yes, it's fun for you.

Galatea. [*Outside.*] It's awfully good-looking, of
course . . .

Madame Pepita. [*Opening the door, which she closed
previously.*] Get out! Somebody is coming.

Catalina. Well, can I go, then?

Madame Pepita. Go to the devil, if that will do any
good.

[Catalina *goes out on the left as* Galatea *enters
on the right. A sewing girl accompanies her, who
retires immediately without speaking.*]

Galatea. [*Sniffing the air.*] Hm! So he has been
here?

Madame Pepita. [*Pretending not to understand.*]
I beg your pardon—

Galatea. [*Immensely pleased.*] Ha! Ha! Ha!
What did he want? I can smell him.

Madame Pepita. I have no idea to what you refer,
señora.

Galatea. How innocent we are! I refer to that
rascal, Augusto. Nobody could mistake that odor of tube-

rose. [*Deeply gratified.*] It would have surprised me if he hadn't come. Probably he wanted to find out whether or not I was alone. Ha, ha, ha! What did you tell him? Suppose he meets the author of his being on the stairs? Ha, ha, ha! [*Becoming serious.*] Well, I ought not to laugh, I suppose. He's been an angel to me—yes, that's a good joke, isn't it? A real angel. What in heaven's name were we talking about, anyway?

MADAME PEPITA. I hope you found something to suit?

GALATEA. Oh, yes! You have wonderful taste.

MADAME PEPITA. [*Bowing.*] Señora!

GALATEA. There's a blue gown that fairly took my breath away, and a lace negligee, somewhat low . . . do you get me? [*Sighing.*] It was fascinating. Imagine me in it!

MADAME PEPITA. Did you notice a mauve *crêpe de chine* teagown, with a jacket effect of *point d'Alençon?* It would be marvelous with your lines. Try it on, and we can mark the alterations.

GALATEA. No, thanks, I don't believe I'll try on anything to-day.

MADAME PEPITA. You won't?

GALATEA. No, I am not interested. You might make me up two or three batiste blouses, perhaps—don't you know? The cheapest things you have—what you use for chemises will do. And send me a bill for four thousand pesetas.

MADAME PEPITA. Four thousand what?

GALATEA. Half for you and half for me. My God, a woman has to live somehow!

MADAME PEPITA. Oh, the bill? But . . .

GALATEA. While you are about it, I don't suppose you'd mind sending it in duplicate?

MADAME PEPITA. In duplicate?

GALATEA. One for the old man and one for the boy. [*Noticing the horrified look on* MADAME PEPITA's *face.*] While a woman's young, she's got to provide for her old

age. What are men for, anyway, except to pay bills?
There are lots of women who enjoy spending money.
Every time they have anything, something else takes their
eye, so off they go and buy. [*Very earnestly.*] But that's
not my style; I've too much sense. The old man is no
good. [Madame Pepita *makes a gesture of dissent.*] I
am merely taking him as an example—no reflections upon
you. Tell me, would you put up with him for a minute
if he never came across? Of course not. [*Imitating in
pantomime the counting of bills.*] But the young fellow is
all right. Besides, what's the use of denying it? I'm
mad over him. But what does he expect? I'm not going
to be the only one who loosens up. Take that from me.

Madame Pepita. If you look at it in that light . . .

Galatea. Light nothing! Look at it as it is.
Suppose now I go in for clothes? Clothes cost money—
you know that; and you can't raise a cent on them afterwards to save your neck. A woman's a fool to spend money
on clothes. [*Contemptuously.*] Jewels are no better.
You have to pay twenty for what you can't sell for ten.
Cash is safer, and land. Every penny I save goes into
land.

Madame Pepita. [*Impressed.*] Then you think well
of real estate?

Galatea. Yes. The next time you run up to Paris,
look out of the window as the train leaves Torrelodones.
You'll see a house on the right, with a fence painted blue.

Madame Pepita. With a tin summerhouse in front,
with a vine on it?

Galatea. Lovely, isn't it? That's me.

Madame Pepita. [*Enchanted.*] You?

Galatea. Drop off if you have time and look me over.

Madame Pepita. Thanks.

Galatea. I'm usually there Sundays, watering my lettuce. [*A pause.*] But probably you have more important
things to do, and I'm taking your time.

Madame Pepita. No, indeed!

Galatea. Oh, yes, you have! I'll look you up later. Remember—two bills. Don't forget! See you later.

Madame Pepita. I shall hope to see you. . . .

Galatea. I've taken an awful fancy to you—indeed, I have!

Madame Pepita. Charmed, to be sure.

[*Both go out. After a moment,* Madame Pepita *returns.*]

Madame Pepita. [*To herself.*] A thousand pesetas, four thousand pesetas, fifteen hundred, two bills—and all for two batiste blouses! God, at this rate I can dismiss the establishment!

[*She goes up to the table and examines the samples that* Alberto *has left. A noise outside. Then, the bell rings and* Don Guillermo *enters, supporting* Catalina, *pale and frightened.* Cristina *and another girl follow immediately.*]

Madame Pepita. [*Alarmed, rushing up to her daughter.*] What is the matter? What has happened, Catalina?

Catalina. [*Very much frightened.*] Nothing, mamma . . . nothing at all.

Don Guillermo. Don't be alarmed, señora.

Madame Pepita. Sir!

Catalina. Mamma, this is Don Guillermo.

Don Guillermo. The young lady has turned her ankle. Perhaps you had better sit down. [*Assisting* Catalina *to an armchair.*] As she was crossing the street, an automobile almost ran over her. Fortunately, it missed . . .

Catalina. There wasn't any danger.

Don Guillermo. Naturally, she was frightened. Have you a glass of water?

Madame Pepita. Squeeze a lime in it.

[Cristina *goes out.*]

Don Guillermo. I should suggest an orange.

[*The* SEWING GIRL *goes out.*]

CATALINA. I'm all right now. I was frightened, that's all.

MADAME PEPITA. Mooning along as usual, were you, with your head in the clouds?

DON GUILLERMO. Don't scold her. Accidents will happen.

CATALINA. [*Insisting.*] Mamma, this is Don Guillermo, the gentleman who lives upstairs.

MADAME PEPITA. [*Brusquely.*] I heard you the first time. [*Affably, to* DON GUILLERMO.] This is a great pleasure. We are much obliged to you.

DON GUILLERMO. Not at all. I was in time to prevent a catastrophe, which somebody else would have prevented had I not been in time.

[*Meanwhile* CATALINA *has taken his hand, affectionately.*]

MADAME PEPITA. Won't you sit down?—Catalina, let go of the gentleman's hand; it embarrasses him.

[CATALINA *lets go of* DON GUILLERMO'S *hand.*]

DON GUILLERMO. [*Sympathetically.*] No, indeed. She is a little nervous. [*The* SEWING GIRL *re-enters with a glass of water, which* DON GUILLERMO *offers to* CATALINA.] Drink this.

SEWING GIRL. We had to put vinegar in it because there wasn't anything sweet in the house.

MADAME PEPITA. That will do.

CATALINA. [*Almost choking, refusing to drink.*] Yes, mamma, because Gregoria finished the orangeade yesterday, when she had that fainting fit, after she had a quarrel with her young man.

MADAME PEPITA. Gregoria a fainting fit? The kitchen cat will be having a nervous breakdown next! [*To the girl.*] Take this away and go back to your work.

[*The* SEWING GIRL *retires with the glass.*]

CATALINA. [*Aside, to* DON GUILLERMO.] Don't you go away.

MADAME PEPITA. What was that?

CATALINA. [*Timidly.*] I asked Don Guillermo not to go away.

DON GUILLERMO. But I must. However, I live only one flight up. If you need me at any time, Guillermo de Armendáriz is my name.

MADAME PEPITA. My daughter tells me that you are a very learned man.

DON GUILLERMO. [*Unimpressed.*] That depends.

MADAME PEPITA. You are a member of the Academy.

DON GUILLERMO. [*Smiling.*] I could scarcely avoid that.

MADAME PEPITA. [*Astonished.*] Avoid it?

CATALINA. He says it's a great pity that I am such an ignoramus.

DON GUILLERMO. I never said that, because you are not an ignoramus.

MADAME PEPITA. Oh, yes she is! But it's not her fault. It's mine—that is, it isn't mine, either. What could I do? I've spent my whole life working for her like a slave, trying to scrape together enough money so that she wouldn't have to go through what I've been through in this world. Tied down as I am to the worry of these miserable clothes, how was I to tend to her education? That's why she's like this, but you needn't think that it isn't a mortification to me, because when God has given you a daughter—or maybe it was the devil—you just want to have her nonplussed ultra, and it's a great grief to me that she isn't. But why am I telling all this to you, when you don't know what it is to have a child? That is, maybe you do know. Anyhow, it's none of my business. I don't mean to be inquisitive . . .

DON GUILLERMO. [*Smiling.*] No, unfortunately I do not know. I am alone in the world. When I was young, I had no time to marry, and now that I am growing old, it is too late. My books are to blame, and they console me for what I have lost, which is no more than their duty.

Since the subject has been mentioned, I wonder if you would allow me to devote a little of my time to Catalina's education?

MADAME PEPITA.   Education?

DON GUILLERMO.   It seems providential—we are good friends already.   We have talked together, and I am fond of her.   She is intelligent.

CATALINA.   [*Greatly astonished.*]   Am I?

DON GUILLERMO.   She will learn quickly; I guarantee it.

MADAME PEPITA.   You give her lessons?   A member of the Academy?

CATALINA.   Certainly, mamma.

DON GUILLERMO.   It will be a pleasure.   Then, I shall feel that my learning is actually of some use in the world.   It has all been rather selfish till now.   What do you say?   Is it agreed?

MADAME PEPITA.   [*Greatly affected.*]   Ah, you have no idea how I appreciate this!   [*Throwing her arms about* CATALINA, *and bursting into tears.*]   My dear, you are to sit at the feet of an Academician!

DON GUILLERMO.   [*Surprised.*]   It hardly justifies the emotion.   It is not so serious.

MADAME PEPITA.   But I feel terribly, because we are dreadfully unhappy.   Naturally, you would never suspect it, but since you're so fond of my daughter, I can tell you.   Besides, everybody knows it, anyway.   We are dreadfully unhappy, right here as we sit, because this poor child has no father.   You imagine that I am a widow . . .

DON GUILLERMO.   Señora, I imagine nothing of the sort.

MADAME PEPITA.   [*Hastily.*]   Well, I'm not, I'm married; that is, I am not married either—I mean, yes I am; but it's just the same as if I wasn't because my husband, that is, the man I thought was my husband—

DON GUILLERMO.   But you owe me no explanations; I am not concerned in the affair.

MADAME PEPITA.   [*Without stopping to draw breath.*]

But I want you to know, so that you won't think . . .
You see, it was this way: My parents were good, honest
people, my mother was lady's maid and my father butler
in the house of the Counts de la Vega de Lezo—you have
heard of them?—but I always had a taste for clothes, so
I went with some French women to be a dressmaker in
Buenos Aires; and when I got there I met the father of
this child. I was young and impressionable then. He
was a Russian—no doubt about that—and we got married,
church and all, but without his settling anything on me,
because it isn't done out there, and I thought he was the
manager of a printing house; but two months afterwards
he turned out to be a duke—yes, sir, a Russian duke, who,
because he was the black sheep of the family, had been
shipped off to America, and then his father died, and he
inherited, and had to go back to his own country. But
that wasn't the worst of it. The worst of it was that he
was a bigamist.

DON GUILLERMO. A bigamist?

MADAME PEPITA. Yes, he was married already in
Russia to a woman of his own rank, and he ran off with
her. So when this poor child came into the world, she
hadn't any father.

DON GUILLERMO. How singularly unfortunate!

MADAME PEPITA. But I kept right on sewing, and
when he got back to Russia, he sent me money, for it is only
fair to admit he was always a gentleman, and then I
came back to Spain, and established myself in business,
and since I've got taste, if I do say it myself, we've gotten
ahead. Besides, now and then he sent me money. But
it's a long time now since he went away, and I haven't
seen him for sixteen years, and my daughter doesn't know
him at all, and she never will, for we don't even know
whether he is alive or dead, and probably he has other
children, anyway; and here I am neither married nor single,
and not even a widow! So you see that I have plenty of
reason for being unhappy.

DON GUILLERMO. Not so much as you think. You have your health, you have your work, an income, a quiet conscience . . .

MADAME PEPITA. Yes, one thing I can say is that my conscience never troubled me.

DON GUILLERMO. What more do you ask? Love played you a trick. Pshaw! In exchange, you have a daughter, a pledge of happiness, a reason for living. You had your illusion of love for a time, but, believe me, even sadder than to have been deceived, is never to have had the opportunity. Hereafter, you must count me as one of your friends. For the present, I must bid you good-bye. You have my sympathy . . .

MADAME PEPITA. Thanks very much. If I can be of any service—

DON GUILLERMO. Perhaps later. Good-bye.

MADAME PEPITA. *Adiós.*

[DON GUILLERMO *goes out. A pause follows.*]

CARMEN. [*Entering.*] *Madame,* the salesman has come with the English samples.

MADAME PEPITA. [*Drying her eyes.*] Show him into the other room. I shall attend to his case immediately. [*To* CATALINA, *who is gazing pensively into space.*] What are you mooning about?

CATALINA. Isn't it sad not to be anybody's daughter, and not to have a father like everybody?

MADAME PEPITA. [*Taking her into her arms.*] You are *my* daughter.

CATALINA. Oh, mamma, we are dreadfully unhappy!

MADAME PEPITA. We are, my child, we are, indeed! [*Moving off a little, and placing both hands on* CATALINA'S *shoulders, while she looks her straight in the eye.*] But remember this: one thing consoles me for all our misfortunes. In my daughter's veins runs noble blood!

CURTAIN

ACT II

CATALINA *and* DON GUILLERMO *are discovered as the curtain rises.* DON GUILLERMO *paces up and down with the air of a person feeling himself thoroughly at home, while* CATALINA *writes at a small table which has been installed near one of the windows to do duty as a desk. It is littered with books and papers, all in hopeless confusion. Presently,* CATALINA *ceases writing, examining the paper on which she has been working as if looking for mistakes. After conscientious scrutiny, she blots it and lays it upon the table, turning to contemplate her inky fingers with an expression half despairing, half resigned. Upon a second inspection, she becomes even more discouraged, as the ink has not disappeared. Finally, running her fingers nervously through her hair, she rubs them upon her apron, and heaves a profound sigh.*

DON GUILLERMO. [*Turning.*] Have you finished?

CATALINA. Yes.

DON GUILLERMO. What are you doing now?

CATALINA. [*Still rubbing her fingers.*] Wiping my fingers. [*Exhibiting her hands.*] I've a little ink on them. [DON GUILLERMO *smiles.*] Writing makes me furious!

DON GUILLERMO. Why?

CATALINA. Because it gets my hands in such a state— it's the pen. I dip it into the ink, and it runs up all over the handle. I use the pen-wiper just as you tell me to, but the more I wipe, the more ink comes off.

DON GUILLERMO. Have patience. It will all come in time. [*Amused.*] The beginning is always difficult. We shall soon see how fast you get on.

CATALINA. [*Discouraged.*] But look at these letters.

The *l*'s are all crooked, and the *m*'s are all pointed. It makes me mad.

DON GUILLERMO. [*Smiling.*] Does it?

CATALINA. Because I know how things ought to be, and, then, I go and do them just the opposite, so, although I know, I don't know, and I get desperate. [*Looking at the paper.*] The *l*'s ought to be straight. Well, I try to make them straight, and they turn out crooked, so what's the use of knowing? Of course, when I'm wrong because I don't know, I'm an idiot, but when I know I'm wrong and then do it, what am I?

DON GUILLERMO. [*Patting her affectionately on the head.*] You are an intelligent young woman, who must work hard in order to overcome the first difficulties, and put what she knows to good use. That is precisely what learning means.

CATALINA. [*After a pause, looking at* DON GUILLERMO *intently.*] Don Guillermo, what use is learning, anyhow?

DON GUILLERMO. Learning teaches us to know.

CATALINA. Yes, I understand that. But what use is it?

DON GUILLERMO. [*Smiling.*] You will soon see. It is useful in many ways, which, little by little, you will discover yourself. Even if it were of no use, it would still be the most wonderful thing in the world, because it is the only thing that is satisfying in itself. When we have once peeped into the Garden of Knowledge, even at the tiniest gate, it is astounding what marvellous voyages we are able to make, and what sights we can see, without taking the trouble of leaving our chairs.

CATALINA. I suppose that's why you never notice what's on your plate at dinner, and laugh to yourself all the time, and walk out on the street without tying your shoes?

DON GUILLERMO. [*Slightly annoyed.*] What a keen little critic we are!

CATALINA. No, I don't mean anything uncomplimentary, only I can't help noticing what you do, because I watch you all the time. You mustn't think I'm criticising. Everything you do seems right to me.

Don Guillermo. [*Greatly pleased.*] Yes, my dear, I know you are sweet and good, and you are very fond of me.

Catalina. Yes, I am. [*Artlessly.*] Are you very fond of me?

Don Guillermo. Don't you know it?

Catalina. [*Sincerely pleased.*] Of course I do. I may be stupid about other things, but not about that. I know you are fond of me, because when I broke that jar the other day in the library, you didn't say one word about it, though it was valuable. That's how I know. I didn't mean to.

Don Guillermo. You have talent, too, for psychology.

Catalina. Now you're making fun of me.

Don Guillermo. I am very fond of you—fonder than you can imagine, fonder than I could have believed possible myself. I love you better than I do art and science put together.

Catalina. [*After a brief silence.*] Are we going to begin this all over again?

Don Guillermo. No, that will do for today.

Catalina. I want to tell you a secret. [*Drawing near, mysteriously.*] We're rich.

Don Guillermo. Who?

Catalina. Mother and I. Who did you think? We've inherited a million. My father died and left it in his will. We got word yesterday, and mother has gone to see the lawyer. Nobody knows except Don Luis; he was here last night when word came. Mother says she is going to retire from business, because she's sick and tired of clothes, and we're going to Escorial to live.

Don Guillermo. To Escorial?

Catalina. Yes, mamma owns property there, and she says she's going to build houses and rent them, and keep one, too, for us to live in, that has a big garden with a grotto, and a fountain in the middle, besides a hot-house where we can grow camelias.

[*The bell rings.* CATALINA *stops short.*]

Here she comes now.

[MADAME PEPITA *enters, attired in a simple tailor-made suit of grey or dark blue; also a mantilla. She is visibly flustered and out of breath.*]

DON GUILLERMO. Good morning.

MADAME PEPITA. [*About to pass without seeing him.*] Oh, excuse me! I didn't notice you. Good morning. I'm so excited I don't know whether I'm on my head or my heels. Has she told you?

DON GUILLERMO. Yes, indeed.

MADAME PEPITA. Terribly sad, isn't it? And to think of my being caught without a stitch of black to my name! No wonder they say: "Go to the Cutler's house for wooden knives." Here I am fussing about other people's clothes, and I look like a fright myself. I wonder what the notary thought when I walked in in colors on such an occasion?

DON GUILLERMO. Don't worry, probably he never thought at all. Sit down. It is a matter of taste.

MADAME PEPITA. [*Sitting down.*] Oh, dear, no! Whatever's right is right, and for my part, I always want to do the correct thing. Poor dear! Think of his remembering us at such a time!

DON GUILLERMO. He has done no more than his duty.

MADAME PEPITA. But so nicely. [*Bursting into tears.*] Ah, my dear, your father was always a gentleman! They tell me the poor man was ill for over two years, not able to move out of his chair. And all the while he was thinking of us, and we were sitting here calm and collected as could be, without suspecting the first thing about it. Oh, my daughter! [*Embracing* CATALINA, *who, as befits the occasion, assumes an expression of supreme anguish.*]

CATALINA. Poor mamma!

DON GUILLERMO. [*Removing* CATALINA.] Come,

come, you must not upset your daughter.   It is not right
to grieve like this.

MADAME PEPITA. [*Between her sobs, artlessly.*] But
I'm not grieving.   I feel I can tell you, because you're so
wise that you understand anyhow.

DON GUILLERMO. [*Smiling.*] In a measure.

MADAME PEPITA.   And that's what makes me feel so
badly, not to be able to grieve as I ought.   Because you
see how the man has behaved to us.   And I did care for
him, yes, I did!   He was the apple of my eye.   And when
it all happened, seventeen years ago, and he left me forever, believe me, it was all I could do to go on living because of my child, and more than once, yes, more than
twice, too, I had a mind to put an end to it all.

CATALINA. [*In tears also.*] Poor mamma!

MADAME PEPITA.   And now he's gone and died, and
they send me word about it! [*Beginning to cry again.*]
Before I can cry the way I feel I ought to cry, I have to
stop and try to remember how it was I was able to cry then.

DON GUILLERMO.   But there is no obligation whatever upon you to cry.   Even if there were, your feelings
are beyond your control.

MADAME PEPITA.   You are right there.

DON GUILLERMO.   To compel ourselves to feel what
we do not feel is hypocrisy, a fraud upon ourselves, because
it mortifies our pride to realize that our feelings do not
measure up to our expectations.   If your feelings do not
prompt you to cry, you ought not to cry.   Tears, unless
they are heart-felt, are injurious.   They do no good to the
deceased.

MADAME PEPITA. [*Exaggeratedly.*] But you don't
know how I loved him!

DON GUILLERMO.   Certainly I do, but your love has
evaporated, like perfume which has stood in a wardrobe for
years.   Today you have been cleaning house; you find the
bottle and it is empty.   The contents are gone, they have

been dissipated, they have ceased to be. You have forgotten him, so why worry? Little by little our bodies change, until, after seven years, not one atom of what we once were remains. Remember, he has been absent sixteen years. Not one vestige now remains of the flesh and blood that glowed and quivered with love for him. You are not the same woman, you are a different woman, who has had nothing whatever to do with that man.

MADAME PEPITA. [*Sentimentally.*] But the soul, Don Guillermo? What of the soul?

DON GUILLERMO. The soul may recall vaguely the emotions which the body has felt, but it cannot continue to feel them.

MADAME PEPITA. [*Very positively.*] Well, anyway, it will be safer to go into mourning.

DON GUILLERMO. And very proper, if it affords you any relief.

MADAME PEPITA. No, on account of what people will say. After all, remember I'm inheriting a million.

DON GUILLERMO. Yes, that fact deserves to be taken into consideration.

MADAME PEPITA. [*To* CATALINA.] Dear, run out and tell Carmen to cut you a blouse from the crêpe we're using for the Baroness's tea-gown. I'm too upset to think of anything for myself.

CATALINA. Yes, mamma. Don Guillermo . . .

DON GUILLERMO. I am going also. It is growing late.

CATALINA. Aren't you coming back to dinner?

DON GUILLERMO. I dined here yesterday, and day before yesterday, and Sunday, too, if my memory is correct; and this is only Wednesday.

CATALINA. Pshaw! What of it? He is coming, isn't he, mamma?

MADAME PEPITA. Of course he is. If he isn't here, I always feel as if there must be something wrong with the table.

Don Guillermo. Well, since you insist. You have my sympathy, as you know, although I believe you are to be congratulated.

Madame Pepita. I appreciate it. [*Greatly downcast.*] We must do the best we can.

Catalina. [*Going to the door with* Don Guillermo, *and taking his hand as if he were her father.*] Don't forget the meringues you promised.

Don Guillermo. I'll bring them along.

[*As* Don Guillermo *and* Catalina *go out, the door bell rings, and they come face to face with* Don Luis, *who enters. Each gentleman displays plainly his discomfiture at the presence of the other. The* Conde *turns his back, affecting indifference, while* Don Guillermo *stares him up and down in disgust, which he does not attempt to conceal. They salute each other, however, the* Conde *remaining frigidly polite, while* Don Guillermo *mutters an acknowledgment between his teeth.*]

Don Luis. Good afternoon, Señor de Armendáriz.

Don Guillermo. Good afternoon. [*Biting off the words.*]

[*Goes out with* Catalina.]

Don Luis. [*After* Don Guillermo *has disappeared.*] Does this good man spend his entire time here?

Madame Pepita. [*Smiling.*] He is giving my daughter lessons.

Don Luis. Ah! [*Apparently to himself, but with the evident purpose of being overheard.*] Such assiduity makes me suspicious.

Madame Pepita. How so?

Don Luis. [*Significantly.*] We may take that up later. At present, more pressing business demands our attention. Have you had time to rest? Have you recovered from last night? [Madame Pepita *nods.*] Have you got the money?

Madame Pepita. Yes.

Don Luis. Where is it?

Madame Pepita. Why, as soon as I received it, I de-
posited it in the bank. The notary went along, because I
was afraid to trust myself in the street alone with so much
money.

Don Luis. Have you any of it about you now?

Madame Pepita. No. Why do you ask?

Don Luis. I fear you are making a mistake. It is a
matter which involves a will. A demand for money may
be made upon you at any time, and I consider it important
that you have sufficient on hand.

Madame Pepita. I thought so, too, but it seems not.
The notary says all the expenses have been paid. My poor
dear arranged for everything off there on his estate, so that
I shouldn't have a thing to do but accept the money.

Don Luis. I appreciate your situation. By the way,
do you happen to have four hundred pesetas? [*Without allowing her time to recover.*] As a first installment upon a
purchase which it is important that you make, a magnificent
opportunity—a piece of property next to your own at Escorial,
which may be had for a song. A friend of mine is in financial
difficulty.

Madame Pepita. [*Interested.*] Is the Conde positive
that it is a bargain?

Don Luis. It is a gift! If you miss this opportunity,
you will regret it all your life, and you will miss it unless
you can let me have four hundred pesetas this very day.
What would I give if I had the money!

Madame Pepita. [*Producing a brand new check book
from her bag.*] Well, I'll sign a check. [*Seating herself at
the table, she begins to make out the check.*]

Don Luis. You certainly are in luck. Money breeds
money. While you are about it, you might make it five
hundred, so as to provide for emergencies.

Madame Pepita. [*Rising, after writing the check.*]
Here it is.

DON LUIS. [*Solicitously.*] Allow me to sign the receipt.

MADAME PEPITA. Oh, not at all! Conde, I should be offended.

DON LUIS. [*Convinced.*] As you wish. Now let me offer you a piece of advice. This confidence, which you place in me, deservedly, extend to nobody else. Be on your guard. You are rich, and the world is full of scoundrels. They will cheat you, rob you, they will swarm to your millions as flies to their honey. Pepita, if you are not careful, your generosity will be taken advantage of. I myself have abused it not a little.

MADAME PEPITA. Oh, don't say that, Conde!

DON LUIS. Yes, Pepita, unavoidably, perhaps, but the fact remains that I have abused it. However, Providence is repaying your kindness with interest. You are rich. [*Suddenly overcome.*] God knows I rejoice with you, although this unexpected good fortune obliges me to renounce a dream—It is a subject, however, which as a gentleman, I prefer not to dwell upon.

MADAME PEPITA. [*Interested.*] A dream?

DON LUIS. [*Loftily.*] Alas!

MADAME PEPITA. But to an old friend? Surely the Conde can tell me.

DON LUIS. Yes, after all, why not? Now that it has become impossible, what difference does it make? Catalina and Augusto—you must have noticed how they have become attached to each other?

MADAME PEPITA. [*Surprised and delighted.*] The Vizconde and my daughter?

DON LUIS. Then you have noticed it?

MADAME PEPITA. No, I hadn't noticed.

DON LUIS. Pepita, you are blind. I have suspected for some time, but now I am certain. He has practically confessed, under compulsion, and it is not surprising. Your daughter is an original creature—unusual, fascinating. And

Augusto's temperament is so artistic! It was inevitable.

MADAME PEPITA. But, Conde, pardon me . . . The Vizconde . . . I thought . . . Is he the sort of man?

DON LUIS. My dear, talk; it is all put on. Disappointment will result in irregularities. Men are naturally that way, anyhow. When he realized that he had become the victim of an impossible passion, for I may say that it never occurred ·to him that I would relent—although you are worthy people, your daughter has no father. We are what we are.

MADAME PEPITA. [*Sobbing.*] Yes, we are.

DON LUIS. However, it is too late now for regrets. When I found myself confronted with a crisis, I was prepared to lay prejudice aside. Adversity has its uses. But you have inherited money.

MADAME PEPITA. Thank God!

DON LUIS. So it is out of the question. You are rich, we are poor. People would think that we were after your money. Never! Never that! Never!

MADAME PEPITA. Why, Conde!

DON LUIS. Never! I could never reconcile myself to such a thing, at least not without a bitter struggle. But my heart aches for my boy. And there is another obstacle.

MADAME PEPITA. Another?

DON LUIS. Which is a great deal more serious. What position does the gentleman on the floor above occupy in this establishment?

MADAME PEPITA. But I have already explained to the Conde that he is giving Catalina lessons.

DON LUIS. But he remains to dinner, he remains to supper, he spends all his time here . . .

MADAME PEPITA. He is devoted to my little girl.

DON LUIS. He is entirely too devoted.

MADAME PEPITA. We are awfully fond of him, Conde.

DON LUIS. That makes it worse.

MADAME PEPITA. He's so gentlemanly and refined.

DON LUIS. No doubt; that is neither here nor there.

The question is not what he is, but what you are. These
visits compromise your reputation. Besides, there are too
many of them. Remember, you are a young and beautiful woman.

MADAME PEPITA. Yes, I'm thirty-seven.

DON LUIS. With a past—although it was not your fault.
With a past! It is another phase which I prefer not to
dwell on.

MADAME PEPITA. Conde!

DON LUIS. Your daughter is grown, yet you persist
in permitting this gentleman liberties which are extended
customarily only to a husband or a father.

MADAME PEPITA. Oh, no! Nothing of the sort. Believe me, there must be some mistake . . .

DON LUIS. Morally, I decline to sanction the situation.
I had hoped that our children might unite, but you must
realize that a name such as mine is peculiarly sensitive to
the breath of slander. I could never tolerate such a dubi-
ous situation—not that I wish to criticise your conduct
or to dictate in any way. No, do as you see fit. Nevertheless, if this gentleman continues his visits to this house,
I shall be obliged to discontinue mine. Interpret it as
you may, I shall retire—regretfully, Pepita, but with
dignity, I shall retire.

MADAME PEPITA. Conde!

DON LUIS. However, I must hurry to place this money
in the hands of my friend. Remember, your interests are
first with me. If you need advice, come to me. But as
it is, I feel that I intrude. Think it over, think it over
very carefully. Do not force me to say good-bye. *Au
revoir!* [*Goes out.*]

> [MADAME PEPITA, *surprised and delighted at the
> prospect of her daughter's becoming a countess, remains
> behind completely dazed.*]

MADAME PEPITA. My daughter? The Vizconde?
Impossible! No, it isn't either . . . Catalina! Catalina!

CATALINA. [*Appearing in the door-way.*] Did you

call, mamma? [*Noticing her mother's agitation.*] Don't
you feel well?

MADAME PEPITA. Yes . . . no, I don't. Come here;
look at me. How would you like to be a countess?

CATALINA. I, a countess? Why?

MADAME PEPITA. Would you or wouldn't you? Answer me at once!

CATALINA. How can I tell?

MADAME PEPITA. Tell me the truth. Are you in love?

CATALINA. I? In love?

MADAME PEPITA. Isn't there any one you'd like to
marry? Are you engaged?

CATALINA. [*Alarmed.*] No, mamma. I'm not engaged.

MADAME PEPITA. But you like some one, don't you?
There is some one you're awfully fond of? Don't you
find him attractive?

CATALINA. No, mamma . . . not exactly attractive.
What are you talking about? Mamma, I don't love anybody.

> [*The bell rings, and* GALATEA *enters like a whirl-
> wind.*]

GALATEA. Where is she? Ah, give me a kiss! An-
other for luck. A hug, too, this time! [*To Catalina.*]
And one for you. [*Embracing mother and daughter in
turn.*] Congratulations! You don't know how delighted
I was to hear it. Think of it . . . a cold million! What?
Pesetas?

MADAME PEPITA. No, francs.

GALATEA. Exchange is at seven and a half. It may
not seem much, but when you figure it up . . . [*Considering
a moment.*] It comes to fifteen thousand duros. I wish
something like that would happen my way. You knew
what you were doing, all right, when you married a Russian. Now don't tell me it was love. I've always stuck
to the home article, Madrid is good enough for me—although I don't suppose I can teach you anything. Anyway,

I'm tickled to death that you've really got the money, because I don't suppose you'll mind so much now about the bill. I've given up hope of the old man, and his son is no better; they simply haven't got it. Not that I care about the boy . . . I'm silly over him, but the old chap ought to pay somehow. Does he think a man can make an ass of himself at his age for nothing?

MADAME PEPITA. [*To* CATALINA, *who is displaying keen interest.*] Catalina, see if the girls are ready to try on your blouse.

GALATEA. Yes, run along. Things will be coming your way pretty soon. [CATALINA *retires.*] She's a lucky girl! God remembers her while she's young; she won't have to go through what you and me have. Look out now that some young whippersnapper don't get after her money. The world's pretty rotten, and I don't know whether a woman's worse off when she has money or when she hasn't any, because what's the satisfaction of marrying a man and then sitting around watching him spend your money on somebody else?

MADAME PEPITA. [*Moistening her lips.*] There are all sorts of men.

GALATEA. And then a few. You've said it.

MADAME PEPITA. It strikes me you're a sensible woman. Why don't you break off with the Vizconde?

GALATEA. With Augusto? Never in the world!

MADAME PEPITA. You're not getting anywhere as it is, it seems to me.

GALATEA. I ought to know that better than you do.

MADAME PEPITA. I say!

GALATEA. I wouldn't give him up if I starved. I could lose everything, but I'd love him just the same. I've thought I'd leave him, sometimes, and march myself off to Paris, where a woman can do something. Out of sight, out of mind, don't you know? There's nothing in this for me. But when the time comes, I can't tear myself away.

MADAME PEPITA. It might be a good idea, though.

GALATEA. No, it simply can't be done. I'd feel as if I was committing murder. I love him more all the time, and it's a shame. Last night I started for the station—

MADAME PEPITA. Did you miss the train?

GALATEA. No, he dropped around. Do you know what I've got in this box? Neckties, to make up. Whenever I feel I can't stand him any longer, I just run out and buy him a handsome present. [*Dubiously.*] Well, I suppose somebody's got to do it.

CARMEN. [*Entering.*] *Madame,* the lady in the Calle de Lista wants you to hurry up those negligees. She says she can't wait any longer.

MADAME PEPITA. Yes, better let her have something for tonight; I'd forgotten all about her. Dear me, life is just one emergency after another!

GALATEA. Congratulations again—I am going. I hear you're retiring from business. If you're selling out cheap, tip me off. I know a good thing when I see one. But don't let me detain you . . .

[MADAME PEPITA *retires.* GALATEA, *after adjusting her hat at the mirror, is about to leave by the other door, when* AUGUSTO *enters.*]

GALATEA. [*Surprised.*] Augusto!

AUGUSTO. Galatea! Are you here?

GALATEA. I was just congratulating Madame Pepita.

AUGUSTO. What were you doing last night?

GALATEA. I was out. [*Smiling.*]

AUGUSTO. But where were you going? You left no word. I searched all Madrid; I was furious. Don't you love me any more?

GALATEA. [*Smiling.*] Search me.

AUGUSTO. Yes, but how about me?

GALATEA. I didn't get very far.

AUGUSTO. What are you doing tonight?

GALATEA. [*Coyly.*] Is it a date?

AUGUSTO. I must have a moment first with Pepita; I shan't be long. You might wait outside in the motor, and then we can go for that ring. I know you've set your heart on it—although I had planned it as a surprise.

GALATEA. I have planned a little surprise for you, too.

AUGUSTO. Do you mean it?

GALATEA. [*Handing him the box of neckties.*] Promise not to look.

AUGUSTO. [*About to open the box.*] What can it be?

GALATEA. Wait until you are alone.

AUGUSTO. [*Kissing her hand.*] You're an angel!

GALATEA. So are you. Peep and see. [*Goes out.*]

AUGUSTO. [*After a discreet, but rapid glance in the glass.*] What can it be? [*Opens the box.*] Cravats! [*Becoming sentimental.*] Although her taste may be bizarre, how she loves me! [*Kissing a cravat.*] And how I love her! [*Rising into transports.*]

　　　[MADAME PEPITA *enters, greatly pleased to discover* AUGUSTO.]

MADAME PEPITA. [*Entering.*] Vizconde! . . . Oh, Vizconde!

AUGUSTO. [*Coming to, hastily bundling up the cravats.*] Pardon me.

MADAME PEPITA. Were you thinking?

AUGUSTO. Thinking? I was trying not to think.

MADAME PEPITA. [*Sympathetically.*] Vizconde!

AUGUSTO. I am in desperate need of seven hundred pesetas. If you cannot let me have them, I shall grow violent. I know you have a million, but I do not ask upon that account. No, I should have had to have them anyway. Life has become insupportable.

MADAME PEPITA. Oh, Vizconde!

AUGUSTO. My heart is broken. What is the good of a heart nowadays? Nobody seems to have one. My heart will be my ruin.

MADAME PEPITA. A tender heart is a priceless treasure.

AUGUSTO. But so expensive! Man cannot exist without woman, woman cannot exist without money.

MADAME PEPITA. Don't let that worry you, Vizconde.

All things come to him who waits, even when it seems impossible. If you are in trouble, come to me. I have the gift of sympathy.

AUGUSTO. So I am coming to you. Can you let me have the seven hundred at once? I am in a hurry, or I should not ask.

MADAME PEPITA. Just a moment, while I write the check.

[MADAME PEPITA *retires.* AUGUSTO *paces back and forth, admiring himself in the mirror. Presently* CATALINA *enters, approaching the table which contains the papers, without noticing* AUGUSTO. *They collide with a violent shock while he is still absorbed in the contemplation of his person in the glass.*]

CATALINA. Oh! Excuse me.

AUGUSTO. Can't you see where you are going?

CATALINA. Can't you see anything but yourself? Puppy! [*Making a face, which he sees in the mirror.*]

AUGUSTO. Let me give you a piece of advice, young lady. Don't you make faces at me.

CATALINA. If you weren't so stuck on yourself, you wouldn't have noticed it.

AUGUSTO. It wouldn't do you any harm to be a little stuck on yourself.

CATALINA. Wouldn't it?

AUGUSTO. Do you take out a license for that poodle effect with the hair?

CATALINA. When it rains, don't forget yours is gummed down and glued.

AUGUSTO. Can't you let me alone?

CATALINA. Who are you, anyway? [*Seating herself at the table, she opens a drawing book in which she proceeds to copy a map.*]

[AUGUSTO *stalks up and down without speaking. They exchange glances of mutual contempt from time to time, until the entrance of* MADAME PEPITA *with*

the check. Highly gratified at finding them together,
she beams upon them with maternal tenderness.]

MADAME PEPITA. [*Entering.*] The poor dears are embarrassed. What a picture they would make! [*To*
AUGUSTO.] The check, Vizconde.

AUGUSTO. Thanks. I shall never forget this—I feel
like another man with this money. I may have to go to
work to repay you, Pepita; love is a great leveler. Ah, for
love's sweet sake! I'm off. . . . [*Rushes out without pay-*
ing any attention to CATALINA.]

MADAME PEPITA. [*Deeply affected.*] For love's sweet
sake! [*Looking at her daughter.*] Poor Vizconde!

ALBERTO. [*Appearing in the doorway.*] May I come
in?

MADAME PEPITA. What is the matter with you?

ALBERTO. No, it's the proprietor, who wishes the
samples of English point, and the gold galloons; they're re-
required.

MADAME PEPITA. God knows what's become of them
by this time.

ALBERTO. We need them to fill an order, just received.

MADAME PEPITA. Very well. Wait, and I'll have
them brought, if they can be found. [*Retires, leaving*
CATALINA *with* ALBERTO. *Both smile, and* CATALINA *con-*
tinues her work.]

ALBERTO. [*Shyly.*] Pleasant day, isn't it?

CATALINA. Yes, very. [*A pause, during which she con-*
tinues working, while he stands a little way off without
removing his eyes from her.] Won't you sit down?

ALBERTO. Thanks. You are very kind. [*Sits down*
at the farther end of the room. Another pause.] Are you
sketching?

CATALINA. [*Smiling timidly.*] No, I don't know how
to sketch; I'm copying a map.

ALBERTO. [*Unconscious of what he is saying.*] Ah! A
map?

CATALINA.   It's the map of Europe.

[*Another pause.* CATALINA *draws busily; then stops and sucks her pencil.*]

ALBERTO.   [*Rising.*] Pardon . . . please don't suck your pencil.

CATALINA.   Eh?

ALBERTO.   It may be impertinent, but it grates upon m. nerve's.

CATALINA.   [*Ready to cry.*] It does look horrid, doesn't it?

ALBERTO.   [*Effusively.*] No! You couldn't possibly do anything that looked horrid, because . . . because . . . well, of course not.

[*Another pause.* CATALINA *draws industriously and breaks the point of the pencil.*]

CATALINA.   Oh, dear, I've broken the point!

[*Taking a penknife, she hacks a fearful looking point after great effort; then inspects it with a sigh.*]

ALBERTO.   [*Impetuously, rising again.*] Pardon. That is not the way to sharpen a pencil. This is the way. [*Rapidly and easily making a perfect point.*] It's very simple.

CATALINA.   [*Admiringly.*] Oh, what a beautiful point! You certainly are a handy man.

ALBERTO.   That's my business.

CATALINA.   Oh . . . yes! You're an artist. Do you really paint pictures?

ALBERTO.   I should like to, but I do not.

CATALINA.   Why not?

ALBERTO.   I am too poor. My mother is a widow.

CATALINA.   [*Interrupting, charmed.*] Just like me!

ALBERTO.   [*Without heeding the interruption.*] Only I have six young brothers and sisters. Mother teaches school in a town not far from here, and she says that only rich people can afford to be artists, so she wants me to be a clerk in "La Sultana," as the proprietor is my uncle. She thinks, when he dies, he may leave the shop to me, since he's a bachelor, and then, naturally we'll all be rich, and we can educate the other children. However, I see no indications . . . but of course that does not interest you.

CATALINA. [*Earnestly.*] Yes, it does; very much.

ALBERTO. I am twenty-two now, and all I do is to carry bundles back and forth to dressmakers and other stupid people who have not the first idea about art. Pardon me . . .

CATALINA. No, you are right. It would be a great deal better to paint pictures.

ALBERTO. [*Enraptured.*] Yes, wonderful pictures, marvellous pictures, such as nobody has ever seen before, palpitating with sunshine and light! Pictures of the sea, the sky—the deep blue Italian sky! Ah, Italy! Rome!

CATALINA. [*Ingenuously.*] Rome is here on the map.

ALBERTO. Rome is in paradise!

CATALINA. Is the sky really so blue there?

ALBERTO. So blue that it is the despair of those who worship her.

CATALINA. Really? I hadn't heard. . . . Funny, isn't it? I've marked the name in blue ink.

ALBERTO. Mark it in gold and precious stones.

CATALINA. Why don't you go if you want to? There's a railroad here, or you can take the boat, across the sea.

ALBERTO. The boat and the railroad cost money, and I have no money.

CATALINA. Oh, don't worry about that. How much do you need?—because we can ask mother for it.

ALBERTO. Mother? No! That would not be right.

CATALINA. Yes, it would. Everybody asks her. Besides, we're rich now. We've inherited a million, and it's in the bank, and all we have to do is sign a paper, and they give us all we want.

ALBERTO. You are kind and generous, but I could never accept it. Thanks just the same; I shall never forget your kindness. I am grateful, really. Could I kiss your hand?

CATALINA.   [*Taken aback, hiding her hands.*]   Oh, no!

ALBERTO.   Why not?

CATALINA.   Because . . . because they're all covered with ink.

ALBERTO.   [*Seizing her hands.*]   What of it?   They are lovely, they are dear and sweet, the hands of a generous woman, who understands, who sympathizes.

CATALINA.   [*After a pause.*]   So you do think you will go to Rome, then, after all?

ALBERTO.   Yes, I shall; I have a plan.   I work all day, but I study at night.   I attend a life class, and when the next competition takes place, I shall enter, I shall win a prize, and then I shall go, no matter what mother says, and when I come back I shall be a great painter.   I wish you could see the marvellous pictures I shall paint in Italy.

CATALINA.   [*Somewhat anxiously.*]   I suppose while you are there you will paint some lovely ladies?

ALBERTO.   Oh, naturally!

CATALINA.   Like the ones you were telling us about . . . with lines, you know, and proportions?

ALBERTO.   'When I am famous, I intend to paint your picture.

CATALINA.   My picture?

ALBERTO.   And win a prize with it.   Yes, indeed!

CATALINA.   But I . . . I . . . At least mother thinks so . . . [*Looking at herself in the mirror.*]   And she's right, too.   I haven't any proportions at all.   [*Almost reduced to tears.*]

ALBERTO.   You haven't?

CATALINA.   And I don't know how to dress or fix my hair.   [*Crying.*]   You can see for yourself.

ALBERTO.   [*Greatly troubled.*]   No, no, indeed!   Not at all!   You are . . . yes, you are, señorita . . . Yes, indeed you are . . . [*Choking, almost ready to shed tears himself.*]   You, you . . . you have character!

CATALINA.   [*Overcome with surprise and delight.*]   I have?

[CRISTINA *enters with two boxes of samples, without noticing* ALBERTO.]

CRISTINA.   So you got rid of it, did you?

ALBERTO.   [*Moving away from* CATALINA.]   It?

CRISTINA.   Oh, are you still sticking around?   Here are your samples, and you needn't bring any more, because Madame Pepita is retiring from business.

ALBERTO.   Thank you so much.

[CRISTINA *goes out.* ALBERTO *is about to resume the conversation, when* DON GUILLERMO *enters, carrying several packages, one of which, apparently, contains a bottle of champagne.* ALBERTO *bows and disappears.*]

Adiós!

[CATALINA *makes no reply.*]

DON GUILLERMO.   [*Stepping to one side to allow* ALBERTO *to pass.*]   *Adiós!*   [*Eyeing him, curiously.*] Here are the meringues.   [*Handing the package to* CATALINA, *who takes it mechanically, and remains standing with it in her hand.*]   Who is the young man?

CATALINA.   [*Almost choking.*]   It's the boy from the silk shop.

[DON GUILLERMO *deposits the packages upon the table.*]

Don Guillermo, is painting a nice business?

DON GUILLERMO.   It is more than a business.   It is an art.

CATALINA.   But is it nice or isn't it?

DON GUILLERMO.   That depends upon how one paints. A good painter has an excellent business.

CATALINA.   But a bad painter?

DON GUILLERMO.   A bad painter, my dear, cannot exactly be sent to jail, but he belongs there.

CATALINA.   [*Alarmed.*]   Not really?   Is it awfully hard to win the *prix de Rome?*

DON GUILLERMO.   It will be in the next competition, as I shall be one of the judges.   I am chairman of the jury.

CATALINA. [*Torn between hope and fear.*] You are?

DON GUILLERMO. Yes.. Why all this sudden interest in painting?

CATALINA. Don Guillermo, when a painter says that you have character, does that mean that you are pretty or the opposite?

DON GUILLERMO. Neither. It means that you have something characteristic about you, something. original, distinguishing you from other people. It means that you are interesting.

CATALINA. But is it a compliment, or isn't it?

DON GUILLERMO. It is the nicest kind of a compliment.

CATALINA. One more question: Does a woman have to be a countess because she's rich?

DON GUILLERMO. [*Alarmed.*] A countess? What makes you ask that?

CATALINA. Nothing, only mother thought perhaps I'd better be one.

DON GUILLERMO. [*Exercised.*] She did? When?

CATALINA. Just now, while you were out, after talking to the Conde.

DON GUILLERMO. Never! There must be some mistake.

CATALINA. Why must there?

DON GUILLERMO. [*Greatly agitated.*] No, you don't have to be a countess. It is absurd, and I shall take care that you don't become one. Never!

CATALINA. What's the difference, anyway? Why fuss so much about it?

DON GUILLERMO. [*Striding up and down, muttering to himself.*] This is too much! Outrageous! I shall make this my business.

CATALINA. [*Timidly and affectionately.*] Why, Don Guillermo? Have I done anything wrong? Are you angry with me? [*Kissing his hand.*]

DON GUILLERMO. No, no. [*With a paternal caress.*]

I was thinking of something else. [*To himself.*] Keep cool! Be calm! [*Aloud.*]   This is my business.

CATALINA. [*Affectionately, hesitating what to do.*] Before you settle down, would you like me to bring your cap and slippers?

> [MADAME PEPITA *enters. She stops short upon discovering* DON GUILLERMO.]

DON GUILLERMO. [*Pleasantly.*]   Well, I am here, you see.   Is dinner ready?

MADAME PEPITA. [*Disconcerted; then frigidly.*]   Dinner? . . .

DON GUILLERMO. [*Handing her a small package.*]   I brought you some nice iced lady-fingers, and a bottle of champagne to enliven the repast.   We are fond of them, so we shall enjoy ourselves in love and good fellowship.

MADAME PEPITA. [*Visibly embarrassed.*]   Yes . . .

DON GUILLERMO. [*Hands* CATALINA *the bottle.*]   Put this on the ice, too.   Oh, by the way, here are some potato chips *à la inglesa.*   They are one thing your cook does not do to perfection. [*Handing her another package.*] Crisp them.   Mind the bottle . . . [CATALINA *goes out. To* MADAME PEPITA, *making himself perfectly at home.*] Well, this house has become a vice with me, Doña Pepita.   You and Catalina have taken complete possession of my heart.   I never cared for a family, but now I could not get along without the illusion of family life which you supply.   One of these days you will be removing me from the door with a broom.

MADAME PEPITA. [*Greatly embarrassed, steeling herself with a determined effort.*]   Don Guillermo, that is exactly what I wanted to speak to you about.

DON GUILLERMO. [*Surprised.*]   Eh?

MADAME PEPITA. [*Scarcely able to articulate.*]   Since my daughter has left the room . . .

DON GUILLERMO. [*Becoming serious.*]   What do you mean?

MADAME PEPITA. To begin with—now don't be offended, it's not as bad as that. That is, it's unpleasant, of course, especially for me, Don Guillermo, because . . . Well, the fact is you've been very kind to us, and all that, and we can never thank you for what you've done and are doing for my daughter's education. I know it can never be paid for, not to speak of your having taken all this trouble, seeing that she's nobody and you are who you are, and know what you do . . . I don't say so because she's my daughter, but a princess wouldn't be a great deal for you to be giving lessons to . . .

DON GUILLERMO. Yes, but come to the point. What do you mean to say?

MADAME PEPITA. Well, Don Guillermo, circumstances alter, you know, so what used to be . . . It does seem too bad, though, doesn't it? It can't go on forever. You know what I mean.

DON GUILLERMO. I certainly do not. Explain yourself.

MADAME PEPITA. Well, we're just two unprotected women, and everybody's so ready to gossip about what is none of their business, and to make things worse than they are, so people might think . . . Especially since I have a past, I'm sorry to say, which is nobody's business, either. Anyhow, when people were coming to this house because I was a dressmaker, it didn't make so much difference who they came to see, but now that I've retired, it don't look respectable . . . [*Swallowing hard.*] Do you understand me?

DON GUILLERMO. I certainly do—better than I could wish. [MADAME PEPITA *heaves a sigh of relief.*] You think, or somebody thinks for you, that my visits may compromise your reputation, or your daughter's?

MADAME PEPITA. Virgins and martyrs, don't be offended, Don Guillermo!

DON GUILLERMO. What hurts does not give offense.

MADAME PEPITA. But—

DON GUILLERMO. You wish me, then, to confine my-self to giving Catalina lessons?

MADAME PEPITA. That won't be so easy, either, I'm afraid, now that we are moving to Escorial to live.

DON GUILLERMO. I have absolutely nothing to detain me in Madrid.

MADAME PEPITA. My daughter is grown, and she will probably marry before long, so, under the circum-stances . . .

DON GUILLERMO. Say no more; I understood from the beginning. I merely wished to hear it stated in plain words. You want to get rid of me.

MADAME PEPITA. No, no indeed! We shall always be glad to see you, whenever you have time. Why not run out some Sunday for dinner?

DON GUILLERMO. [*After a pause.*] I see only one drawback to your plan; it won't work.

MADAME PEPITA. It won't?

DON GUILLERMO. [*With dignity and restraint.*] I shall not give up Catalina.

MADAME PEPITA. [*Alarmed.*] Don Guillermo!

DON GUILLERMO. [*Smiling.*] Don't take it so hard. As you say, it sounds worse than it is. [*Deeply moved, but assuming a satiric tone, in order to conceal his emotion.*] I have spent the forty-five years of my life so completely shut off from the world, that I have scarcely become ac-quainted with myself. Now that I look back, I realize that I have wasted my time. My mother was wrapped up in me, and watched over me until a few years ago, so that I never had occasion for another woman's love. I grew up a selfish old bachelor, salted down in my books. But the strange part of it is, that while I have never cared for women, I have always been fond of children, no matter how ugly or dirty they might be, as they stumbled along. I yearn to take the little dears by the hand, to teach and pro-tect them. Love between men and women is a relation of equals, it may even imply inferiority on the part of the man. Perhaps I am proud—it is one of my failings; but I have never felt like kneeling before a woman, though I have often had a desire to hold a loving creature in my arms. [DON GUILLERMO, *in reality, has been talking to himself, his eyes fixed upon the floor, but, when he arrives at this point he suddenly becomes aware of the presence of* MADAME PEPITA, *and turns toward her.*] I beg your pardon . . .

MADAME PEPITA. [*Vastly impressed, but without understanding one word.*] Pardon me.

DON GUILLERMO. Since I have known Catalina, this desire has become concrete. She is everything to me. I could not say whether she is quick or dull; I am not sure whether she is beautiful or plain; I can not even tell you the color of her eyes; but I feel that she is my daughter, much more than she is her father's, yes more, certainly much more than she is yours.

MADAME PEPITA. But it seems to me . . .

DON GUILLERMO. Much more. You brought her into the world, but I have brought a new world to her, fresher, more striking, materially and spiritually, than the old. I have rejuvenated myself so as to bring my mind down to her level. I talk like a child so as to companion with her innocence, and I should gladly forego all the joys of this world and the next, merely for the pleasure of holding her hand while she writes.

MADAME PEPITA. Why, Don Guillermo!

DON GUILLERMO. [*Firmly.*] No, I cannot surrender the child. She requires protection which is absolutely disinterested and sincere. Perhaps you may need it, too. I know what I am doing . . . although you would be entirely within your rights if you put me into the street.

MADAME PEPITA. I shouldn't think of such a thing.

DON GUILLERMO. I should not question your decision. Your point of view is as proper as it is absurd. Legally, I have no right to paternity. My position is extra legal, yet it can be recognized and reduced to legal status; and the sooner it is done, the better for us all. Don't stare at me—I am not crazy. Desperate diseases demand desperate remedies. The pill is a bitter one, but I shall swallow it. You are a woman of courage yourself.

MADAME PEPITA. What in heaven's name are you talking about?

DON GUILLERMO. I must be accepted in this house as a husband and a father, otherwise I shall not be free to act —I shall be hampered. Why not face the facts? We must marry, and conform to the conventions of society, however inconvenient. I am willing to marry you.

MADAME PEPITA. You?

DON GUILLERMO. [*Visibly worried.*] You, yes and I . . . if you are agreeable.

MADAME PEPITA. [*Speechless with amazement.*] You and I?

DON GUILLERMO. You and I. Pardon my abruptness—you never occurred to me before, I mean, in the light of a wife.

MADAME PEPITA. But you knew that I had been married?

DON GUILLERMO. [*More and more disturbed.*] Be that as it may, this would be a marriage of convenience, pure and simple.

MADAME PEPITA. Pure and simple?

DON GUILLERMO. A moral necessity; love does not enter into it. But we shall be spared embarrassment. You are rich, while I am not poor, which will be sufficient to silence evil tongues, although the opinion of others has no influence with me. I have means to support myself and to permit me to indulge in some pleasures, so money will not be lacking. If you will marry me, I offer to defray the household expenses like a good husband, while you dispose of your million in any way you think convenient. I shall not even take note of its existence. I am a famous man—my name appears in the papers. I have the entrée of the Palace, and a place of honor at all Court ceremonies, which, naturally, you will share with me. You will be entitled to a reserved seat at the functions of the Academy; the doorkeepers will bow whenever you appear. You will be the distinguished wife of an illustrious author, of an eminent critic, who is one of the glories of his country. Whenever a monument is unveiled or a cornerstone laid, you will be among those who remain for refreshments, and if photographs are taken for *La Ilustración* or *Blanco y Negro* you will be immortalized with me in the group.

MADAME PEPITA. But . . . are you in earnest?

DON GUILLERMO. [*Offended.*] Do I look like a man who would treat marriage as a joke?

MADAME PEPITA. If that is the case . . .

DON GUILLERMO. Your fondest dreams will be realised. One of my ancestors crossed the sea with Hernán Cortés, and undertook the conquest of America. He proved so adept at killing Indians that His Majesty conferred a coat of arms upon him, which I have somewhere under cobwebs at home. You are at liberty to dust it off, since you are partial to nobility, and to display it upon our notepaper, so that people can see who we are.

MADAME PEPITA. [*Deeply affected.*] Don Guillermo!

DON GUILLERMO. And on the door of our automobile too, for we shall have one. We shall get along faster, it is permissible for a man nowadays to blow his own horn. [*Greatly excited, striding to and fro, until, finally, he comes face to face with* MADAME PEPITA.] Well, what is your answer?

MADAME PEPITA. It would be very nice, of course. Protection means so much to a woman, especially when it's a celebrated man. But Catalina . . .

DON GUILLERMO. With due respect to the Slav aristocracy, Catalina will be far better off as the stepdaughter of a Spanish gentleman than as the natural daughter of a Russian duke. She will be more marriageable, too, and it is no compliment to myself.

MADAME PEPITA.   No, of course not.   But . . . I must
say you don't seem enthusiastic.

DON GUILLERMO.   I know what I am doing, and that is
enough.   You are not responsible.

MADAME PEPITA.   But how do you suppose that I feel?

DON GUILLERMO.   My reasons are disinterested, so forgive me; I am anxious, too, to have you satisfied.   I am nervous, upset . . . I appreciate what you are.   Besides, I am a
gentleman, who respects the sex.   I do not love you—I
shall not pretend that I do—but whatever I have is yours.
You will never regret having accepted my name.   [*A
pause.*]   That is, if you do accept it.

MADAME PEPITA.   [*Vastly moved.*]   Certainly.   What
else can I do?   But I wonder what my daughter will say.
I shall never have the courage to face her.

DON GUILLERMO.   Leave that to me.   [*At the door.*]
Catalina!   Catalina!

CATALINA.   [*Outside.*]   I'm coming.   [*A pause.   DON
GUILLERMO and MADAME PEPITA wait, but CATALINA does
not appear.*]

MADAME PEPITA.   [*Impatiently.*]   Catalina, are you
coming or are you not?

CATALINA.   [*Outside.*]   Yes, I'm coming.   [*After a
moment she enters, not yet quite fastened into a flamingly
audacious gown, which scarcely permits her to walk.   In
the attempt, she entangles herself in the train.*]   Did you
call?

MADAME PEPITA.   But . . . What have you been doing?

CATALINA.   Dressing.

MADAME PEPITA.   What in the devil's name have you
got on?

CATALINA.   It's the latest model.   I picked it out myself.   I'm seventeen now, and I'm no Cinderella any more.
I have lines and proportions, and it's time to show my character.   [*Looking at herself in the mirror, turning half
way round and tripping over her train as she does so.*]

MADAME PEPITA. [*Staring at her, completely stupefied.*] You? In that dress? [*With sudden inspiration.*] Praise God, it's the Vizconde! A miracle of love!

CURTAIN

ACT III

Garden of a country house at Escorial, hopelessly modern and in bad taste. A fountain in the middle contains the familiar group of two children huddled together beneath an umbrella. This masterpiece is zinc, painted to look like marble. The ground is neatly sanded. At the rear, a wall separates the garden from that of the adjoining house. Morning glories cover the wall, vying in luxuriance with a number of fruit bearing vines, while, above the wall, the tops of the trees of the neighboring garden may be seen. The façade of the house is upon the left. The building is an absolutely modern, two-storied structure, boasting a flight of steps, a glass baldaquin, a balustrade decorated with urns which are too large for it, and a crystal ball which hangs from the baldaquin in such a manner as to reflect a view of the garden. Half a dozen wicker chairs are scattered about between the fountain and the house, as well as a small wicker table, on which a sewing basket reposes, also of wicker ware.

The garden extends some distance toward the right, the street gate being a little farther on.

The morning is a bright, sunny one.

When the curtain rises the stage is empty. After a moment, DON LUIS *appears above the wall, followed shortly by* AUGUSTO. *They wear light outing suits and broad-brimmed straw hats, and ascend cautiously by means of a step-ladder from the neighboring garden.* DON LUIS *carries a sharp-pointed stick in one hand.*

DON LUIS. [*To* AUGUSTO, *who has not yet appeared.*] Up, my son! You ought to be ashamed of yourself not to be able to climb a wall at twenty-five.

AUGUSTO. [*Appearing above the wall, in obvious ill*
215

humor.] I am able, but ascensions among wall flowers do not appeal to me.

Don Luis. You fail to appreciate the delights of coun‑ try life. Give me air, fresh air! What a morning for filching one's neighbor's figs! [*Extending the stick toward a fig tree, whose top obtrudes between the wall and the house.*] Aha! The biggest one—it's for you. Now, my turn . . .

Augusto. [*Placing the fig on a leaf, which serves as a substitute for a plate.*] Why not ask Pepita for them? She would hand them over already picked. It would be more convenient.

Don Luis. The pleasures of the chase, my boy. [*Re‑ citing.*]

"Flérida, sweeter far
Than fruits of neighbor's garden are!"

Augusto. [*Impatiently.*] Bah!

Don Luis. Besides, by removing Pepita's figs, we de‑ prive that literary husband of hers of their enjoyment. He has been eying them for the past week, watching them ripen to sweeten his lunch.

Augusto. You'll lose your balance and topple over.

Don Luis. Don't worry about me. [*Drawing back a little.*] Some one is coming.

[Catalina *is heard calling in the house.*]

Catalina. Papa! Papa!

Augusto. The daughter! Down quick!

Don Luis. Never retreat under fire.

[Catalina *enters from the house and crosses the garden. She has discarded short dresses, and now wears a simple, smart morning frock instead.*]

Catalina. [*Looking about.*] Papa! He isn't here.

Don Luis. Good morning, little rosebud.

Catalina. [*Startled.*] Eh? [*Looking up at the wall.*] What are you doing up there?

Don Luis. [*Affably.*] Waiting for you.

Catalina. Me?

Don Luis. To tell you how charming you are.

Catalina. Awfully sweet, I am sure. You almost scared me to death. [Goes off at the left.]

Augusto. Ingratiating creature.

Don Luis. Yes. Wait until you are married.

Augusto. Still harping on that, eh?

Don Luis. I am more enthusiastic than ever.

Augusto. I could not endure the sight of her, painted and gilded.

Don Luis. You place your expectations too high. Don't be so deucedly romantic. She is pretty, and will learn to wear clothes, to develop personality. Suppose you don't love her? After all, that is not expected. Marry with your eyes open, like other people.

Augusto. But she can't endure the sight of me, either.

Don Luis. What of it? You are young and dress well—that ought to satisfy her. You are noble, besides.

Augusto. I have no money.

Don Luis. After you are married, you will have as much as your wife.

Augusto. That follows, naturally.

Don Luis. Naturally. My son, we are confronted with a crisis. We have not a penny in the world, and this Academician is insufferable. Pepita may become disillusioned at any moment, and the girl fall in love with another. We subsist as by a miracle. It is absolutely essential that you propose today—sacrifice yourself. What the devil! If I were in your place, if I were twenty-five, I should sacrifice myself with alacrity. [Losing his balance in his excitement, he is about to tumble into the garden.]

Augusto. Be careful or you'll fall! Climb down.

Don Luis. Perhaps it would be best. We are in no position to argue. Lend me a hand . . . Oblige me this time, and take the stick. What do you care? Steady the ladder . . . [Disappearing.] Marriage usually steadies a man, anyway.

[*As soon as they are out of sight,* Catalina *and*
Don Guillermo *are heard upon the left.*]

Catalina. [*As she becomes audible.*] I searched
through the garden for you. How did you manage to
slip out?

Don Guillermo. [*Smiling.*] Now that you have
grown to be a young lady, not to say a coquette, you spend
all your time dressing. I could not wait.

Catalina. Yes, I am a young lady. How do you
like my gown?

Don Guillermo. Very pretty. You look well in it.

Catalina. Do you think it's a good thing for a woman
to fuss over her looks, or don't you think so?

Don Guillermo. If she is clean and healthy, and
there is nothing false about her, I see no occasion for her
to fuss.

Catalina. [*Smoothing her hair, uneasily.*] I suppose
you're going back to Madrid pretty soon, aren't you?

Don Guillermo. Now that the competition is over,
there is nothing to take me back. Your protegé will win
the prize.

Catalina. [*Her heart in her throat.*] Honestly?

Don Guillermo. Yes, he is certain to be a great painter
some day.

Catalina. Then will he have to go to Rome?

Don Guillermo. Assuredly. How are the figs, by the
way? I wonder if they are ripe yet. They hang so high
that we shall have to climb the tree for them. Get me
a basket.

Catalina. [*Taking a basket from the table.*] Put
some leaves in the bottom to make it look nice.

[*They retire behind the corner of the house, under the fig tree. After a brief interval,* Madame
Pepita *enters, breathlessly, from the street, hatless, but
carrying a parasol.* Andrés, *a village lad, evidently
impressed but lately into the family service, follows.*]

MADAME PEPITA. Ask Paco to help you unpack the crate.

ANDRÉS. Yes, señora.

MADAME PEPITA. Then you can go to the mason's and tell the head man to come here at once. Oh, and be sure you count the bags of lime and the bricks that the workmen bring very carefully, because the number they charge me for is outrageous. The way I am spending money here is something wicked.

ANDRÉS. The Conde says that he don't need any help to count bricks; he says he's managing your property himself, and he don't want me around when he counts the lime, either.

MADAME PEPITA. [*Looking about, indignant and surprised.*] But where are the benches? What have you done with the benches? Didn't you set them out?

ANDRÉS. Just as you said, but as soon as you left we took them away again. because. . . .

MADAME PEPITA. Because what?

ANDRÉS. The gentleman told us to.

MADAME PEPITA. My husband?

ANDRÉS. Your husband.

MADAME PEPITA. Why?

ANDRÉS. Because . . . because he said they were monuments of vulgarity.

MADAME PEPITA. [*With suppressed ire.*] Very well.

ANDRÉS. Is there anything else?

MADAME PEPITA. [*Venting her spleen.*] Only get out of my sight!

ANDRÉS. Excuse me. [*Goes out.*]

MADAME PEPITA. [*Pacing up and down.*] Monuments of vulgarity! Monuments of vulgarity! [*In mingled rage and despair.*]

[DON GUILLERMO enters.]

DON GUILLERMO. Apparently we raise figs for the neighbors. We are conducting a charitable institution. [*Dis-*

covering Madame Pepita, *and altering his tone.*]   Hello!
I didn't see you.

Madame   Pepita.   [*Sweetly.*]   Why?   Is   anything
wrong?

Don Guillermo.   Yes, our figs are gone.   We have
lost six—six fat ones, oozing honey.

Madame Pepita.   The sparrows must have eaten them.

Catalina.   [*Entering behind* Don Guillermo, *deeply
dejected.*]   No, mamma, it wasn't the sparrows; it was
the Conde and his son.   I saw them on the wall with a
long stick.   They said they were looking for me, which I
knew, of course, was a lie.

Madame Pepita.   Of course.   They are nothing if not
polite.   [*Wishing to cut short the conversation.*]

Catalina.   I thought you ought to know, because they
are there all the time.   Yesterday, they reached through
the fence in the garden patch and stole all our raspberries,
and they threw a stone into the poultry yard day before
yesterday and frightened the chickens, so one flew over
the wall into their yard, and they never sent it back, because they ate it, if you want to know what they did with
it.

Madame Pepita.   How perfectly silly!   Run in and
set the table for lunch as fast as you can.   We expect company.

Catalina.   Again?   Are they coming to lunch again
today?

Madame Pepita.   Why not?   Run in and do as I say.

Catalina.   Yes, mamma.   [*Waving to* Don Guillermo *from the top of the steps.*]   Wait for me!   I won't
be long.

Don Guillermo.   [*Waving back.*]   I'll be there before you.

Madame Pepita.   [*Going up to* Don Guillermo.]
Don't you like it?

Don Guillermo.   Certainly.

Madame Pepita.   Do you mind their coming to lunch?

Don Guillermo.   This is your house; invite whom you please—you are at liberty to do so.

Madame Pepita.   I should be sorry if you didn't like it, because I always feel that Don Luis and Augusto are members of the family.   However, if you object . . .

Don Guillermo.   It is a matter of complete indifference to me.

Madame Pepita.   Don Luis has some important business to talk over.   They were coming anyhow.

Don Guillermo.   Relative to the purchase of the adjoining property from one of his friends?

Madame Pepita.   [*Slightly embarrassed.*]   No, this is about some mines.   The Conde felt terribly because that investment turned out the way it did.   But this is different. It's a stock transaction.   A big company has been formed to take in everybody.   If you care to see a plan of the mine . . .

Don Guillermo.   No, thank you.

Madame Pepita.   Aren't you interested?

Don Guillermo.   No.   I have no desire to interfere in the management of your estate, nevertheless I advise you to be cautious.   Receive this gentleman with the proper warmth, only be careful to confine your expansions to the sentimental sphere, where they are not dangerous.   When he and his son install themselves as tenants, rent free, in the very first house that you build, leaving us to stand around and wait for the paint to dry on the second, I say nothing. But don't let your affections run away with your principal.   I warn you; you are heading straight for ruin in the arms of your friend.

Madame Pepita.   [*Sentimentally.*]   Everything Don Luis does seems wrong to you.

Don Guillermo.   If you are going to cry over it, I shall retire.   Lose your money and enjoy yourself.   I am willing.

Madame Pepita.   [*Verging toward tears.*]   It is awfully hard to please everybody.

Don Guillermo.   You are under no obligation to please me.

Madame Pepita.   [*As before.*]   But I'm sure I'd like to.   [*Sighing.*]   That is, if such a thing is possible.

Don Guillermo.   [*Surprised.*]   What is the trouble now?

Madame Pepita.   [*Assuming a martyred air.*]   Nothing.   Although . . . We had better talk of something else. [Don Guillermo *stares at her.*]   You had those benches taken away that I had set out.

Don Guillermo.   Oh, is that what you have against me?   Yes, I did.   Pardon my interference in your domestic arrangements, but for once it was too much for me.   Artificial stone!   Imitation trees!   I cannot abide the abominations.   They are . . .

Madame Pepita.   [*Interrupting.*]   Monuments of vulgarity!   Is that it?

Don Guillermo.   Worse!   They are immoral.

Madame Pepita.   Immoral?   I cannot see how.   There were no statues on them.   [*Staring at him as if he were crazy.*]

Don Guillermo.   What is there immoral in a statue? It's the deception of the thing.

Madame Pepita.   [*Failing to understand.*]   Deception?

Don Guillermo.   Yes, benches which pretend to be stone and make believe to be wood, when they have never even seen a forest or a quarry—they dissemble their true nature, they are impostures.   This door, which looks like mahogany when it is miserable pine, these solid marble children who at heart are hollow zinc, these bars and gratings which pass for wrought iron and are the cheapest of calamine—they are impostures, cheats, perpetual lies!   In a word, they are immoral.   Furthermore, they are ugly.

Madame Pepita.   But if all our furniture has got to be genuine, it will cost a fortune.

Don Guillermo.   Then go without; don't counterfeit.

These everlasting frauds, which deceive nobody but ourselves, create an atmosphere of deception.   How do I know
that a woman who swathes her neck in cat's fur which is
dyed to look like sable, will not as easily deceive her husband if she has the opportunity?

MADAME PEPITA.   Don't suggest such a thing!   Suppose
somebody should hear?

[ANDRÉS *enters.*]

ANDRÉS.   Señora, the crate is unpacked.   Do you want
us to bring it in, or what shall we do with it?

MADAME PEPITA.   Yes, bring it here.   [ANDRÉS *retires.*
MADAME PEPITA *turns to* DON GUILLERMO.]   I'm so glad
it came, just when we were talking about art.   You'll like
this when you see it.

   [ANDRÉS *and a second youth enter.   Between them,
   they carry a life-sized figure of a hideous negro, seated
   in a chair, smoking a cigarette.*]

ANDRÉS.   Where shall we put it?

MADAME PEPITA.   [*Ecstatically.*]   Set it there.

   [*The boys set the negro carefully upon the ground.*]

DON GUILLERMO.   [*Clasping his head with his hands.*]
Merciful Powers!

MADAME PEPITA.   [*Delighted.*]   Do you like it?   [*Discouraged.*]   You don't like that, either!   [*Sinking into a
chair and beginning to cry.*]

DON GUILLERMO.   But, Pepita!   Don't cry, please!   It's
not worth it, really.

ANDRÉS.   Shall we leave it there, Señora?

MADAME PEPITA.   I don't know.   Anywhere.   Throw
it down the well!

DON GUILLERMO.   No, stand it in the hall.   It was
intended for the hall, was it not?

MADAME PEPITA.   [*Through her tears.*]   Yes, for the
hall.

DON GUILLERMO.   Put it where it belongs.   [*The boys
mount the steps and stagger into the house.*]   Don't feel so
badly.   [*Relenting.*]   It's too awful!   If you like it, I am

satisfied; only don't cry. I must go to the city—on business—I may have time yet to run to the station and catch
the express. Forgive me . . . Catalina! What has become of Catalina?

CATALINA. [*Appearing at the window.*] Did you
call?

DON GUILLERMO. What do you say to a stroll to the
station?

CATALINA. I'll be ready in a minute; I've finished the
table. Wait under the pine tree.

DON GUILLERMO. Bring your hat along. It's growing
pretty hot.

> [DON GUILLERMO *withdraws;* CATALINA *waves to*
> *him from the window. As soon as he has disappeared,*
> *her mother calls her.*]

MADAME PEPITA. Catalina!

CATALINA. Yes, mamma.

MADAME PEPITA. Come here; I want to speak to you.

> [CATALINA *leaves the window, descends the steps,*
> *and goes up to her mother.*]

CATALINA. What is it?

MADAME PEPITA. Sit down.

CATALINA. What is the matter with you? You're all
excited.

MADAME PEPITA. No, my dear; I have been discussing
art with your father.

CATALINA. I knew it was something awful.

MADAME PEPITA. Sometimes, my dear, a woman does
feel sentimental.

CATALINA. [*Impressed.*] Yes, mamma.

MADAME PEPITA. And, my dear, it is my duty to warn
you. We have invited to lunch—

CATALINA. The Conde and his son.

MADAME PEPITA. But I didn't tell you that they're not
coming merely for lunch.

CATALINA. Aren't they? What else do they want?

MADAME PEPITA. They, or rather we, expect you and

Augusto to arrive at an understanding. We are anxious to have it settled.

CATALINA. Settled?

MADAME PEPITA. Yes, your engagement.

CATALINA. My engagement?

MADAME PEPITA. Don't be silly. You know what I mean, though you're so coy about it. Augusto—I mean the Vizconde—is willing to marry you. It's an honor.

CATALINA. No!

MADAME PEPITA. Yes. He has consented.

CATALINA. Never!

MADAME PEPITA. Never?

CATALINA. I don't love him.

MADAME PEPITA. How do you know whether you love him or not, when you've never been in love? You will find out after you're married.

CATALINA. I shall never love him.

MADAME PEPITA. I don't see why. He is young and handsome, and dresses well.

CATALINA. He frizzles his moustache with an iron.

MADAME PEPITA. To make it curl.

CATALINA. A man's moustache oughtn't to curl unless it curls naturally. It must be geniune. Truth is more important than anything else in the world.

MADAME PEPITA. You, too!

CATALINA. Yes, me too, mamma.

MADAME PEPITA. [*Rising nervously.*] This a pretty state of affairs. [*Seizing* CATALINA *and shaking her, greatly incensed.*] Catalina, this is shocking nonsense, the chatter of a silly little parrot! You are going to marry Augusto because it's the best thing you can do. Besides, he's a fine fellow, and he's crazy about you. You'll be a countess, then, which has been the dream of my life. I only wish I was in your place. He is good enough for you, anyway, considering who you are.

CATALINA. I'm my father's daughter—Don Guillermo's daughter, remember that.

MADAME PEPITA. Don't you come that on me.

CATALINA. But, mamma, he loves me and he is kind to me, and I love him. If you insist on my marrying, I'll run and tell him, and he'll protect me, and you'll find out then whether or not I marry.

MADAME PEPITA. You'll marry because I tell you to— and be very careful how you say I will and I won't to me. You silly girl, do you know what you are doing? Making faces at your happiness! I suppose you've got some snip of a prince tucked away up your sleeve?

CATALINA. No, I haven't got any prince there, and you needn't think you can work off any Vizcondes on me, either.

MADAME PEPITA. Wait! You forget you're unmarried. What good is an unmarried woman, anyhow? That's the reason she's unmarried. Your happiness is at stake, and some day you'll thank me for it. A mother's duty is to protect her children.

CATALINA. Yes, and so is father's! I'm going to tell father.

MADAME PEPITA. Oh, let up on father!

CATALINA. Let up on father?

MADAME PEPITA. Yes, your mother is talking now, and your mother comes before everybody else in the world. It would be nice, wouldn't it, if a man who has known you only two or three weeks . . .

CATALINA. I won't have you talk like that about father! [*Beginning to cry.*] You don't love him!

MADAME PEPITA. [*Loftily.*] Whether I love him or not, is none of your business.

[DON LUIS *and* AUGUSTO *appear at the left.*]

DON LUIS. Do we intrude?

MADAME PEPITA. [*Composing herself.*] Oh, no! Come in! Come right in! [*To* CATALINA.] You stay here with me.

CATALINA. But father?

MADAME PEPITA. To hell with father! Send word out you're engaged.

DON LUIS. We anticipate, perhaps, but I am impatient to conclude that transaction.

MADAME PEPITA. Ah, yes! About the mines?

DON LUIS. Yes. [*Glancing significantly toward* AUGUSTO *and* CATALINA.] About the mines. We might look over the plans in the house, where it will be more convenient.

MADAME PEPITA. No doubt something of the sort would be best.

DON LUIS. Meanwhile the young people may enjoy themselves in the garden—until luncheon.

MADAME PEPITA. Yes, it will not be ready for a long time.

CATALINA. [*Pulling at her mother's skirts.*] No, mamma.

MADAME PEPITA. Don't be so damm Gothic! [*To the* CONDE.] After you.

DON LUIS. Precede me.

[*They mount the steps and disappear into the house, closing the door behind them.* AUGUSTO *and* CATALINA *remain alone. They look at each other, but say nothing. After an interminable silence,* AUGUSTO *ventures a remark as gracefully as the state of his feelings will allow.*]

AUGUSTO. Would you care to take a little walk?

CATALINA. You don't call it walking, do you, in the garden?

AUGUSTO. I do.

CATALINA. I do not.

AUGUSTO. You do not?

CATALINA. Walking is climbing mountains, and scrambling over rocks, and crashing through the underbrush. I adore walking.

AUGUSTO. I do not.

CATALINA. Oh! Don't you like mountains?

AUGUSTO. When I hunt.

CATALINA. Do you like to hunt?

AUGUSTO.   I do.

CATALINA.   I do not.

AUGUSTO.   You do not?

CATALINA.   It's silly for a grown man to spend all day killing poor little animals, who have never done him any harm.   It would do you a great deal more good to stay home and read a book.

AUGUSTO.   Do you like to read books?

CATALINA.   Very much.   Do you?

AUGUSTO.   I do not.

CATALINA.   [*Aggressively.*]   Well, what do you like?

AUGUSTO.   I like horses and dogs.

CATALINA.   Oh, I thinks dogs are disgusting!   They jump all over you, and upset things, and eat everything there is in the house.   Besides, they have fleas.   I would rather have a canary; it's pretty and it sings.

AUGUSTO.   You don't call that singing—shrilling because it is shut up in a cage?   I hate anything that's in a cage.   Canaries are in the same class with yellow novels and romantic girls.

CATALINA.   [*Delighted.*]   Don't you like romantic girls?

AUGUSTO.   I don't like any kind of girls.

CATALINA.   [*Enchanted.*]   You do not?

AUGUSTO.   I like women who have spirit and nerve, blood and fire, who know something, and are not ashamed to show it.   They may laugh at a man, and have no use for him twenty-three hours out of the twenty-four, but in the one hour that they do, they make him live, or they take his life away.   I forgot I was talking to you. . . .

CATALINA.   Oh, don't stop on my account.   I suppose you mean something superior?   Well, I am afraid I'm dreadfully romantic, and I haven't got much fire in my blood—not a bit of it, in fact, although sometimes I do get hot when I think . . .

AUGUSTO.   Of a man?   Is it some man you already

know, or one you would like to know? Tell me, what sort of man would you like for your husband?

CATALINA. Now, don't be offended. I would like a real man, not as elegant as you are, but one who seems like a man, and who knows something—about art, for instance, and is willing to travel—to Rome, if necessary, and become famous. He might be a painter. I don't care whether he is noble or not; he might belong to the people —no, not to the people, either, but his mother might be a school teacher—

AUGUSTO. [*Seizing both her hands.*] Really? You are an angel!

CATALINA. What?

AUGUSTO. [*Transported.*] An archangel, an extraordinary woman!

CATALINA. [*More and more alarmed.*] Oh! It is true, then. You do want to marry me?

AUGUSTO. No, positively I do not.

CATALINA. Then why do you say all these things?

AUGUSTO. That's it exactly—because I don't want to marry you, because you don't love me, because you love somebody else.

CATALINA. I do not.

AUGUSTO. Yes, you do, though you may not know it. I have no idea who he is—apparently a painter or something of that sort, thank God! Now don't be offended; I don't love you either, although I think better of you than I did, and I am grateful beyond measure. Thank you again, oh, thank you! Thank you! [*Kissing her hands.*]

CATALINA. [*Allowing him to kiss her hands, so completely indifferent that she attaches no importance to it.*] It certainly is a great relief to us both. But wait till mamma hears!

AUGUSTO. [*Distressed.*] And papa!

CATALINA. [*Tapping the ground with one foot.*] She says I ought to take you because you are a vizconde.

AUGUSTO. Yes, and then, you know you are rich. But I'd rather throw in my title for nothing.

CATALINA. And you could have all my money. However, that is impossible.

AUGUSTO. I fear so. What shall we do?

CATALINA. Think of something; you're a man.

AUGUSTO. I? I can't think.

CATALINA. [*Having an inspiration.*] No, we had better ask father. He's not awfully enthusiastic about it, either. Come and find him—or, perhaps, I had better go alone; you can slip out by the orchard gate. Mother and Don Luis will believe, then, that we are still together. How do you like that?

AUGUSTO. Perfect! Hurry and separate and fool them both.

CATALINA. Hurry, while I get my hat. [AUGUSTO *runs out behind the house. As* CATALINA *reaches the steps, she notices her mother's parasol, which leans against a chair, where it has been forgotten.*] This parasol will do. What's the difference? [*An automobile horn is heard.*] An automobile! [*Distressed.*] Who can it be? [*Hesitating.*] Oh, well! Never mind. [*As she is disappearing,* GALATEA *enters.*] Oh, Madame Galatea! [*Going up to her pleasantly.*] How do you do?

GALATEA. [*Frigidly.*] How do you do?

CATALINA. [*After looking at her.*] Something is the matter—Mother is inside. Won't you step in?

GALATEA. Thanks. I've business with you, first.

CATALINA. With me? Won't you sit down?

GALATEA. [*Walking nervously to and fro, looking about in all directions.*] I'm easier as I am.

CATALINA. [*Curiously.*] Perhaps you have lost something?

GALATEA. [*Brusquely.*] Yes, and you have picked it up.

CATALINA. I?

GALATEA. My dear, think it over, or all these sweet dreams of yours may turn out to be nightmares.

CATALINA. [*Amazed.*] Nightmares?

GALATEA. Depend upon it, as long as I'm alive, that man is never going to marry anybody but me.

CATALINA. [*Astonished and shocked.*] What man?

GALATEA. So you want me to stage this little scene, do you?

CATALINA. I? What scene? Unless you make it a good deal plainer, I shan't understand one word you say.

GALATEA. You want me to make it plainer, eh?

CATALINA. Yes, make it plainer.

GALATEA. Well, is this plain enough? You think you're going to be a damn countess.

CATALINA. Why, I never heard of such a thing!

GALATEA. What are you doing with Augusto, any-way?

CATALINA. Oh! So it's Augusto, is it? Is that what you're so mad about? Do you want to marry him?

GALATEA. That's my business.

CATALINA. I think so, too. Well, if you love him, and he loves you, go ahead and marry him. Count me out of it.

GALATEA. Don't you love him?

CATALINA. No, and I never did. I can't stand a man who parts his hair with a ruler.

GALATEA. [*Offended.*] Parts it with a ruler?

CATALINA. Yes, that's what he does. And he wears corsets and rouges—although you do yourself, so you've nothing on him there, as far as that goes.

GALATEA. [*Uncertain whether to be pleased or not.*] But there must be some mistake. I thought—I heard that you . . .

CATALINA. Perhaps. I heard it myself, but you can't always believe what you hear.

GALATEA. No, but when you're fond of a man . . .

CATALINA. Are you fond of him, honestly?

GALATEA. I'm fond of him all right.

CATALINA. It is hard for me to believe it.

GALATEA. However, I understand your position. A woman cannot get along without love. She may suffer, she may wish she was dead, and worry until she has not one hair left on the top of her head, but, after all, when you come down to it, love is love. There's nothing else like it.

CATALINA. [*Absorbed.*] I feel as if you might be a great help to me. Have you been engaged very long?

GALATEA. [*Depressed.*] I've never been engaged.

CATALINA. Never engaged?

GALATEA. And it's too late now. I was starving, and needed the money.

CATALINA. Do you really mean you were hungry?

GALATEA. [*Smiling at her innocence.*] Oh, that was a long time ago. But I could starve all my life for that man. You're a lucky girl! Some day you will have a sweetheart yourself, and be engaged. You'll understand, then, what love means.

CATALINA. [*Earnestly.*] I hope I will.

GALATEA. [*Preparing to leave.*] We all go through it. However, there is no need for you to worry.

CATALINA. Are you in a hurry? Won't you wait for Augusto?

GALATEA. No, I guess he's safe with you. But remember! . . . [*Goes out.*]

CATALINA. Don't forget, yourself. [*Puzzled, watching* GALATEA *as she disappears.*] She's in love. Just imagine it! Ah, before you can be in love, you have to find somebody who is willing!

[ALBERTO *enters. He is dressed as an artist, by which it is to be understood that he wears a flowing tie and broad-brimmed hat.*]

ALBERTO. Good morning. [*Advancing.*]

CATALINA. [*Startled and happy.*] Oh!

ALBERTO. Don't be afraid. [*Disconcerted himself.*]

CATALINA. But . . . I didn't know you were there.

ALBERTO. [*Dreadfully embarrassed, but making an effort to maintain his dignity.*] Yes . . . that is . . . I was in the street, looking for you.

CATALINA. For me?

ALBERTO. [*Apologetically.*] No, not for you—for Don Guillermo. I wish to thank him. Don't you know?

CATALINA. Ah, yes! Of course!

ALBERTO. The gate was open, so . . . But I frightened you?

CATALINA. [*Hesitating.*] Then you did win the prize?

ALBERTO. Yes, thanks to Señor de Armendáriz.

CATALINA. That wasn't the only reason. The picture had to be good, too.

ALBERTO. It wasn't bad, although they said the subject was a little worn out.

CATALINA. Jacob wrestling with the angel.

ALBERTO. Yes, I should never have won the prize on that. The other pictures were good, too—there were two or three good ones; but Don Guillermo preferred mine, because . . .

CATALINA. Because why?

ALBERTO. Because . . . because he thought the angel looked like you.

CATALINA. [*Overcome.*] The angel?

ALBERTO. [*Apologizing.*] Yes, but you mustn't think that I did it on purpose.

CATALINA. [*Disappointed.*] Oh, didn't you?

ALBERTO. No, I just had you in mind. I seemed to see you, that was all. Your head is so characteristic—and your curls, and your wonderful eyes! After I had seen you, and we had talked a little—it came to me as a revelation, just like that.

CATALINA. [*After a pause.*] I suppose you are awfully anxious to go to Rome, aren't you?

ALBERTO. Awfully.

CATALINA. [*After another pause.*] You must be very happy.

ALBERTO. Yes; that is, I should be, very—because I have done what I set out to do. It is my career. Italy is my dream!

CATALINA. [*Sadly.*] I know.

ALBERTO. But, then, I am sorry to go. Honestly, I should rather not. [*Manifestly embarrassed.*]

CATALINA. Why not?

ALBERTO. [*Repenting his indiscretion, before it is too late.*] Because . . . because I am awfully fond of Madrid.

CATALINA. Oh! Are you?

ALBERTO. However . . .

CATALINA. [*Hopefully.*] However?

ALBERTO. However, I am fond of it, and so are you, although you don't live in Madrid any more.

CATALINA. No, I live in the country.

ALBERTO. Yes, in the country!

CATALINA. Are you fond of the country?

ALBERTO. I am fonder of it than I am of Madrid.

CATALINA. Are you? Why?

ALBERTO. Because . . . [*Catching himself.*] There are so many trees in the country.

CATALINA. Are you fond of trees?

ALBERTO. Very—if you are.

CATALINA. [*Touched.*] Oh, yes indeed! [*Restraining herself.*] If you are.

ALBERTO. I am fond of everything that you are, because . . . because you have such excellent taste.

CATALINA. I? What makes you think so?

ALBERTO. Because . . . [*Throwing restraint to the winds.*] Because you have such beautiful eyes!

CATALINA. [*Overwhelmed.*] Have I?

ALBERTO. [*Embarrassed.*] No, excuse me. Yes, you have. They are blue.

CATALINA. Do you like blue eyes?

ALBERTO. Immensely.

CATALINA. [*Coquettishly.*] But my eyes are not blue. That is, they are not entirely blue.

ALBERTO. No, not entirely.

CATALINA. Can you see any green in them?

ALBERTO. Yes, green—decidedly; but it makes no difference to me.

CATALINA. Of course it makes no difference to you.

ALBERTO. [*Fervently.*] Absolutely not.

CATALINA. What do you care what color my eyes are, anyway?

ALBERTO. That is quite different.

CATALINA. Is it?

ALBERTO. Yes. [*Hopelessly embarrassed.*] If you were nothing to me, of course I shouldn't care. Pardon my saying so, but you can never be nothing to me. You could not be indifferent.

CATALINA. Oh! Couldn't I?

ALBERTO. [*Impetuously.*] Never! I must tell you— I know it's not right, but I am very unhappy. You are rich and I am poor—only a poor artist. All I have is my future—a hope of glory, merely a hope, that is all. It is little enough to offer a woman in exchange for happiness.

CATALINA. [*Wishing to appear oracular.*] It may seem little enough to you, but it's an awful lot right now to me.

ALBERTO. No!

CATALINA. Because I have money, you think I must be hard to please, and want the earth, besides. Men always think they know so much, they imagine that they are the only ones who have ideals, or can dream about the future, and things that can never be. Well, let me tell you, women do it, too. Though they may be ignorant, they are just as anxious to go to Rome as men are. [*She begins to cry.*]

ALBERTO. [*Deeply moved.*] Catalina!

CATALINA. [*Without raising her eyes.*]   Here am I.

ALBERTO. [*Drawing nearer.*]   Catalina!

CATALINA. [*Discovering* DON GUILLERMO, *who enters.*] Papa!

DON GUILLERMO. [*Without noticing* ALBERTO.] Hello! Are you here? I was waiting for you.

CATALINA. [*With a tremendous effort.*]   Alberto is here, papa.

DON GUILLERMO.   Alberto?

ALBERTO. [*Advancing.*]   Alberto Jiménez y Vergara, sir, at your service.

DON GUILLERMO. [*Slightly surprised.*]   Ah, yes! I am delighted . . .

ALBERTO.   I have come to thank you for . . . for . . .

CATALINA. [*Interrupting.*]   For his prize.   [DON GUILLERMO *makes a deprecatory gesture, indicating that it is not to be mentioned.*]   And while we are about it, I thought I would tell you that he has asked me to go to Rome with him.

DON GUILLERMO. To Rome? With him? Impossible!

CATALINA. [*Blushing.*]   We can get married before we go.

DON GUILLERMO. Outrageous!   [*To* ALBERTO, *angrily.*]   I demand an explanation, sir.

CATALINA.   It was all my fault.

DON GUILLERMO.   Your fault?

CATALINA.   Yes, he was poor, so he was afraid to ask me, because I am rich, so I had to ask him. It's the same thing, anyway. I love him, and he loves me.

DON GUILLERMO.   This is too preposterous.

CATALINA.   And if you won't let us marry, I am going to die, or shut myself up in a convent.

   [*While* DON GUILLERMO *and* CATALINA *are speaking,* DON LUIS *and* MADAME PEPITA *enter from the house.* MADAME PEPITA *listens in amazement, and turns, unable to restrain her indignation.*]

MADAME PEPITA. [*To* CATALINA, *seizing her by the arm.*] What is all this nonsense?

DON GUILLERMO. [*Calmly.*] They are in love and want to get married.

CATALINA AND ALBERTO. [*In unison.*] Yes, we want to get married.

MADAME PEPITA. But Augusto?

DON LUIS. Yes, what about Augusto?

CATALINA. [*Heroically.*] He doesn't love me and he is out of it. He is in love with another woman.

MADAME PEPITA. You don't know what you are talking about.

CATALINA. He is in love with Galatea. She's just been here, and she swears Augusto will never marry any one else as long as she is alive.

MADAME PEPITA. Galatea? That shameless hussy?

DON LUIS. Leave her to me. I shall attend to her case.

DON GUILLERMO. [*Interrupting.*] No, it has been attended to already.

DON LUIS. We shall see.

DON GUILLERMO. As long as your activities in this house were confined to checking up lime and bricks, I remained silent; I hesitated to arouse my wife. Now, however . . .

DON LUIS. Do you dare to insinuate . . . ?

DON GUILLERMO. [*Paying no attention to the interruption.*] As I am infinitely more interested in Catalina's happiness than in her mother's bricks, I shall not tolerate any further interference from you.

DON LUIS. Then you imply, sir . . . ?

DON GUILLERMO. That the time has arrived for you to go. Remove yourself! We are not in the habit of discussing family affairs in the presence of strangers. [*Turning his back.* MADAME PEPITA *is struck dumb.*]

DON LUIS. Very well! I shall retire. What shocking bad taste! Pepita, you will regret this. You will think of me when I am gone and you are pining away, alone with this man. Remember! You have my sympathy. [*Goes out.*]

MADAME PEPITA. [*To* CATALINA.] Because Augusto may have made a few slips, is that any reason why I should permit you to—

CATALINA. [*Interrupting.*] Certainly, mamma.

MADAME PEPITA. [*Looking scornfully in* ALBERTO'S *direction.*] With that man?

CATALINA. Certainly, mamma.

MADAME PEPITA. My daughter, the daughter of a Russian duke, marry a clerk, who is a retailer?

CATALINA. He's an artist.

DON GUILLERMO. In a few years, he will be famous— I guarantee it. He will paint pictures, win medals, and in the course of time be elected to the Academy—[*Sadly.*] perhaps in my place. Some families seem predestined to glory. You will have a great man for your husband, as your mother has had before you.

MADAME PEPITA. [*Sighing.*] All the same, a title would have done no harm, if we could have had it thrown in. I don't want anybody to say I am an unnatural mother.

CATALINA. [*Embracing her.*] Nobody ever accused you of that, mamma.

ALBERTO. We are much obliged to you for what you have done.

MADAME PEPITA. [*Deeply affected.*] Children are a constant source of anxiety.

ALBERTO. But I must not miss my train. I am nervous. If there is nothing I can do . . . Madame Pepita, Don Guillermo . . . I can never thank you sufficiently.

DON GUILLERMO. My wife deserves no thanks.

MADAME PEPITA. God help us both!

ALBERTO. *Adiós,* Catalina.

CATALINA. *Adiós.*

[*They look at each other, too embarrassed to move.*]
ALBERTO. I must be going . . .

CATALINA.   Yes, you really must.

ALBERTO.   If I am to return—the very first thing in the morning.

CATALINA.   Be sure you don't forget!

[DON GUILLERMO *smiles.*]

ALBERTO.   [*Confused.*]   I am going.   I am going now . . . *Adiós!*

[*Disappears.* CATALINA *gazes after him, without daring to follow.*]

DON GUILLERMO.   Run along and see him off, if you want to.   Everybody is willing.

[CATALINA *runs out.*]

MADAME PEPITA.   Well, she seems happy, I must say. This has been a great day.   She is going to leave us.

DON GUILLERMO.   [*Pacing up and down, as he repeats his wife's words.*]   Yes, she is going to leave us. [*Suddenly realizing their significance.*]   Going to leave us? True!   She is going to leave us!

MADAME PEPITA.   The poor dear!

DON GUILLERMO.   [*Startled, staring at his wife as if discovering her for the first time.*]   And I am left alone with this woman!

MADAME PEPITA.   [*Coyly.*]   Guillermo . . .

DON GUILLERMO.   What luck!   [*Fiercely.*]   Catalina is going to marry—naturally, she will live with her husband.   Then what will become of me?   I have nothing to detain me here.   There is no time to lose!   I have an invitation to visit Egypt to conduct excavations.

MADAME PEPITA.   Not in Egypt?

DON GUILLERMO.   Yes, of long standing.

MADAME PEPITA.   But you can not go alone?   [DON GUILLERMO *nods.*]   What is to become of me?

DON GUILLERMO.   [*Uneasily.*]   You?   [*She assents.*] You can stay behind—the trip would be too fatiguing. Besides, you could never make up your mind to leave all these objects of art.

MADAME PEPITA.   [*On the verge of tears.*]   True, I

forgot. Aren't they lovely? I know you only want to get rid of me.

DON GUILLERMO. Nonsense! How could I?

MADAME PEPITA. It mortifies me to think that my husband—

DON GUILLERMO. Although, strictly speaking—

MADAME PEPITA. But you grow fond of a dog when you live with him. After my experience with that man, it never occurred to me that I could love another. But my heart is tender, and I couldn't help seeing what you were. You happened along, and after all, you are my husband, though I am not the one to say it, and I am your wife, and . . . and I love you!

DON GUILLERMO. Pepita, do not prevaricate.

MADAME PEPITA. No, I love you! I wish to God that I didn't, but it's too late now, and I love you. [*Bursting into tears, she sinks into a chair.*] And there you are!

DON GUILLERMO. [*Dumbfounded.*] Pepita! But, Pepita! Come, come, I had no idea . . . [*Going up to her.*] Don't cry now. You unman me.

MADAME PEPITA. [*Sobbing.*] I am nobody, and you are a philosopher, and you belong to a different class, but I love you! I don't care whether you love me, only it isn't my fault. Don't go away, because I can't bear it. I have lived alone all my life, without anybody to take care of me—my first husband ran away, but I had my daughter, and I shared her with you because you said you needed her. But now she is leaving me, and if you leave me, too, you take the heart out of my life!

DON GUILLERMO. Pepita!

MADAME PEPITA. There is nothing left.

DON GUILLERMO. Please forgive me. A man may be an egotist, but not to that extent. I was not thinking of you. You are alone in the world, you have been deserted; but so have I. I do not ask you to love me; it is more than I could wish . . .

MADAME PEPITA. But you deserve it.

DON GUILLERMO. I know. You have no idea what it means to a man to have a wife at his side. Old age is coming on, when it is sad to be alone. No, I cannot refuse the offer of a generous woman's hand.

MADAME PEPITA. [*Sitting up.*] Guillermo, this is so sudden!

DON GUILLERMO. [*Stifling a sob.*] We might spend our honeymoon in Egypt and conduct explorations by the way.

MADAME PEPITA. Guillermo! [*And they fall into each others arms.*]

[CATALINA *enters, flushed and confused with the remorse of the first kiss. Her eyes open wide as she discovers her mother with* DON GUILLERMO. *After hesitating a moment, she smiles discreetly, smoothing her disordered hair.*]

CATALINA. Papa and mamma! [*Tiptoeing out.*] Something new.

CURTAIN